Fifty Years Have Flown

The History of Cork Airport

Farmers Cross

by Bernard O'Donoghue

My mother took to farming like a native,
as if she'd not grown up by city light;
she always said the front row in heaven
would be filled exclusively by farmers.

She'd married into it. Then, as if things
were not bad enough, three days after he died
that cold March Sunday, a cheque he'd dated
on the day came back to us, explaining

'Not honoured: signatory deceased.'
His subscription to the *Irish Farmers' Journal.*
But he hated farming: every uphill step
on the black hill where he'd been born and bred.

So she flew out for good and back to England,
from the new Airport near Cork, where the lights
fought a losing battle with the fog
at Farmers Cross. 'Why on earth,' everyone

was asking, 'build it on a hill? Why not keep
to lower ground east of the city? Wasn't it plain
to God it couldn't prosper there? That they'd
always said it was a hard farm to work.'

From Bernard O'Donoghue, *Farmers Cross* (Faber & Faber, 2011)
— sincere thanks to Bernard for permission to use his poem.

Donal Ó Drisceoil and Diarmuid Ó Drisceoil

Fifty Years Have Flown

The History of Cork Airport

The Collins Press

FIRST PUBLISHED IN 2011 BY
The Collins Press
West Link Park
Doughcloyne
Wilton
Cork

British Library Cataloguing in Publication Data

O Drisceoil, Donal.
Fifty years have flown : the history of Cork Airport.
1. Cork Airport—History.
I. Title II. O Drisceoil, Diarmuid.
387.7'36'0941956-dc22

ISBN-13: 9781848891302

Design and typesetting by Burns Design
Typeset in Sabon
Printed in Italy by Printer Trento

CONTENTS

FIFTY YEARS HAVE FLOWN since Cork Airport opened for business in October 1961. In that time, it has established itself as an indispensable thread in the economic, social and cultural fabric of Cork and its surrounding region. This book not only traces the airport's often turbulent history, but also provides extensive background chapters that cover areas such as: the development of aviation and Cork's part in it; the airport's long 'prehistory' of elaborate plans and broken promises; the protracted process of choosing a site; and the frustrating delays in completing a project that seemed dogged by bad luck. However, despite being a late arrival, the airport was finally born, and Cork joined the 'modern' world, just as Ireland was opening up its economy, applying for EEC membership and RTÉ was beaming its first programmes into Irish homes.

There's an old joke about Heathrow in London being the only building site in the world with its own airport, and Cork Airport in its early weeks and months was still very much a building site. However, it soon came together and, despite its perennial fog problem, established itself not only as a gateway to the wider world for the people of Cork and neighbouring counties, and a valuable entry point for tourists and business visitors, but as a thriving social hub in its own right. In the early days people in their thousands flocked up the hill to the airport on Sundays to catch a glimpse of a plane or just to 'hang around'. The airport restaurant hosted a Saturday night dinner dance that was the highlight of Cork's social calendar and it became a popular venue for weddings, parties and social gatherings of all kinds. The small scale of the airport facilitated a strong 'family' bond amongst workers in all sections of the operation, and friendships and relationships were forged that have lasted a lifetime. The good atmosphere established at the outset gave Cork a reputation as a friendly airport, which has lasted to this day.

The illustrations that accompany the text capture the evolution of the airport through the decades: the crowded viewing balcony, the variety of aircraft, airport workers and buildings, and passengers – famous and otherwise. Statistics are provided, long-term trends are analysed and the airport's broader economic impact is detailed. The book also deals with the tragedies that have touched the airport over the years, such as the Tuskar Rock crash of 1968, the 1985 Air India disaster and the 2011 crash of the Manx2 flight from Belfast. But it also captures, in word and picture, the happier times, and tries to give the reader an appreciation of the special qualities that make Cork Airport distinctive.

It began life under the Department of Transport and Power, before coming under the Aer Rianta umbrella in 1969 and currently operates under the Dublin Airport Authority. Its fifty years have been ones of steady progress and growth, though there have been a number plateaux, blips and setbacks. Passenger numbers grew from 60,000 in its first year to over 3 million in 2007. The airport showed a financial surplus for the first time in 1985, and passed the magic 1 million passengers mark in 1996. Modernisation and upgrades in the 1990s and

2000s saw Cork go from being very much the Cinderella of the three major Irish airports to being the state-of-the art poster child of Irish aviation. The break-up of Aer Rianta and the thorny question of who is responsible for the airport's debts cast something of a shadow over the place as it enjoyed its boom years during the Celtic Tiger and moved into its spectacular new terminal and, as it celebrates its golden jubilee in 2011, the clouds of recession are hovering ominously overhead. But, as this book shows, Cork Airport has weathered such storms successfully before, and all the indications are that it will do so again.

The late Michael Barry, an aviation enthusiast who worked at the airport for many years, wrote two fine books on the history of the airport to mark previous anniversaries in 1986 and 2001. We would like to acknowledge the contribution his research has made to our work, and the roadmap it provided. Many others have also helped in a wide variety of ways: Kevin Cullinane (Marketing Manager at Cork Airport); Tina Quinn (H+A Marketing & PR); John Borgonovo; Deirdre Clancy; Kieran Collins (Heffernan's Travel); Mike Cronin; Linda Crowe and Gillian Culhane (Aer Lingus); Aidan Forde (*Irish Examiner*); Anne Kearney (*Irish Examiner*); Mick Lynch; Brian Magee (Cork City and County Archives); Mary McCarthy; Eibhlín McGrath (Cork Airport); Harry Moore; Órlaith Ní Challanáin; Tony O'Connell; Aonghus Ó Drisceoil; Des O'Driscoll (*Irish Examiner*); Colman O'Mahony; Ted and Betty O'Sullivan, and everyone at The Collins Press.

We also thank the staff at the Boole Library, University College Cork; the Cork City and County Archives; the Cork City Library Local Studies Department; the Cork Harbour Commissioners; the Imperial War Museum, London; the National Archives of Ireland; the National Archives (UK), Kew, and the National Library of Ireland.

This book would be much the poorer were it not for the photographs of Gabriel Desmond who was most generous in providing a large number of images from his fifty years of photography at the airport.

Thanks also to those we interviewed: Mary Blyth, Dan Callanan, Brendan Clancy, Kevin Cullinane, Frank Darcy, John Drennan, Donie Harris, Lilibeth Horne, Pat Keohane, Denis McCarthy, Mary Murphy, Barry Murphy, Ogie O'Callaghan, Joe O'Connor, Tom Russell and Ray Shanahan. We also thank those who spoke to us but did not want to be named. The laws of libel, amongst other legal restraints, mean that much of the 'hidden history' must remain out of print; at least it means we can continue to travel safely through Cork Airport!

Finally, a special 'thank you' to our families, Orla, Kim and Fionn, and Miriam, Méabh and Aonghus for their patience and support.

DONAL Ó DRISCEOIL & DIARMUID Ó DRISCEOIL

Cork, 2011

Lord Carbery (John George Evans Freke) in the cockpit of his Morane-Saulnier monoplane in 1914.

1

AVIATION IN IRELAND
THE CORK CONNECTION
1784–1939

A VIEW OF THE BALLOON OF Mr SADLER'S ASCENDING

With him and Captain Paget of the Royal Navy from the Gardens of the Mermaid Tavern at Hackney on Monday Aug 12 1811

A. The Balloon | B | The pipe that fills it
C. The Car | D | The Netting.

The Balloon ascended at 3 O. clock in the afternoon, and descended safe near Tilbury Fort in Essex at 30 Minutes part four.

E. Mr Sadler | F | Cap.t Paget
C. The Mermaid Gardens.

James Sadler flies his hot-air balloon over Hackney in London. His son, Windham, was the first person to fly a balloon over Cork.

F ROM THE DAY in 1784 when an unmanned balloon was launched near the Mardyke, through the adventures of the colourful aviator Lord Carbery, the wartime activities of the British and Americans, the use of planes during the Civil War, the establishment of the Cork Aero Club, to the spectacular flying circuses of the 1930s, Cork has been an integral part of Irish aviation history. However, as we note in this chapter and detail in Chapter 2, the opportunities to develop a commercial airport in the county were repeatedly spurned, and it was at Shannon rather than Cork, as many had hoped, that the country's first state-backed commercial airport was opened just before the outbreak of the Second World War.

Lighter than air: early ballooning in Ireland and in Cork

In the late eighteenth and early nineteenth centuries Irish adventurers were replicating the experiments of balloonists in Britain and France. The world's first manned balloon flight was on 21 November 1783 when Jean-François Pilâtre de Rozier and François Laurent d'Arlandes flew over Paris for twenty minutes in a Montgolfier hot air balloon. Richard Crosbie is usually credited with being the first person to fly in a balloon in Ireland, having made his first flight on 19 January 1785. Crosbie, who came from County Wicklow, made a number of balloon ascents in Dublin and attracted huge crowds to watch his flying exhibitions. He attempted a crossing of the Irish Sea from Dublin in 1785 but had to abort the flight before he even left the Irish coast. In May of that year he persuaded a lighter man to take his place in the basket for a rearranged flight but the balloon ditched in the sea a short distance northeast of Howth Head.

The first recorded balloon flight in Cork was on Saturday 27 March 1784. The event was described in the *Hibernian Chronicle* of the following Monday:

Last Saturday about four o'clock, the Air Balloon which had been exhibited at the Great Room in George's-street for charitable purposes, was let off from a field adjoining the Mardyke, amidst a numerous concourse of Ladies and Gentlemen, who testified their approbation of the execution with the loudest huzzas on its ascension to the clouds, which took up about a few minutes, when it totally disappeared. Its flight was in a Northerly direction and if the inflammable air does not speedily evaporate we may suppose by the velocity of its ascension that it has ere this traversed many miles.[1]

On the following Thursday, 1 April, the same newspaper recorded the subsequent fate of the balloon and the consternation it caused when it came to earth near Macroom:

Last Saturday evening at six o'clock the Air Balloon which was launched from a field near the Mardyke at four the same evening, was seen by two men at Coopers-hill mountain near Macroom, distant about eighteen miles. When first they saw it their amazement was very great, one thought it was the Devil appearing in the clouds, taking the tube for the Infernal's tail, the other supposed it an Angel coming to warn wicked sinners of the day of Judgment being at hand. However, they endeavoured to pursue it, but to little purpose as it went faster than they could run; but as the wind ceased it fell down between two rocks. They then brought it home and had a number of villagers to see the wonder, but not having any other light to examine its contents, they applied a rush made of bog deal so close that a spark fell on it, which discharged the Inflammable air with such an explosion, as to affright all the spectators and made them conclude it really contained the Devil. One man was burned in a shocking manner in the face and a woman slightly, some fainted and others ran away to give notice to their friends of the approach of the diabolical Spirit.

In 1812 James Sadler, a confectioner by trade and regarded as England's first 'aeronaut', came to Ireland. On 1 October of that year he attempted a balloon crossing of the Irish Sea from Dublin. He managed to get east of the Isle of Man but was rescued from the sea, having had to ditch before reaching the Welsh coast. Sadler's son, Windham, became the first balloonist to cross from Ireland to Britain by air when he reached Holyhead after a six-hour flight from Dublin on 22 July 1817. A little later another balloonist, John Hodsman, also completed a successful flight across the Irish Sea, and Joseph Simmons flew the reverse route and landed in County Kildare.

Earlier in his flying career Windham Sadler made the first recorded manned balloon flight over Cork on 2 September 1816, taking off from the central square of what is now Collins Barracks on the north side of the city. A correspondent of the *Freeman's Journal* described the spectacle:

When we contemplate the grandeur and sublimity of his ascension, the vast machine with which this aerial voyager entered upon his dauntless course – the brilliant and crowded concourse – the sensation of the moment – all combined to produce an effect which baffles description. As the balloon ascended, Mr. Sadler, standing up in his car, saluted the astonished multitude, by waving his hat to them, and as it rose higher, did the same with his flags, which could be easily discovered as he passed over the city ... and after having thrown out some of the ballast, the ascent became quite rapid ...; every eye being anxiously turned towards it, as from the direction of the wind, being about due north, it seemed to take a direct course towards the sea, and by thus increasing the apparent danger, heightened the feelings of those who beheld it. In a few moments it was again lost sight of; and after waiting for some time, in hopes of catching a glimpse at it, but in vain, the people returned to their respective homes, with every good wish for Mr. Sadler's safety.[2]

The same edition published a letter written by Sadler to his father after he had landed that evening: 'I am happy to say, I had an excellent descent within a quarter of a mile of the beach of Robert's Cove. I shall be at Mr. Hodder's, at Fountainstown, where the balloon and car are; send directly some conveyance for my return.' Five days later the newspaper printed Sadler's own account of his flight, giving us the earliest first-hand 'bird's-eye' description of the Cork region: 'the city and coast extending towards Bantry to the west, and that of Waterford to the east I distinctly perceived, whilst the Harbour of Cork and the interior country, with its various mountains, was a view sublime in the extreme'.[3] His flight lasted a little over thirty minutes in all.

The novelty of ballooning waned somewhat following these historic firsts, and even though flights continued people were much less inclined to part with their money to watch exhibitions. From the 1840s ballooning developed largely as a sport.

The Wright brothers made the world's first successful flight in 1903 near Kitty Hawk, North Carolina.

Harry Ferguson made Ireland's first flight on 31 December 1909. AER LINGUS

Heavier than air

In the late nineteenth century there were experiments with fixed-wing gliders, flapping wing and helicopter-type aircraft. Professor George F. Fitzgerald of Trinity College Dublin, for example, conducted a number of experiments with gliders in the mid-1890s, but never managed to get himself airborne. It was the development of the internal combustion engine that made the first powered flights in heavier-than-air machines possible. Whereas the pioneers of ballooning in the eighteenth and nineteenth centuries tended to be men of some means or aristocrats looking for adventure, those who eventually made powered flight a reality were keen mechanics, skilled tradesmen with an almost boyish dream to fly. The Wright brothers were the sons of a clergyman and had a keen interest in mechanical inventions from boyhood. Their experiments turned to flying when their father gave them a gift of a toy helicopter designed by Alphonse Penaud. They made their living making and repairing bicycles but continued experimenting with kites and gliders, eventually developing the design of aircraft wings with ailerons, movable sections that could be used to vary their inclination, thus giving a pilot a greatly increased measure of control. Their first successful flight was on 17 December 1903 near Kitty Hawk in North Carolina, USA. As Orville Wright wrote:

The flight lasted only 12 seconds, but it was the first in the history of the world in which a machine carrying a man had raised itself by its own power into the air in full flight, had sailed forward without reduction of speed, and had finally landed at a point as high as that from which it started.[4]

Those magnificent men (and women) in their flying machines …

Within six years of the Wright brothers' first flight a garage mechanic in Ireland was replicating their success. His name was Harry Ferguson and his plane became the first heavier-than-air machine to be successfully flown in Ireland. This was a monoplane with its engine in the nose, and on 31 December 1909 at Hillsborough, County Down, he flew it a short distance at an altitude of about 12 feet. Ferguson continued to experiment and within a few months was measuring his flight distances in miles. He was the first aviator to carry a passenger, usually his assistant mechanic, Joe Martin, and in August 1910 Miss Rita Marr, from Liverpool, became the first female to be carried as a passenger in a plane in Ireland. In 1912 Ferguson abandoned his interest in aviation and turned his mechanical abilities to the development of agricultural tractors, and the Ferguson name, one that might well have become as famous as Lockheed, Fokker or Douglas in aviation, became synonomous with the slower, earthbound machines.

Around the same time, also in the north of Ireland, Lilian Bland of Carnmoney, County Antrim, was conducting her own experiments. She produced a working glider and then added an engine, supplied by Alliot V. Roe, founder of the Avro aircraft firm, to power her craft. Miss Bland christened her biplane *Mayfly* and she successfully flew her creation in August 1910 at Randalstown, near Lough Neagh. By the end of 1910 she was advertising her 'Irish Biplanes' for sale at a cost of £250, excluding engine. Like Harry Ferguson, Bland also abandoned aviation within a short few years, but in her case it was her father's fears for her safety that dissuaded her. A number of other enthusiasts were also building planes and experimenting with different designs in Ireland in those years. In Portlaoise, for example, a father-and-son team of motor-car mechanics named Aldritt built a monoplane in 1912, but there is no evidence that it was ever flown. The Aldritts' work attracted the attention and help of a local teenager, James Fitzmaurice, who later became an Irish Air Corps officer and a member of the team that completed the first successful east–west flight across the Atlantic in the *Bremen* in 1928.

By 1909 there was sufficient interest in aviation in Ireland to prompt a group of enthusiasts to found the Irish Aero Club in November of that year. In 1910 the group, by then called the Aero Club of Ireland, organised a two-day air display at

Leopardstown Racecourse near Dublin on 29 and 30 August. Three airmen and their planes were brought from England for the event – Bertram Dickson and Cecil Grace came with Farman biplanes, and Armstrong Drexel brought a Blériot monoplane. Flying demonstrations were given and passengers were carried by Drexel in his plane. Huge crowds came on both days and the club made a profit of over £400 on the event. Two weeks later Robert Loraine, an actor and aviator, attempted a crossing of the Irish Sea in a Farman biplane, powered by a 50 hp engine. He took off from Holyhead in Wales and intended landing in Dublin's Phoenix Park. He managed to cross the Irish Sea, but engine trouble and other problems forced him to ditch into the sea a few hundred yards off Howth, near Dublin. He swam ashore and his plane was retrieved by a passing coaster.

In April 1912 the Irish Sea was successfully crossed for the first time by a powered aircraft. Denys Corbett Wilson, an Englishman who lived in Kilkenny, and his Irish friend, Damer Leslie Allen, left Hendon, near London, in two Blériot monoplanes on 17 April. Allen overnighted at Crewe and flew westwards over Holyhead and out to sea towards Ireland the following day. He was never seen again. Wilson flew to Fishguard in stages and on 22 April he left the Welsh coast and flew across to County Wexford in an hour and forty minutes, becoming the first person to complete an aeroplane flight across the Irish Sea.

The Aero Club of Ireland organised the first air race in Ireland in September 1912. The total prize money was £600, a huge sum for such an event, and it was planned that the planes would race from Leopardstown Racecourse to Belfast. So great was the advance public interest in the event that the Great Northern Railway had planned to run a special open saloon train to allow passengers to view the race as it progressed. As a result of poor weather only four planes took off to race, and only two of those made much headway, eventually abandoning their flights near Newry,

County Down. They were piloted by H. J. D. Astley and James Valentine and they shared the £300 first prize. Astley successfully flew from France to England a week later and on 21 September he returned to Ireland to take part in an air display in Belfast that was arranged to compensate the public partly for the disappointing outcome of the earlier air race. Unfortunately, Astley was killed at the display when he crashed, watched by a crowd estimated to number 30,000.

Looping the loop and defying the ground: Lord Carbery, Cork's greatest aviator

The story of Lord Carbery, Cork's first and probably greatest aviator, reads like an Edwardian *Boys' Own* adventure. He was born John George Evans Freke in 1892, the only child of the ninth Lord Carbery, Algernon William George, and his wife Mary (née Toulmin). He had a very comfortable upbringing in the family's ancestral home at Castle Freke in west Cork, and in England, and on his father's death in 1898 he became the tenth Lord Carbery. In 1906, at the age of fourteen, Lord Carbery showed his adventurous spirit when he travelled to Cork and bought a motor car. As aviation began to capture the popular imagination and the interest of those with a spirit for adventure and the means to indulge it, Carbery acquired an aeroplane and was awarded his Pilot/Aviator certificate in July 1913. He very quickly made a name for himself as a daring pilot and his aerial adventures were covered in the press in Ireland and Britain. Shortly after qualifying for his flying certificate he made news when he flew the English Channel. *Flight* magazine noted:

The honour of being the first peer to pilot an aeroplane across the Channel has fallen to Lord Carbery, who although he only took his certificate three weeks ago, surprised London on Sunday morning by arriving from Paris on

his Morane-Saulnier monoplane. He left Buc at 6 a.m., his monoplane ... being loaded with a supply of the Paris edition of the *Daily Mail*. He made two stops on the way, one in France and the other in England, and arrived at Hendon shortly after noon ... Lord Carbery's *nom de vol* is M. Cardery.[5]

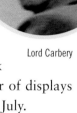

Lord Carbery

He took part in many air races and displays. On 6 June 1914, for example, he flew his Morane-Saulnier monoplane with twenty-three others at an aerial derby at Hendon near London, and two weeks later he flew in a London-to-Manchester air race. He travelled home to west Cork shortly thereafter and gave a number of displays of flying in his native county in early July.

On the afternoon of Sunday 5 July 1914, Lord Carbery gave an exhibition of flying in Clonakilty, organised by the local agricultural society, on the outskirts of the town. Over 3,000 people watched the displays and the Cork, Bandon and South Coast Railway ran special trains to the town for the event. The 'youthful, daring and very capable aviator' performed the first 'loop-the-loop' in Ireland that day and thrilled the crowd with other courageous feats, as the *Cork Examiner* of the following day reported:

Lord Carbery's monoplane, a Morane-Saulnier machine, was situated in a special enclosure, and the mechanics in charge were kept busy answering the many questions which were put to them, and incidentally in preventing the less thoughtful members of the crowd from doing any injury to the monoplane ... The flying machine having been inspected and examined, it was moved from its enclosure and wheeled to the centre of the left-hand side of the ground ... To clear the field and allow the aviator sufficient room to get his machine in motion did not appear a very easy task, but the people were as anxious to see the flight as were the promoters for the success of the fixture. The members of the Agricultural Society, who were asisted by the men of the R.I.C., had little trouble in getting the huge throng to move back the required distance. Shortly after 4.30 everything was in order for the great event, and at seventeen minutes to five Lord Carbery boarded the machine ... Five minutes later, amidst breathless silence, the machine darted forward. It ran along the ground for about fifty yards, then slowly and very gradually rose in the air against a fairly strong south-westerly breeze ... With the machine still soaring, Lord Carbery went off in a south-westerly direction for a couple of miles, when he circled to the left, and passing back over the astonished thousands in the Show Ground, he circled the town, and on the return journey he looped the loop. The admiration of the spectators found vent in the great applause which this daring feat evoked. Lord Carbery brought the machine nearer to the earth with a dead leaf fall, but when within one hundred feet or so, he again rose, and struck off against the wind once more. Having looped the loop again he went through a number of evolutions, including an exhibition of spiral descent, and the dead leaf drop.

He landed after performing a number of other thrilling feats and 'he was taken and placed on a chair, which was borne on the shoulders of cheering enthusiasts'. He was carried through the crowds 'who had witnessed one of the most successful flights that has been given at any aerodrome, and what was unquestionably the finest yet given in Ireland, where for the first time an aviator looped the loop'. Lord Carbery gave two further displays of flying that afternoon before departing 'to the loud and prolonged cheers of the

spectators'. He was given a share of the gate receipts of the Clonakilty exhibition and he donated the £16 to a fund that had been set up to help organise a branch of the National Volunteers in the town. In his accompanying letter he wrote: 'In politics I am personally a supporter of the Irish Party and absolutely dissociate myself from the Unionists'.[6]

The following Thursday he was in Cork to give an exhibition of flying at the university's sports ground at the Mardyke. This was billed as 'Aviation Day' and was the centrepiece of a series of events organised in the city for Cork Week. Lord Carbery was available to bring passengers, one at a time, on a short flight over the city for £5, while £25 would enable the more adventurous to experience a 'loop-the-loop' with the intrepid young pilot. The advance publicity for the event, the first display of flying ever given in the city, brought great crowds to witness the spectacle: 'Then came the great bustle, as all roads led to the Mardyke. Motors whizzed past with gay occupants; the jaunting cars carried their happy quota; the trams laboriously brought more than their complement, and the sturdy pedestrian cheerily followed his way'.[7] The Mardyke grounds were soon full and the local newspaper's correspondent complimented the organisers for not screening off the grounds from those unable or unwilling to pay the entrance fee:

Thus persons with the tenacity to hold on to vantage points on the Wellington Bridge, near the tram terminus on Sunday's Well and along the Ferry Walk in particular, had all the pleasures of the occasion, if not the proud privileges. The gradual rise of Strawberry Hill made a fine free grandstand for a mass of people. In fact to the north of the grounds was a sea of faces.[8]

Above: Aviation Day, 9 July 1914, at the Mardyke in Cork. Spectators examine Lord Carbery's aircraft. *IRISH EXAMINER*

Below: Lord Carbery, left, with his mechanic at the Mardyke in Cork, 9 July 1914. *IRISH EXAMINER*

Lord Carbery's Morane-Saulnier monoplane. *IRISH EXAMINER*

Before the first flight, the Lady Mayoress presented Lord Carbery with a small green flag bearing the Irish harp, which he fixed to his plane. Having taken off 'to the accompaniment of ringing cheers' he circled the enclosure a few times and gave a display of 'steeplechasing' and 'spiral switch-backing'. He was unable to perform the much advertised 'loop-the-loop' as a mist had developed, which brought the cloud ceiling down to about 400 feet, disappointing many of the spectators and the *Cork Examiner*'s correspondent, who wrote that the exhibition 'consequently became a little monotonous'. He landed after about five minutes and on his second short flight he carried his first passenger of the evening, a Patrick Casey of Cork, who waved a white handkerchief to the crowd as Lord Carbery managed to take off on his second attempt. He subsequently did five further passenger flights of about six minutes' duration each, and his second passenger, Miss L. E. Townsend, was 'the first lady

to take a seat in an aeroplane at a flying exhibition in Ireland'.

The following day Lord Carbery travelled to England by sea to take part in an air race from London to Paris and back. He flew a Bristol Scout A biplane, which he had bought for £400 without an engine, in the race. He had it fitted with an 80 hp Le Rhône nine-cylinder engine. Unfortunately, on the return leg from France, he was forced to ditch in the English Channel, but luckily the sea was calm and his plane suffered only minor damage. The plane stayed afloat and Carbery and his aircraft were hoisted aboard a tramp steamer that was in the vicinity. 'I never wetted my clothes. It was not even necessary to change them,' he told a *Daily Mail* reporter.[9] The steamer changed course for Folkestone and HMS *Vincent* took the peer and his plane on board, after which the commander of the vessel entertained him to dinner. Within a week the tireless adventurer was back in Ireland looping the loop at displays in Waterford and Bray. *Flight* magazine reported that Lord Carbery gave a free flying exhibition in late July 1914 in the grounds of Castle Bernard, near Bandon, in his native west Cork. He looped the loop and did the dead-leaf drop and on landing 'he was given a most enthusiastic reception, and was presented with an address by the local branch of the Irish National Volunteers'.[10]

On 4 August 1914 Britain declared war on Germany and Lord Carbery travelled back to England again where he enlisted in the Royal Naval Air Service. His service record shows that he enlisted on 19 August 1914 and was given the rank of Flight Sub-Lieutenant, and was later promoted to Flight Lieutenant. He left the service in September 1918, 'invalided from wounds'.[11] In 1920 his first marriage ended in divorce and he also renounced his title, changing his name to John Evans Carbery. He sold his ancestral home at Castle Freke and moved to Kenya where he continued to live life to the full, often outraging the staid ex-pat British community there with his behaviour. He married twice more, in 1922 and 1930, and died in 1970.

Aviation in Cork 1914–21

AIRSHIPS

In September 1913 a detachment of six planes of the Royal Flying Corps (precursor of the Royal Air Force) flew in stages from Scotland to Rathbane near Limerick to take part in a series of training manoeuvres with the British Army. This was the first use of military aircraft in Ireland. Britain declared war on Germany in August 1914, and in the first years of the conflict no units of the Royal Flying Corps (RFC) or of its sister force, the Royal Naval Air Service (RNAS), were deployed in Ireland. By 1915 German U-boats were exacting a heavy toll on British shipping, especially in the

so-called Western Approaches, an area of sea that included the southern and southwestern coastal waters of Ireland. The British Admiralty decided to use airships to counteract the threat posed by German submarines. A number of airship stations were established on the southwestern and western coasts of Britain, and in early 1916 a substation to that at Pembroke in Wales was opened at Johnstown Castle near Wexford. Similarly a station on Anglesey had a substation at Malahide Castle, County Dublin. Airships became a familiar sight over St George's Channel and the Irish Sea during the war, patrolling for submarines and providing escorts for troopships and other vessels.

By 1917 German U-boats were sinking an average of 100 vessels per month and it was felt that an airship base was needed closer to the southern and southwestern Irish coast. A decision was made to build a full airship base near Killeagh in County Cork. A site of over 300 acres was acquired for the base, in the townlands of Ballyquirke, Knochnaskagh and Ballindinis, and construction work began in 1918. The base was to store and maintain two Coastal Class and two 33 Class airships, which were over 60 metres in length, requiring huge sheds, electricity generating capacity, quarters for officers and men, canteens, stores, garages, a railway siding and connection to the Cork–Youghal railway line, and all the other necessities for a fully functioning wartime airship base. By the time the armistice that ended the war was signed in November 1918, construction at the

A Coastal Class airship of the type that patrolled the south and east coasts of Ireland during the First World War. A large airship base was being built near Killeagh, County Cork, when the war ended in 1918.

11

A Curtiss H-16 seaplane is launched at Aghada in Cork Harbour in 1918. US NAVY

Killeagh airbase was well advanced and indeed continued for some months after the cessation of hostilities. Work was eventually halted in August 1919 and the Killeagh base never became operational. At the end of 1922 the site became the responsibility of the new Irish Free State. When security was relaxed there was an ongoing problem of building and other materials being stolen and in 1925 charges were brought against sixty-seven farmers for possession of articles said to have been taken from the base.[12] There were occasional suggestions that the Killeagh site should be developed as an aerodrome for the new state's fledgling army air corps or for civil aviation purposes, but the notion was not pursued. In 1928, for example, Midleton Urban Council requested the government to consider the site as an aerodrome or airship station but the reply from the Minister for Industry and Commerce stated 'that the question of the establishment of an aerodrome for the South of Ireland will not arise until definite proposals for an air service are put forward by some responsible company founded for that purpose'.[13]

SEAPLANES

The USA declared war on Germany in April 1917 and Britain's new ally quickly brought its influence to bear on both offensive and defensive strategies. The Americans saw the importance of reducing the successes of the German submarine campaign and the United States Naval Air Service (USNAS) set about establishing a number of seaplane bases at key locations on the Irish coast. Aghada in Cork Harbour was chosen as the headquarters for the seaplane initiative and the necessary facilities were built here and at three other locations – Lough Foyle, Ferrybank in Wexford, and Whiddy Island in Bantry Bay. All the bases were ready by August 1918 and the first seaplanes, Curtiss H-16 twin-engined biplanes (known as 'Large Americans'), were assembled at Aghada and sent to Wexford to begin operations. It was planned to station eighty seaplanes in all at the four bases, but by the war's end in November 1918 only forty-three had been delivered. Of the 2,879 officers and men of the USNAS stationed in Ireland, about 1,500 were based at Aghada, which was an assembly station

The seaplane slipway built by the US Navy at Aghada is now part of the facilities at the Lower Aghada Tennis and Sailing Club.

for the seaplanes as well as a training and operational base, and twenty-eight seaplanes were based there by November 1918.

As the bases were operational for less than three months it is difficult to assess their contribution to the war effort. In all, only 247 flights, adding up to 761 hours of flying, were completed by planes from the four bases in that period, about one third of those being done by seaplanes from the two County Cork bases. The only fatality associated with seaplane personnel occurred on 22 October 1918 on Whiddy Island, when a crewman of one of the planes based there was killed when his plane crashed.

THE RAF IN IRELAND AND CORK

No units of the RFC or of the RNAS (merged in April 1918 to become the Royal Air Force) were deployed in Ireland in the early years of the First World war. The success of German submarines against British shipping, however, led to the establishment of airship and seaplane bases in Ireland from 1916, while the rapidly growing need for an air force capable of winning dominance in the air over the Western Front saw a huge expansion in military, as opposed to naval, aviation. In this connection, sites for the development of aerodromes in Ireland, essentially for training purposes, were selected in the summer of 1917 and by mid-1918 the first of these, at the Curragh, was brought into use. A number of others became available during 1918 also: Collinstown, Baldonnel, Gormanston and Tallaght. These were designated as training depots and another nine or so outlying aerodromes were also developed in different parts of the country, including one at Fermoy, County Cork. Within months of the opening of these airfields the war was over and the RAF infrastructure in Ireland was consequently greatly reduced. In May 1918 No. 106 Squadron, which had been formed the previous September at Andover in England, was relocated to the new aerodrome at Fermoy, but it was disbanded in October 1919. By that time,

Hangars at the Fermoy aerodrome.

with demobilisation and consolidation, Baldonnel had become the headquarters for what was left of the RAF in Ireland.

While the RAF was being reduced to a peacetime strength during 1919, the Irish War of Independence was beginning to impact on the remaining British presence in Ireland and the escalation of hostilities in 1920 led to a decision to re-form and redeploy some RAF units there. During the 1919–21 period planes were based at Baldonnel and at the outlying aerodromes at Castlebar and Oranmore in the west, and at Fermoy in Cork. The RAF also had the use of another forty-three airfields of varying standard, as well as about sixty other landing sites, the latter often on the estates of sympathetic Anglo-Irish gentry.[14] Aircraft did not play a major role in the conflict, planes being initially used for patrol and reconnaissance, for transporting senior army personnel, and occasionally for aerial photography and pamphlet drops. As the postal system became increasingly vulnerable to IRA attack and infiltration in mid-1920, the British army set up its own airmail service using the planes of the RAF, connecting the principal garrisons in Ireland and also extending to bases in outlying areas, especially in the south and southwest where violence was

greatest. A landing ground near the military barracks at Ballincollig was the base for this mail service in the Cork area, from where the RAF No. 2 Squadron, under Major Butler, delivered mails in increasing numbers: the number of flights increased from thirty-eight in August 1920 to 109 in May 1921.[15]

There were occasional losses of aircraft. On 13 August 1920 a plane made a forced landing near Kanturk and a detachment of ten soldiers from the town went to secure the scene and protect the pilot and his observer. A local IRA unit attacked the soldiers and in the gun battle one soldier was killed.[16] On 11 February 1921 a plane on a mail run from Fermoy to Oranmore was forced to land near Kilfinane, County Limerick. *The Cork Examiner* reported that '. . . the machine was fired at by a party of men and brought to the ground'. If that were true then this would have been the first aircraft shot down in a conflict in Ireland. While the pilot went to seek assistance 'a large number of civilians were immediately on the scene and the officer was forcibly seized and taken away to an unknown destination'. The plane was then burned. The captured officer was later released unharmed.[17]

14

In April 1921 a military aeroplane, bringing letters and dispatches for the Crown forces at Bantry from the Cork district met with a serious accident when landing on the appointed field, close to the police and military barracks in Bantry. The machine struck a large mound in the field and was disabled. It was later removed to the military barracks.[18]

The Fermoy aerodrome was the base for RAF operations in County Cork and in the south of Ireland generally, the most violent and active region during the War of Independence. There were no proper repair facilities at Fermoy and as the planes, mostly Bristol Fighters, were in need of constant maintenance and repair, it was difficult to maintain a sufficient number of aircraft in a full state of readiness for all calls on their services. In March 1921 Lewis machine guns were fitted to the previously unarmed RAF planes in Ireland, but there is no evidence of planes being used in armed engagements.

Civil War: the Irish Army Air Service over Cork

Following the truce in July 1921 and the signing of the Anglo-Irish Treaty the following December, the RAF began to withdraw from Ireland. With the occupation of the Four Courts in Dublin by anti-treaty republicans, pressure from Britain was brought to bear on Michael Collins and the Provisional Government to deal effectively with the anti-treaty forces. The British offered the use of planes for an attack on the occupied Four Courts and a number of aircraft were flown from Aldergrove to Baldonnel to be equipped for such an action. In the event they were not used.

As the negotiations for what became the Anglo-Irish Treaty got under way in London in November 1921, two IRA volunteers (both former RAF pilots) purchased a five-seater Martinsyde Type A Mark II passenger aircraft at Croydon and had it shipped back to Baldonnel, where it did not arrive until June 1922. These two men, Charles Russell and Jack McSweeney, drove the

Men of the Irish Army Air Service at Fermoy Aerodrome during the Civil War 1922–23. AER LINGUS

Charles Russell, right, and Jack McSweeney drove the development of aviation in Ireland in the early 1920s.
AIR CORPS

development of aviation in Ireland in the early years of the state, with the full support of Michael Collins, Russell having responsibility for civil and McSweeney for military aviation. They were both given the rank of Major General. An Air Council was established, made up of representatives of various government departments, with Russell also a member, and it met on a number of occasions in 1922 in an effort to progress aviation matters.[19] The Irish Army Air Service came into being in the spring of 1922 (renamed the Army Air Corps in 1924) and it occupied Baldonnel aerodrome as its headquarters in April of that year, British forces having vacated it two months before. McSweeney set about acquiring aircraft for the new state's air force and by the end of 1922 the force had thirteen aircraft and forty personnel,

including fourteen pilots, all of whom were former members of the Royal Flying Corps or Royal Air Force.

The new air force saw some action during the Civil War of 1922–23. The aircraft were used for reconnaissance, ground support, enemy harassment and occasional strafing. Leaflet drops were also undertaken in areas held by the anti-treaty IRA. Planes flew on reconnaissance missions over Passage West, Rochestown and Cork city on 9 and 10 August 1922, for example, following the taking of the city by the Free State army. Michael Collins, Commander-in-Chief of the Free State Army, was in County Cork less than two weeks later to get a first-hand impression of the war situation at what was then the interface between the two opposing forces. He was keen that Fermoy aerodrome would be occupied by a unit of the new air force to support the struggle in the south. On the evening of 22 August the following message from Collins was received at the wireless station at Portobello Barracks in Dublin: 'Tell Russell that Fermoy [is] suitable for landing. Ask him if he will fly over Macroom to Ballyvourney to Inchgeelagh, Bandon to Dunmanway ... most anxious to have these places reconnoitred'.[20] Collins was killed that same evening shortly after 8 p.m. by an anti-treaty IRA unit at Béal na Bláth, between Bandon and Macroom.

Fermoy aerodrome was reoccupied on 1 October 1922 by Free State forces and four aircraft and crews were posted there. For the rest of that year and into the early months of 1923 the planes at Fermoy patrolled railway lines, provided air escorts to military convoys and conducted reconnaissance of the areas in north and west Cork, and counties Tipperary and Limerick, where anti-treaty forces still held out. In December 1922 a small air base was established at Tralee to give similar cover in County Kerry. The Fermoy aerodrome was closed on 14 April 1924, nearly a year after the end of the Civil War, but was used occasionally in the 1930s and during the Second World War for Air Corps bombing and airfiring training.

An *Irish Times* account of an ambush in west Cork in December 1922 graphically illustrates how aircraft were sometimes used in armed actions during the Civil War. Λ party of about sixty 'Irregulars' ambushed two lorries of Free State soldiers between Drimoleague and Dunmanway, killing one. Being outnumbered and pinned down the soldiers sent for reinforcements. Some time later an Air Service plane flew over the scene and

> bombs were dropped from the aeroplane and the ambush party was filled with consternation. It was then observed that they were splitting up

and that men were scampering in ones and twos toward the wood, seeking any shelter it might afford. The plane, however, circled the wood and raked it with machine gun fire ... The dramatic employment of air force against attacks on national troops has made a great impression here in Cork.[21]

The only Irish Air Service airman to be killed on active service was an observer in a plane that crashed near Fermoy on 25 June 1923.[22] Another plane was lost on 8 September 1922 near Macroom, when an anti-treaty unit destroyed it after it was forced to land due to engine trouble.[23]

After the end of Civil War hostilities and the closure of the Fermoy aerodrome, aviation in the Cork area more or less ceased, the only planes seen over the city in succeeding decades being those of the air circuses that visited in the 1930s and the occasional private aircraft. There were a number of people in Cork who saw great potential in the development of aviation and they were to struggle for almost forty years before their dream of an airport in Cork was eventually realised.

Transatlantic aviation: Cork's hopes dashed

During the years of the First World War the science and practice of aviation made great advances, driven principally by the military demands of the warring parties. The great advantage conferred on the side with superior air power was recognised as the war advanced, and aircraft progressed from being observation and reconnaissance craft to being virtual weapons in themselves, capable of engaging other craft in 'dogfights', bombing and strafing the enemy on the ground. Aircraft were developed for different purposes, had an ever-increasing endurance and became safer and more reliable. After the war many demobilised pilots found work with the new and developing

W. T. Cosgrave, President of the Executive Council of the Irish Free State (head of government), second from left, with the three pilots of the *Bremen* who made the first east–west flight across the Atlantic in 1928: (l–r) Baron Gunther Von Hunefeld, Colonel James Fitzmaurice and Captain Hermann Koehl. AER LINGUS

commercial airlines, flew air taxis, carried mail and often joined 'air circuses' that thrilled and entertained crowds wherever they toured. In the post-war years hydrogen-filled airships were seen as having the potential to satisfy the need for long transatlantic crossings, while large seaplanes, or flying boats, and land planes also competed for attention in the race to satisfy the demand for safe and quick long-distant flight.

Aviation was still a novelty for most people in the two decades after the war, and the adventures of the airmen and airwomen who pioneered long-distance flight in those years frequently made headlines. The successful pilots became world-famous and they were fêted and celebrated by a public ever-hungry for heroes. In 1919 John William Alcock and Arthur Whitten Brown completed the first non-stop crossing of the Atlantic, landing near Clifden, County Galway, and in 1927 Charles Lindbergh made the first solo west–east flight across the Atlantic. The following year the *Bremen* became the first plane to fly the Atlantic from east to west. The flight began in

Ireland and one of the three crew was Irishman James Fitzmaurice, a former RAF pilot and Commanding Officer of the Army Air Corps (later the Irish Air Corps). Amelia Earhart and Amy Johnson were the world's most famous female fliers in the 1930s, but their achievements have been somewhat overshadowed by the tragic nature of their deaths: Amelia Earhart disappeared in 1937 on a west–east flight around the world, while Amy Johnson was killed when her plane crashed into the River Thames in London in 1941. Tragedies like these highlighted the dangers of air travel, but the adventurers who were pushing the limits of aviation and breaking records were also showing where commercial airlines could develop new routes. The dramatic loss of the *Hindenburg* airship in New Jersey in May 1937 hastened the end of any realistic hopes for the future of airships for passenger transport, while at about the same time the first transatlantic proving flights by seaplanes were showing that the future of such air travel could lie with the so-called flying boat.

Ireland's position at the western extremity of Europe – its 'unique position as an Atlantic springboard' – made it a key player in the various plans for transatlantic air routes in the 1920s and 1930s.[24] Pan American Airways was investigating the possibility of such routes from 1929 and by the early 1930s several sites in Ireland were being examined as potential bases for transatlantic seaplanes. Cork figured greatly in these plans and a number of public bodies in the Cork area, as well as highly motivated and visionary public officials like the Cork County Surveyor Richard F. O'Connor, campaigned vigorously to have Cork Harbour chosen as the Irish terminus for transatlantic seaplane traffic (see Chapter 2). Other locations examined included Kenmare Bay, Tralee Bay and Valentia Island in County Kerry, as well as Galway Bay, the Shannon Estuary and a number of lakes also. The speedy carriage of mails to and from Europe was the principal consideration in those early plans, potential passenger traffic being then of subsidiary importance. In December 1935 representatives from Ireland, Britain, Canada and Newfoundland met at Ottowa and agreed to cooperate in a programme to develop transatlantic air services, with a northern route by way of Ireland being given preference over more southerly options. Agreement was later reached with the USA on the proposal and Pan American Airways was to develop and operate the west–east route, while Imperial Airways would operate in the opposite direction. Ireland would become a hub, a centre to and from which mails and passengers would be carried and distributed, a gateway between Europe and America. In 1936 the Shannon Estuary was chosen as the Irish base for transatlantic air traffic, much to the disappointment of those advocating the merits of Cork. A government memo later noted that 'in spite of apocryphal tales of the inspired manner of the selection of the Irish terminal', there had in fact been a protracted, careful process of inspection and elimination by an expert committee appointed by the government.[25] An airport was to be built at Rineanna on the northern shore of the estuary that would be capable of handling land planes, combined with a seaplane base adjoining that location. As an interim measure Foynes, on the southern shore of the estuary, was chosen as Ireland's transatlantic seaplane base pending the completion of facilities at Rineanna, now Shannon Airport.

Foynes had good natural facilities and these were improved and developed as preparations were made for the first proving flights. The need for the best possible weather information led to the establishment of the Irish Meteorological Service in December 1936, with a base at Foynes. While work progressed on what was to become Shannon Airport, Foynes received its first transatlantic seaplane flights in June 1937. These proving and experimental flights continued through the following two years. The first cargo of mail was carried from Foynes across the Atlantic on 20 July 1938 by an Imperial Airways composite aircraft, a large flying boat which carried a smaller seaplane 'piggyback'. The smaller plane carried the cargo and it launched from the larger aircraft in mid-Atlantic and flew on to Montreal, thereby completing the first commercial transatlantic flight. The first seaplane, or flying boat as larger seaplanes are sometimes known, to carry passengers from the USA across the Atlantic was the Pan American Boeing *Yankee Clipper*. This flight landed at Foynes on 28 June 1939 carrying eighteen passengers, a crew of eleven and a cargo of mail. Ten weeks later Europe was at war and while the Foynes airbase continued to be used during the six years of hostilities, its use was much restricted. Many of the flights through the base carried Allied government officials on war business, diplomats, high-ranking military in civilian clothes, and, no doubt, an assortment of spies and agents from all sides, some of whom

Above: The Imperial Airways composite aircraft in Foynes, which carried the first transatlantic cargo of mail. NATIONAL LIBRARY OF IRELAND

Below: Local people travel out to view the Imperial Airways flying boats at Foynes, July 1938. NATIONAL LIBRARY OF IRELAND

The *Iolar*, a de Havilland 84 Dragon, was the first Aer Lingus plane. AER LINGUS

would have also belonged to the former categories. In 1945 scheduled transatlantic seaplane flights ended as land planes took over the routes and the seaplane base at Shannon Airport was never built.

Shannon Airport received its first flight on 18 May 1939, an Air Corps aircraft, and its first scheduled civilian flight was a Sabena aircraft that landed there on 11 July 1939. Aer Lingus operated its first scheduled flight from Shannon to Dublin in 1942 (the airport at Collinstown was opened in January 1940) and up to that date most civilian planes using the airport were shuttle flights, mostly operated by the British Overseas Airways Corporation (the successor to Imperial Airways, formed in April 1940), supporting the seaplane services at Foynes. With the ending of the Second World War a large number of long-range, high-capacity aircraft became available to the civil commercial airlines for adaptation to passenger use. The war had speeded up technological advances in all aspects of aviation and in the later 1940s and into the following decade air travel

became more accessible and affordable to so many people that the era of the great transatlantic liners began to come to an end. Land-based aircraft now had the range and capacity for Atlantic crossings and Shannon entered its golden era as a major stopping-off point in air travel between Europe and America.

As well as the developments at Foynes and Shannon in the 1930s, Irish aviation was making great strides forward on other fronts also. After a long gestation Aer Lingus, Ireland's national airline, began operations on 27 May 1936 when the *Iolar*, a de Havilland 84 Dragon, took off from Baldonnel with five passengers and a parcel of *The Irish Times* and flew to Bristol. This route was later extended to London. The new airline also inaugurated routes to the Isle of Man and Liverpool in its first year. The outbreak of war in 1939 severely limited the services and expansion of Aer Lingus, and some of the planes acquired by the airline were disposed of during the war years. After 1945 the delayed growth of the airline resumed. In December 1936 the Irish government had announced that the old aerodrome at Collinstown, some ten kilometres north of the city, was to be developed as an airport for Dublin. The development was financed jointly by the government, Dublin Corporation and Dublin County Council. The new airport was officially opened on 19 January 1940 and Aer Lingus moved its base of operations there from Baldonnel. Ireland now had two modern airports, but the people of Cork, and the southern region generally, were still being frustrated in their efforts to have an airport built there.

Air circuses in Cork

While civil aviation was being developed in the years after the First World War, the interest of the general public in flight and planes was maintained by a number of touring air shows or circuses. Many former wartime pilots found work with these circuses and the more daring the pilots and the displays, the larger the crowds that came to watch. Sir Alan Cobham managed the most famous and successful of these air circuses in Britain and Ireland in the 1930s, and he toured extensively in both countries as well as in Europe. Cobham had been a pilot with the Royal Flying Corps during the First World War and later became internationally famous for his feats as a pilot. He was involved in a number of commercial ventures, all related to aviation, and he worked tirelessly to promote its commercial potential in the 1920s and 1930s. He was knighted in 1926 following a successful return flight to Australia from England, undertaken in an effort to show the feasibility of scheduled flights on that route. In 1928 he undertook a series of flights in a flying boat and completed a circumnavigation of the continent of Africa, again with the intention of highlighting the potential for commercial aviation

on that continent. Cobham's air circus was a commercial venture in itself, but it was also part of Cobham's mission to raise the public awareness of aviation. Between 1932 and 1935 Cobham's air circus drew over 4 million paying spectators at various locations and carried nearly 1 million passengers on pleasure flights.

Cobham first planned to bring his air circus to Ireland in July 1933 and in the spring of that year he had a number of potential sites near centres of population in the country surveyed by an associate, Captain J. R. King. Ten locations were chosen and the tour took place between 1 and 17 July under the auspices of the Irish Aero Club, visiting Kildonan near Dublin, Waterford, Ballincollig near Cork, Limerick, Clonmel, Galway, Bundoran, Derry, Belfast and Dundalk. Cobham was very efficient in marketing his air circus and took full advantage of all opportunities to advertise and promote his show. There was a great public appetite at the time for spectacles such as his and the *Cork Examiner* newspaper ran a competition in conjunction with the visit, offering forty lucky readers a free flight in Cobham's Handley Page Clive Air Liner, 'the largest aeroplane yet seen in the Irish Free State'. The Lord Mayor, Seán French, drew the winning coupons and he also accorded Sir Alan Cobham and his team a civic welcome on the first day of the air display at Ballincollig.

The display at Ballincollig was held near the military barracks on 5 and 6 July on a site that was used as an occasional aerodrome. A newspaper report captured the excitement:

The first of the 'planes came over the city a little after 11 o'clock, circled gracefully a few times, and then made straight for Ballincollig Aerodrome. It was but a mild introduction to what was to follow.

A quarter of an hour afterwards another distant humming brought the citizens to their

Seven aircraft of Sir Alan Cobham's Air Circus fly over the County Cork countryside, July 1933. *IRISH EXAMINER*

doors, windows and rooftops. First came a single 'plane, then another, and another, until the remainder of the fleet was overhead. Business was completely suspended. Necks were craned skywards, first here, then there, as one machine after another called for attention. One in particular got all eyes following its eerie capers ... Upwards it shot, looped the loop, turned turtle, carried on upside down, thrilled the spectators by diving for the church spires, and straightening out just at the crucial moment ...

Over the northern side of the city came the Autogiro, the newest type of flying machine, and a decided novelty in these parts. Over the centre of the city it poised almost stationary, its long surmounting blades revolving gracefully. Then it too followed the trail to the aerodrome.[26]

Later that afternoon all twelve aircraft of the Cobham air circus flew in formation over Ballincollig before the various individual displays. Some were used for bringing members of the public on short flights and 'the demand for flights by the public was astounding'. The more courageous took the opportunity to sample some aerial acrobatics:

The young boys and little girls veritably clamoured for a joy-ride. Neither was there the slightest difficulty in finding passengers to taste the thrills of aerial stunting ... all appeared to relish being hurtled about in space. Probably the hair-raising acrobatic performances had more effect on the spectators than on the immediately-concerned passengers.[27]

23

Above and previous spread: the Cobham Air Circus at Ballincollig, County Cork, 5 and 6 July 1933. *IRISH EXAMINER*

There was also a more serious side to Cobham's presence in Ireland, and in Cork in particular, as he continued his mission to promote aviation. He delivered a lecture on this and on his own experiences on 6 July to a large crowd at Cash's department store on St Patrick's Street. At that time Cork County Surveyor, Richard F. O'Connor, and other individuals and public bodies were petitioning central government to site an airport in Cork. O'Connor had drawn up detailed plans for an airport near Belvelly and Cobham was asked for his views on the proposal. He visited the site on 6 July and gave his enthusiastic approval for the plan, remarking that the Belvelly site would be 'a magnificent aeroplane and seaplane base' (see Chapter 2). A deputation from Ballincollig also met with Cobham seeking his support for the development of the aerodrome there for civil aviation, but they were to be disappointed – 'I don't think the idea can be considered seriously … The Ballincollig 'drome can be continued with until another site near Cork has been brought to a state of perfection', was Cobham's judgment.[28] The Cork City Manager, Philip Monahan, and some elected members of the city's corporation saw potential for the Ballincollig site as a municipal aerodrome and took a lease on the site from the Office of Public Works. Their plan, however, came to nothing. Cobham's air circus moved on to Limerick and on Friday 7 July the chief flying instructor of the Irish Aero Club, William R. Elliott, and a passenger were killed when Elliott's plane crashed during the display there. Elliott had also been part of the two-day air display at Ballincollig.

Another air display was held at Ballincollig on 6 and 7 August. Midland and Scottish Air Ferries from Britain was planning to operate a scheduled air service from Cork to Dublin, then onwards to Liverpool and organised the displays in conjunction with the Irish Aero Club and the Air Corps at the Phoenix Park in Dublin and at Ballincollig to promote their venture. Two crashes at the show in Dublin resulted in the deaths of three participants and the withdrawal of the Air Corps from the Ballincollig show. Nevertheless, the event went ahead and attracted spectators in their thousands. Midland and Scottish Air Ferries began its service between Baldonnel and Liverpool a week later on 13 August 1933, the first scheduled air service between Ireland and Britain, but abandoned the project only six weeks later. The Cork-to-Dublin leg of the service never operated.[29] Sir Alan Cobham was back in Ireland with his air circus again in September 1933 and held two shows in Cork, one at Fermoy on 15 September and the other at Mallow Racecourse on 27 September. The series of air shows held in the Cork area during the July to September period, coupled with the attendant publicity and the ongoing campaign for an airport in Cork, did much to further the awareness of aviation and its potential in the region.

Aero Clubs

One of the principal objectives of the Irish Aero Club was the establishment of commercial scheduled air services within Ireland, and between Ireland and other countries. The club was instrumental in bringing the various air shows to Ireland in the 1930s and its planes and some of its members performed at those shows. When Sir Alan Cobham was in Cork in July 1933 he said: 'I advise you people down here to form a branch of the Irish Aero Club in Cork, stimulate municipal interest, and keep it stimulated in civil aviation, which will mean a great deal to you in the future.'[30] In April 1934 the Cork Aero Club was formed following a meeting at the Imperial Hotel. Richard F. O'Connor, Cork County Surveyor and ardent proponent of aviation, was chosen as the club's president. At that early stage club flying was based at the Fermoy aerodrome. To celebrate the formation of the club an air show was held at Fermoy on 24 June 1934. The aerodrome site at Ballincollig had been taken on a lease by Cork Corporation in 1933 with a view to having it approved as a municipal aerodrome. The plan, as noted above, came to nothing and the site was offered to the Cork Aero Club in 1934, but the Department of Industry and Commerce would not grant the site a licence as they deemed it unsafe.[31] In July of that year the Cork club acquired a site at Farmer's Cross, across the road from the present entrance to Cork Airport, and quickly established itself as an active club.

The Irish Aero Club had planned an Irish Aviation Day for August 1934, but the events were cancelled. However, they were more successful the following year and the club organised a series of air shows in cooperation with the Army Air Corps and Sir Alan Cobham's air circus. Sunday 12 May 1935 was declared National Aviation Day and the first show took place at Phoenix Park in Dublin. The following weekend, 18 and 19 May, the show was in Cork at the new airfield at Farmer's Cross and ten of Cobham's planes, as well as one belonging to the Irish Aero Club, again thrilled the crowds. By the end of 1935 Cobham could see that the era of the travelling air circus was coming to an end and he sold his company to C. W. A. Scott. Scott's smaller air circus toured until early 1937, but was then wound up. He toured Ireland in May and June 1936, and four displays were organised in Cork between 16 and 20 May – at Cobh, Farmer's Cross, Mallow and Fermoy.

There was one further touring air show in Ireland before the outbreak of war in 1939. During the summer of 1937 the Irish Aero Club and Aircraft Demonstrations Ltd organised a fifty-day tour of the country, including six shows at venues in County Cork in June and July. Crowds were not as big as at the shows of previous years but aviation matters had progressed significantly in Ireland since Cobham had first toured four years before: the seaplane base at Foynes for transatlantic traffic was being developed; new airports were being built at Shannon and Dublin; Aer Lingus, the national airline, had come into being in 1936; and there was a general recognition that aviation was key to economic development, especially in an island country like Ireland. This made the failure of the government to act on the numerous plans and promises of an airport at Cork all the more frustrating.

Pleasure flights from Farmer's Cross airfield were often organised at weekends during the summer. *IRISH EXAMINER*

A LONG APPROACH
THE 'PREHISTORY' OF CORK AIRPORT

1921–57

ORK WAS KNOWN ACROSS THE WORLD as a transatlantic liner port of significance, and a number of forward-thinking individuals and public bodies realised in the late 1920s and early 1930s that it was in a prime position to exploit the possibilities in the rapidly developing area of air transport. While the idea of a land airport was always present in discussions and plans, emphasis was initially on the potential for a seaplane base, as it was believed that seaplanes would be the leading type of plane that would be used in transatlantic travel. In 1928 Lufthansa had expressed interest in using seaplanes for first-class mails from America to Europe by linking them to transatlantic liners at Cobh, and in the same year Imperial Airways carried out tests on seaplanes in Cork Harbour.[1] Wealthy individuals were already making the connection, so to speak, hiring seaplanes from England to fly them on to Europe after arrival by liner in Cobh in the late 1920s.[2] There was no lack of interest from commercial airlines in the possibilities offered by Cork Harbour, especially in relation to transatlantic traffic, but the constant obstacle was the lack of interest or commitment from the Irish government in helping to finance the construction of suitable airports or seaplane bases. Imperial Airways wanted to begin a scheduled service between Cork and Cherbourg in France but was blocked by the government, and informed Cobh Urban District Council (UDC) in August 1928 that, while it was still interested, the government and/or the local authorities would have to give financial backing and guarantees. Over the following three decades, despite continuous planning, lobbying and promises, the dream of a Cork airport was constantly frustrated. As the *Cork Examiner* noted on the day that the airport finally opened in 1961, 'despite the intensity of all the efforts and the enthusiasm and the energy, plan after plan came to nought, mainly due to the apathy of officaldom'.[3]

From the late 1920s the Cork Harbour Commissioners promoted the idea of an airport in Cork.

Cork Harbour Commissioners

Given the centrality of the harbour to the thinking about a proposed airport in Cork, it was appropriate that it was the Cork Harbour Commissioners who made the early running, inviting retired Irish Air Corps officer and prominent advocate of an Irish air service, Colonel Charles Russell, to address them in September 1928. (As early as 1921, Russell had paid the director of the London/Paris Air Service 'for a study of the viability, including costs, of "the commercial possibilities of an air service between Cove and London"'.[4]) Russell believed that those who held that a proper 'terminal Customs Aerodrome' at Cork was not essential were 'denying the rapid progress of World Commercial Aviation' and the need for Ireland to be part of it. He suggested an airport at Lakelands on the outskirts of the city and a seaplane base in the lower harbour.

Russell had no doubt about the commercial viability of airports and air services – the problem lay in getting an initial subsidy, which was difficult due to official and public fears about the safety of air travel. He felt there was a need for education about the safety of air transport and travel, but that ultimately the best demonstration was the actual safe operation of regular air services. Russell said Imperial Airways would be interested in investing in the commercial air development of the south of Ireland to the tune of £50,000, provided the government guaranteed the airport; an additional £30,000 would need to be raised in Ireland (on a second visit he mentioned £150,000 as the necessary sum, as an enlarged scheme would be more feasible). He believed that the government, Cork city and county local authorities, Cobh UDC, the Harbour Commissioners and the liner companies should all contribute, but he seemed frustrated at the

reticence to invest not only on the part of the government and public bodies, but also private Irish investors.[5] While Russell suggested a site at Lakelands, others, such as J. C. Foley, President of the Irish Tourist Development Association, pointed to the airship base at Killeagh, which had been partly constructed by the British, as a possibility.[6]

Harbour Commissioner and chair of Cobh UDC, Seamus Fitzgerald, followed Russell's address with a motion that the harbour engineer be directed 'to prepare a full report on the suitability or otherwise of the Port for the landing and taking off of aeroplanes or seaplanes'. The engineer, James Price, completed his report for the meeting of 10 October 1928. It stated that the best site for aeroplanes was a large field of flat land south of the railway line, just east of Little Island station, and for seaplanes, the piece of foreshore at the west end of the Five Foot Way near Whitepoint, Cobh. If an amphibian form of plane was used, the report concluded that the Cobh site would be the best option. The Commissioners carried a motion requesting the government to make an aerial survey of Cork and its environs with the object of facilitating local enterprise in the establishment of 'aeroplane and seaplane bases for commercial, passenger and mail services'. Cork senator Benjamin Haughton moved the same motion in the Senate. Haughton spoke of Cork's 'humiliation' and 'grievance', because of the situation whereby a seaplane or aeroplane or airship arriving off Cork Harbour would have to 'proceed to the neighbourhood of Dublin to comply with the Customs regulations'. He argued that that 'there is no more suitable place for a seaplane base obtainable either in Great Britain or in any other part of the world than the great port of Cork affords'. Haughton urged the survey of the suitable sites around the harbour area in the light of the rapid investment in airports already

A Lufthansa seaplane moored near Cobh, October 1934. *IRISH EXAMINER*

under way in Britain and France. Seconding the motion, another Cork senator, J. C. Dowdall, mentioned that a considerable amount of surveying had already been done by the British and Americans during the war, the latter having established a seaplane base at Aghada in east Cork, which he suggested as suitable for development.

The prospects of much-needed government support, however, were remote. The Minister for Industry and Commerce, Patrick McGilligan of Cumann na nGaedheal, had established a committee to investigate the development of air transport in Ireland. It reported that a nationally operated air service would require significant financial assistance in its early years, prompting the financially strapped and fiscally conservative Cumann na nGaedheal government to back off. Major James Fitzmaurice of the Air Corps, who had taken part in the first east–west transatlantic crossing aboard the *Bremen* from Baldonnel in 1928 and was linked to Russell's plans for commercial air development, resigned from the Air Corps in disgust. He noted in his unpublished autobiography that the government had 'showed not the slightest interest' in developing air transport and that 'Ireland seemed to me to be a land in which only the gombeenman could make good'.[7]

Despite the lack of interest on the part of the government, Corkonians continued to push and plan for an airport. The Harbour Commissioners invited the famous British aviator Sir Alan Cobham to address them in January 1929. He praised their forward thinking, said a combined aerodrome and seaplane base would be best, and confirmed that 'Cork is in a unique position as an airport for services to England, the Continent and eventually to America'.[8] A subcommittee to deal with aviation matters was established by the Commissioners, and it maintained pressure on the Department of Industry and Commerce. Another report, this time by the Cork Harbour Engineer and Cork Harbour Master entitled 'Aircraft station near Cork Harbour' in August 1929, concluded that Cork Harbour could be made 'the best seaplane station in Ireland – two-and-a-half hours by plane from London, and in the route of all Liners for Liverpool, Southampton and Continental Ports', and that it would be commercially viable.[9] Russell stayed in contact, enquiring about an experimental flight from Cobh to Paris in early 1930, while the US company O'Connor Transatlantic Airways made a survey of the port and found it entirely suitable.[10] Like all the other surveys and plans, nothing came of it. Dutch airline KLM sent a representative in 1931 to evaluate the possibility of a transatlantic airbase in the harbour; the representative was 'highly interested', but complained in his report about the slowness of the authorities in furthering the project.[11]

Richard F. O'Connor, Cork County Surveyor, who had the vision of Cork Harbour as a transatlantic airbase and who drew up detailed plans for an airport at Belvelly.

Richard F. O'Connor and 'the great Cork airport' plan

The scheme that attracted most attention in this era was that of Cork County Surveyor Richard F. O'Connor. It was featured in the leading British aviation magazine *Flight* in July 1933 and received widespread coverage in the national media. 'The unique geographical position of Cork Harbour as the most westerly Harbour in Europe', began O'Connor's text, 'on the track of the North Transatlantic Steamship Routes and equipped to accommodate large liner traffic makes it the obvious site for the North European terminal Airport'. He argued that 'Cork Airport should be set up at once if advantage is to be taken of the present Liner traffic, so that air routes will be established before the seaplane crossing of the

Atlantic becomes practical business.' The first objective of the scheme was to gain control of English and continental transatlantic mail services, with a proportion of passenger and light goods traffic following.[12] He believed that unless an Irish port could establish itself quickly as 'the principal European terminal airport for Transatlantic traffic in competition with the claims of Plymouth, Southampton and Cherbourg', then Ireland would be 'wiped off the map'.[13]

The initial projected routes in O'Connor's plan were:

(1) Cork–Dublin–Belfast–Glasgow, serving Scotland,

(2) Cork–Dublin–Liverpool, serving the English Midlands, with an airplane line to Hull, the projected seaplane base connecting with the Scandinavian countries,

(3) Cork–Rosslare–Pembroke–London, connecting with the existing airlines to the continent, and serving the south of England,

(4) Cork–Cherbourg (seaplane service), a direct service to France.

O'Connor suggested that the saving in time alone would attract traffic: as an example he pointed out that mails carried on eastbound liners passing Cobh every Friday reached London too late for delivery during office hours on Saturday; by air service, this mail would be delivered on Saturday morning.

In the longer term, O'Connor believed, correctly as it turned out, that airplanes would eventually prevail over seaplanes as the dominant form of air transport. With this in mind, his main proposal was for an aerodrome, the best site for which was on the tidal mudflat east of Belvelly Bridge, between Great Island and the mainland to the north. After reclamation, there was scope to

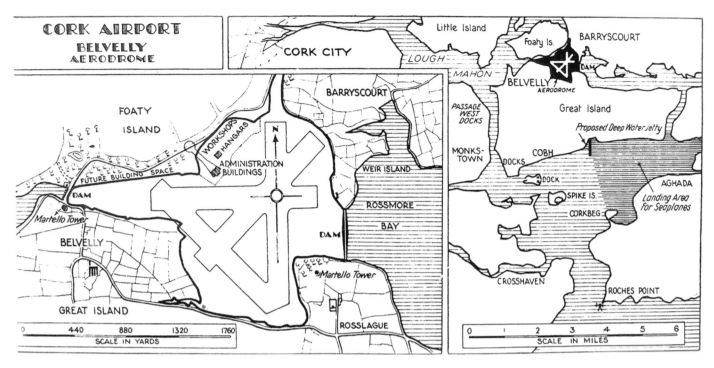

Above: Richard F. O'Connor's plans for an airport at Belvelly, published in *Flight* magazine, 20 July 1933.

Below: The site of Richard F. O'Connor's proposed airport, looking eastwards from Belvelly Bridge.

construct runways of up to 1¼ miles in length and extensive room for the future extension of airport buildings. The site had been examined from land and air by several experienced aviators, including Colonel Russell, who were all agreed 'as to the great possibilities of the site as likely to form the safest landing ground in Europe'. The proposed site was 5 miles by road from Cobh and 10 miles from the city centre of Cork. His proposed site for a seaplane base was the large stretch of water east of a line from Cuskinny to Corkbeg, which was off the main channel, of relatively uniform depth, and provided 2 to 3 miles of water for landing and taking off.

On 6 July 1933, Sir Alan Cobham, in Cork with his air circus (see pp. 22–7), delivered a lecture at Cash's department store on St Patrick's Street. He said that the reception he had received in Cork convinced him of the 'air-mindedness of its people', and that the probability was that Cork would become 'a big air centre'. He visited Belvelly that morning and regarded it as 'magnificent': 'Cork must go ahead, and you must be determined to make it go ahead, and become a huge airport, with air liners arriving from all parts of the world'. He pointed to the example of the rapid development of air facilities in Africa, 'and Ireland should be able to develop just as quickly'.[14] The following October another world-famous aviator, Charles Lindbergh, was over Cork in a seaplane, conducting an aerial survey of the site at Belvelly on behalf of Pan American Airlines, on foot of an invitation from O'Connor. At the Cork Harbour Commissioners meeting the next day, chairman R. Wallace referred to the visit and said that less than £1,000 would complete the seaplane base partially developed by the American navy. The meeting ended with notice of a motion from Martin Corry TD, to the effect that a sum not exceeding £4,000 be set aside for the development of the Belvelly site as an airport.[15]

'Nobody's child'

O'Connor followed up his initial July 1933 scheme with three further sets of plans over the next ten months, all of which were lodged with the Board of Works. The estimated cost, which was vetted by the Board, was £20,000 for reclamation of the Belvelly site and £30,000 for erection of buildings and equipment. He suggested that half the initial £20,000 be provided by central government (through a relief grant), with the remainder split between Cork Corporation and County Council. Cobh-based Fianna Fáil TD Hugo Flinn, who was parliamentary secretary (junior minister) with responsibility for the Board of Works (Fianna Fáil had come to power in March 1932), had taken a keen interest and, according to O'Connor, 'it was cut and dried, ready to go ahead', but with the rather significant proviso – 'if the money was available'. In February 1934 O'Connor told the Department of Industry and Commerce that the difficulty with progressing his project was that 'it was "nobody's child"'. None of the interested local bodies could do much to forward the scheme until such time as the central government threw its weight behind it. 'It is not too much to expect', a frustrated O'Connor told the department, 'that our Government imitate the small state of Iraq.'[16] A departmental official was sympathetic, though he argued that O'Connor was overemphasising the importance of transatlantic traffic, and should concentrate on internal and cross-channel routes. Pointing to the rapid development of airports in all sizeable towns in Britain and Germany, he admitted that 'The Irish Free State is probably the only European country without landing-grounds at the principal towns', and that it was not even possible for private planes to land in the south, with all the lost tourism potential that entailed. He agreed that the best cross-channel air route was from Cork via Bristol to London, but suggested that the Cork local authorities make the running with regard to the establishment of adequate landing grounds.[17]

O'Connor noted in early May 1934 that 'I have been trying to move heaven and earth to get our local people to build my aerodrome at Belvelly'.[18] The result was the establishment of the Cork Airport Joint Local Authorities Committee in that month. O'Connor told the inaugural meeting that Dutch carrier KLM had examined Cork and declared it potentially 'one of the most suitable connecting places between future Atlantic services and the European Continental air lines'. German airline Lufthansa told him that if Cork Harbour had a good connection and facilities it would have a special attraction, and it intended later that year to fly to Cork. (A Lufthansa seaplane landed in Cobh in October 1934). Britain's Imperial Airways saw Cork–London as 'unquestionably' one of the most attractive routes within what they called the British Isles, and the company would welcome any developments.[19]

The Cork Airport Committee, as it came to be known, was made up of representatives of the various local bodies, initially, Richard F. O'Connor; Seamus Fitzgerald of Cobh UDC and newly elected to the Senate for Fianna Fáil; Philip Monahan, the Cork City Manager; and Eugene Gayer, Manager, Cork Harbour Commissioners.

It continued to maintain sporadic focus on the need for an airport over the following several years. In the meantime, O'Connor was busy, in partnership with C. P. McCarthy, a chartered accountant, and Captain W. P. Delamere of the air-training school at Baldonnel, in planning an Irish commercial air company.[20] He submitted his proposals to the government in July 1934. The proposed company was to be called 'Aerlingus Éireann, Teoranta', the name being a corruption of the Irish words for air (*aer*) and fleet (*loingeas*). Like other national airlines, O'Connor's company would need government subsidy in the initial stages; he also suggested that the government should bear the lion's share of the cost of the necessary construction of airports, as his proposed transatlantic terminal airports in Galway and Cork would be principally of national, rather than purely local, use. Until the construction of a suitable airport at Dublin, he suggested the airline would use Baldonnel aerodrome as its initial temporary base. As 'the great airport in Cork, on which this scheme principally depends for connection with Trans Atlantic services', would take two years to construct, a temporary landing strip needed to be built in Cork for the transfer of mails, and so on. He included full costings in his plan, which included suggested flights between

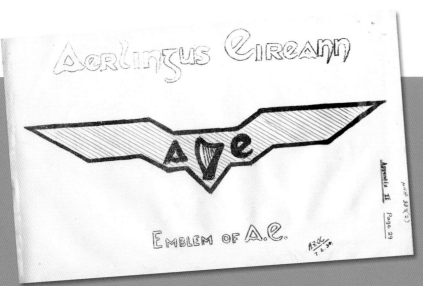

Richard F. O'Connor suggested that Ireland's national airline should be called Aerlingus Éireann and he produced this proposal for its logo in 1934. CORK CITY AND COUNTY ARCHIVES

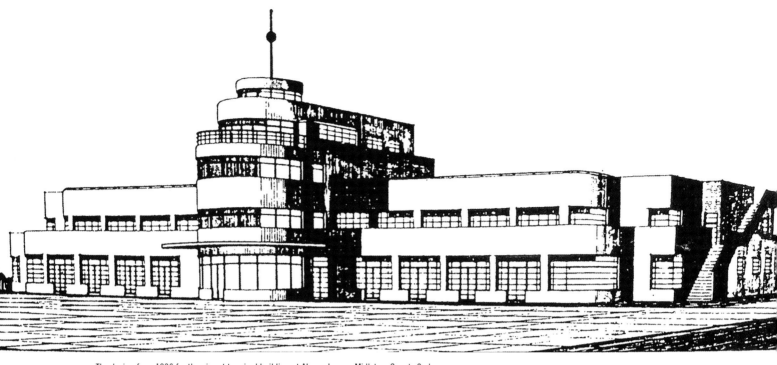

The design from 1936 for the airport terminal building at Ahanesk, near Midleton, County Cork.

Cork and Dublin, Liverpool and London.[21] O'Connor was appointed to serve on a preparatory board to push the idea of an airline company forward, but when Aer Lingus was established in early 1936, he remarked to his family that 'They have dropped my scheme but taken my name'.[22] Aer Rianta was established the following year to oversee the development of aviation in Ireland, and plans for the development of airports in Dublin and Shannon proceeded; 'the great airport in Cork', however, remained as far away as ever.

'I wonder if Cork has got the plague'

Corkonians continued to promote the county's claims for the remainder of the decade. In April 1935 Senator Seamus Fitzgerald wrote to Minister for Industry and Commerce Seán Lemass regarding a visit to Cork and Cobh of representatives of Imperial Airways, who met with the USA Lines shipping company and agreed on the feasibility of a chartered service from Cork to Croydon, where a link with continental airlines would be made. Fitzgerald said that as the Ballincollig aerodrome was not approved of, and the Aero Club's field at Farmer's Cross was too small, the City Manager was willing to expand the latter if the Minister would license an aerodrome there.[23] Lemass, however, was unwilling to entertain the idea, and admitted in the Dáil the following month that an airport in Cork was not a matter of national importance at that time.[24] The Cork Airport Committee kept plugging, and in March 1936 commissioned London-based aviation consultants Chamier, Gilbert-Lodge & Co. to report on seaplane and aeroplane bases in Cork. They reported in June 1936, noting the site at Rushbrooke Docks as most suitable for a seaplane base, but doubting the suitability of O'Connor's original Belvelly site due to engineering problems, and supporting another suggested location, at Ahanesk, about 1 mile southwest of Midleton.[25]

Dublin airport, opened in 1940. AER LINGUS

In the meantime, in May 1936, Aer Lingus began its service from Baldonnel aerodrome to London via Bristol. Over the summer, services were provided to the Isle of Man and Liverpool. In April and May 1936, Major F. Leo Crilly ('an Ulsterman who committed the indiscretion of being born in England') of Crilly Airlines in London visited Cork to survey the possibility of establishing air services between it and Britain. He proposed a daily Cork–London link, and even had plans for an aircraft factory. Crilly was informed by the department that the government was 'unable to entertain his proposals' because of the government's intention to establish a national airline service from various locations at the earliest possible date.[26] Minister for Industry and Commerce Seán Lemass told the Dáil in February

1937 that Aer Lingus services from Cork to the south of England and Wales were 'matters for consideration in the very near future'. Industry and Commerce inspectors rejected the proposed seaplane site in Cork Harbour, but approved of the Midleton site provided certain work was carried out. In the meantime, a transatlantic seaplane base was established in Foynes, County Clare, in 1936, which remained in operation until 1945, when the era of the seaplane was effectively at an end, together with the seaplane hopes of Cork Harbour. The state began work on the construction of two airports – in Collinstown, Dublin, for general civil aviation, and Rineanna, County Clare (Shannon), for transatlantic flights. O'Connor and the Airport Committee kept up the pressure on the government, seeking financial support for the

Seamus Fitzgerald, who was a prominent advocate of an airport for Cork from the 1920s. As a member of Cobh UDC and the Cork Harbour Commissioners, he was active in the Cork Airport Committee that kept the idea on the agenda, and later campaigned in his role as a Fianna Fáil Senator and TD. He also served on the boards of Aer Lingus and Aer Rianta.
CORK CITY AND COUNTY ARCHIVES

'Midleton Aerodrome', but to no avail.[27] Money was easily found for airports in Dublin and Shannon, but not for the southern capital, complained East Cork Fianna Fáil TD Martin Corry in April 1937: 'Again I wonder,' he told the Dáil, 'if Cork has got the plague.'[28] As far as the government was concerned, Cork's local authorities and public bodies needed to make the running on the construction of an airport; only then would the state consider the level of support it would offer.

Right up until the outbreak of the Second World War in 1939 the agitation continued, spearheaded by the Airport Committee, which met with Lemass and his officials, as well as Hugo Flinn and the Board of Works, on a number of occasions. In July 1938 a deputation to Lemass

headed by Seamus Fitzgerald (who had by this stage been appointed to the board of Aer Lingus) argued that, as the government was funding the construction of the Dublin and Shannon airports with little or no contribution from the respective local authorities, why could the major portion of the cost of an airport in Cork not be borne by central government also? Cork airport, no less than the other two, would serve national more than local needs.[29] The government held out on the need for what Fitzgerald described as 'large financial subventions from Cork Public Bodies'. In 1938 an Aer Lingus development plan envisaged a Cork–Paris route in pool with Air France, to begin in 1940, indicating an expectation that an airport would be built.[30] In 1939 the government approved the proposal to establish an airport at

Cork. The estimated cost was £92,000, with the state providing 45 per cent and local authorities meeting the balance.[31] With Shannon and Dublin airports taking shape, it seemed that Cork's time had finally come also. However, the outbreak of war in September 1939 saw Cork airport fade into the future yet again.

'A project for post-war development'

Limited services had begun in Shannon in the summer of 1939, and Dublin Airport opened in January 1940. Ireland's first internal air service, between Dublin and Shannon, commenced in August 1942, prompting *The Irish Times* to opine that,

> ever ambitious, Cork, doubtless, will be stirred by the very real promise of this up-to-date transport to take energetic steps for the provision of a landing ground within easy reach of the city. Plans for a Cork airport have been mooted many times; but their realisation seems to be as far away as ever.[32]

The new service did indeed revive Cork's ambitions, and local authorities, public bodies and business interests all called for the issue to be put back on the agenda.[33] The Airport Committee was reconvened, and plans were made to identify a temporary site that could be used to link Cork into an internal air network, pending the construction of a permanent airport. Seamus Fitzgerald was elected to the Dáil in the July 1943 election, and informed the Harbour Board in September that the Airport Committee had adjourned further consideration until surveys had been carried out.[34] These were done by engineers from the Office of Public Works in 1943. They reported in detail on three sites, which they said were the only possible ones within a 15-mile radius of Cork city. A departmental committee appointed to consider the

matter eliminated one of these – in the townland of Lahardane, 3 miles north of the city in the direction of White's Cross – leaving two potential sites: one near Midleton, 12 miles east of the city, and the other at Ballygarvan, 5 miles south of the city, close to the existing airfield at Farmer's Cross.[35] Lemass told Fitzgerald that before a final decision could be made, it was necessary to collate data over an extended period, and he cautioned the Corkman not to say anything in public so as not to arouse expectations; the construction of an airport at Cork, the minister told a presumably unsurprised Fitzgerald, 'will necessarily be a project for post-war development'.[36]

The reports received by the Department of Industry and Commerce described the Midleton site at Ahanesk as being situated in a saucer-like depression, which would present difficulties in the construction of runways, while surrounding high ground 'would leave something to be desired' with regard to approaches for air navigation. However, it was felt that it would be possible to provide a satisfactory airport on the site if necessary. The Ballygarvan site was on a hilltop of about 500 feet above sea level, adjacent to the main Cork–Kinsale road. Much heavy cutting and filling would be necessary, but it was felt that the approaches were considerably better than in Midleton. However, meteorological testing at both sites showed Midleton to be far more suitable. The meteorological observation station at Ballygarvan was closed in late 1947, and the linking-up of the station at Midleton with the local telephone exchange in December of that year raised local hopes that the Midleton site would host Cork's airport.[37] However, Lemass had told the Dáil only three weeks previously that the 'decision as to the most suitable site will be based not only on the meteorological data but on consideration of the type of air transport operations which are likely to be served by an airport at Cork'.[38] The continuing delays were met with understandable frustration

Ahanesk, from the south, one of the sites proposed for Cork's airport.

in Cork, from where demands for government action continued to issue forth.

Meanwhile, an extended airfield was opened at Farmer's Cross in 1948 by the newly formed Cork Airways Company, which was granted a restricted licence to operate private and charter flights. Cambrian Air Services wanted to operate a daily service between Cork and Cardiff, but permission was refused by the new inter-party government that replaced Fianna Fáil in February 1948. In the Dáil in February 1950, Liam Cosgrave, parliamentary secretary (junior minister) at Industry and Commerce, defended the decision to reject the Cork company's application to operate scheduled services, and also shot down any hopes of a change in thinking at government level with regard to a state-supported airport in Cork: 'There is no intention of establishing any new aerodrome at the moment and it is unlikely in the foreseeable future.'[39] A year later Fianna Fáil was back in power, Lemass had resumed his Industry and Commerce portfolio, and almost 300 planes had used the Farmer's Cross airfield.[40] The continuing pressure from the Cork Airways Company via Cork TDs and other interests for a licence to operate a commercial airport at Farmer's Cross helped to force the government's hand. Lemass announced in November 1951 that Aer Rianta had been commissioned to prepare a report on the issue, and continued to resist pressure to grant a licence for scheduled services to Farmer's Cross on the basis that it did not possess the facilities to justify it. Privately, however, officials in the Department of Industry and Commerce admitted that demands from Cork could not be ignored for much longer and unless a proper airport was built,

A group photographed at the official opening of the Cork Airways Company airfield at Farmer's Cross, 9 May 1948. (L–r): George Heffernan, Director, Cork Airways Company; Lt Col. W. J. Keane; James Hickey TD; E. Gayer, Cork Harbour Commissioners; Liam Cosgrave TD, Parliamentary Secretary at Industry and Commerce; Michael Sheehan TD; unknown; Dan Cullinane, Director, Cork Airways Company; Senator Richard Anthony; E. O'Neill; W. Cullinane; Patrick Lehane TD. *IRISH EXAMINER*

the Minister feels that eventually he will be forced to grant the applications by the Cork Airways Company and the Cambrian Air Services. The grant of permission to the last-mentioned company for the operation of regular cross-Channel air services would make difficult the continued refusal of applications by other British Companies and very severe competition with Aer Lingus may result.[41]

The estimated cost of construction was now £1 million, with £60,000 budgeted for annual running costs.

Decision time – finally

East Cork TDs maintained the pressure for Midleton, and it was suggested in the press and the Dáil that Lemass had intimated to Fianna Fáil figures from the area in late 1952 that the Ahanesk site was favoured.[42] This is likely, as he had advised the government in October 1952 that the advantages of Ballygarvan (better approaches, better runway potential, closeness to the city) were outweighed by the 'extremely bad meteorological conditions', and concluded that 'if Cork is to have an airport from which regular services can be operated, it should be at Midleton'.[43] The other relevant ministers and departments (Defence and External Affairs) had no objections to the proposed project; opposition came from only one, predictable, departmental quarter – the notoriously frugal Department of Finance and its long-serving Secretary, J. J. McElligott (dubbed 'the "Dr No" of Irish economic policy' by economic historian Cormac Ó Gráda due to his 'relentless anti-spending negativism'[44]). McElligott believed the case for an airport at Cork – 'which would serve only a small area of the south, the remainder being more conveniently served by the airports at Limerick [*sic*] and Dublin' – had not been demonstrated to his minister's satisfaction. He argued that the prospects for internal air traffic were poor and that the existing rail and road connections with other cities and the other airports made the costs of a third facility unjustifiable. With classic Finance logic, he argued that 'it would indeed be cheaper to give free return train fares from Cork to Dublin to Cork citizens flying from Dublin to London than to provide an airport at Cork'. McElligott pointed out, correctly, that when an airport for Cork was approved in 1939, it was on condition of sharing the costs with the local authorities. Even if this still were the case, the project, with the massive inflation of costs since – up to tenfold – would represent an unjustifiable 'draw' on the country's capital resources.[45] Aer Rianta was also less than enthusiastic, arguing against heavy expenditure on a new airport for fixed-wing aircraft on the basis of pessimistic forecasts about potential traffic. It even suggested, supported by the Aer Lingus Board, that a service of twin-engined twenty- to thirty-seat helicopters might suit the needs of Cork.[46] On further investigation it discovered that helicopters of this size, suitable for commercial operations, would not become available for ten years or more, and, moreover, the development of helicopter air services internationally had been slow. Aer Lingus envisaged annual passenger traffic over the first ten years at approximately 30,000–60,000 people, and referred to the competition that might be expected from improved rail services between Cork and Dublin. The objections of Finance and Aer Rianta were noted and ignored, and on 18 November 1952 the government decided in principle that an airport be provided at Cork for scheduled air services and that detailed plans be drawn up.[47]

'Ballygarvan is the better of the two'

As almost ten years had elapsed since the original site inspections, an expert group of technical officers from Industry and Commerce, together with an Aer Lingus representative, was appointed to proceed with the selection of an airport site in Cork. It reported in July 1953. A range of potential sites was examined at Little Island, Glanmire, Douglas, Lakelands (near Blackrock), Ballincollig, Ovens, Blarney and Farmer's Cross, as well as Ballygarvan and the Midleton site. The group reported that they found 'no valley or low ground site superior to Midleton, and no hill site superior to Ballygarvan', and that the choice was between these two, as previously indicated. They were unimpressed by the Midleton site, primarily due to the hills of up to 600 feet on the north and northwest approaches, which they considered would be 'frequently hazardous'. Furthermore, the distance of 12 miles to the city rendered it 'very inconvenient' and 'would impose a severe handicap on the development of air services'. The group concluded that 'from the points of view of suitability of ground for the necessary runways, clearness of approaches and feasibility of installing lighting and radio aids', Ballygarvan was the best site available. There remained the thorny issue of the meteorological conditions, which had previously seemed to discount Ballygarvan in favour of Midleton. The group concluded, however, that 'the clear approaches to Ballygarvan mitigate considerably the disadvantages of the prevalent low cloud and poor visibility'. They reanalysed the meteorological data from the site and concluded that 'while a large proportion of instrument landings would be necessary, it would be possible to operate with safety and with reasonable regularity from Ballygarvan if runways were fully equipped with radio and lighting aids'. In conclusion, the report noted that while the combination of meteorological and topographical conditions in the Cork area made it unfavourable to the establishment of an airport, and that neither Midleton nor Ballygarvan were particularly 'good sites', they felt that 'on the balance, Ballygarvan is the better of the two'.[48]

The writing seemed on the wall for Midleton. An interdepartmental committee that had been considering the issue met on 16 October 1953 (coincidentally, eight years to the day before Cork Airport was officially opened) to consider various estimates and reports, technical and administrative, and decided that 'a submission would be made to the Government recommending the construction of an airport at Ballygarvan'.[49] In November 1953 Lemass admitted to the Dáil that while meteorological considerations from the 1947 survey had suggested the suitability of the Midleton site,

> Meteorological conditions are only one of the factors that will determine the decision. In fact, the most important consideration must be its location in relation to the City of Cork ... meteorological considerations are less important now than they were in 1947, because various navigational aids which have been developed in the meantime permit of safer operations in adverse meteorological conditions than would have been possible then ... Technical and commercial considerations will determine its site.[50]

An Industry and Commerce memo to government outlined how 'Ballygarvan's natural shortcomings as an airport site can be mitigated by artificial aids to a point where it is not markedly inferior to Midleton. That being so, Ballygarvan's proximity to Cork city must, in the Minister's view, be the determining factor.'[51] On 12 January 1954 the government decided that an airport would be built at Ballygarvan, consisting of two runways of 4,500 and 3,800 feet respectively. On the recommendation of the Minister for Defence, it was decided that the airport should be planned in such a way that the main runway could be extended to 6,000 feet 'if that should be found necessary for military reasons'.[52]

Politics and procrastination

The announcement of the decision to provide Cork with an airport might have been expected to boost Fianna Fáil's prospects in the upcoming by-election in Cork city, where its candidate was Seamus Fitzgerald, who had been a prominent advocate of the Cork airport cause for many years. However, a range of issues, predominantly the appalling state of the economy, saw Fianna Fáil lose out to Fine Gael in this and another by-election in Louth. Taoiseach Éamon de Valera decided to call a general election. Despite bringing in an election budget in April, Fianna Fáil lost out in the May election and the second inter-party government (comprising Fine Gael, Labour and Clann na Talmhan) came to power, with John A. Costello as Taoiseach. The county's severe balance of payments deficit and the need to postpone a number of capital projects, such as hospital building, as well as the severe losses being made by Aer Lingus, led the new government to long-finger action on the Cork airport project. Ongoing talks with the British to amend a 1946 Anglo-Irish air agreement to facilitate the operation of a full airport in Cork provided cover for the government's procrastination throughout 1955 and 1956. In October 1956, the Minister for Industry and Commerce, Labour's William Norton, told the Dáil under questioning that the 'Cork Airport project is under active consideration at present, following the conclusion of the new air agreement with Great Britain, but I cannot, at this stage, say when it will be possible for me to make any announcement on the subject'. When Fianna

Fáil's Jack Lynch asked 'whether or not there is agreement amongst the members of the Government as to the future of this project', Norton refused to answer.[53] According to an east Cork journalist writing in the *Southern Star*, 'the saga of the airport is a tale of political three-card juggling in which the right card is always turned up by the party in power and the other two cards by the opposition and the taxpayers'.[54]

It appears that Minister for Health T. F. O'Higgins and Minister for Finance Gerard Sweetman, both of Fine Gael, were amongst those opposed, with the latter submitting a memo to government in December 1956 (having withdrawn it in early 1955 pending the conclusion of the Anglo-Irish discussions) opposing the Cork airport project.[55] The memo pointed to the drain on resources represented already by Dublin and Shannon, and outlined how 'the economics of providing an airport at Cork … are patently unsound', particularly given the government's policy of 'ensuring that capital investment is directed only to projects likely to yield a direct and worthwhile benefit to the national economy'. It was argued that the need for an airport at Cork 'has been assumed rather than demonstrated' and Sweetman recommended that 'the Government should resist the local pressure for a State owned and operated airport at Cork and reject the proposal or, at least, postpone it indefinitely'.[56] At a government meeting of 15 January 1957,

(1) it was agreed, in principle, that an airport should be constructed at Ballygarvan, Co. Cork ; and

(2) it was decided that action to give effect to the decision … should be taken at such a time as may be determined, by the Government, as being appropriate in the light of the financial situation.[57]

It seemed as if Cork would never get its airport. In the meantime, the Cork Airways Company continued its campaign to have a licence granted to it to operate scheduled services,[58] and beyond this, for the Farmer's Cross airfield to be developed into a full commercial airport (though, admittedly one that could facilitate only smaller planes such as Vikings, which carried thirty-six passengers), rather than spending the estimated £1 million in starting from scratch on a site only half a mile away. The company's proposal was supported by Cork Corporation, but consistently resisted by the Department.[59]

The country's 'financial situation' continued to deteriorate, with unemployment, emigration and the balance of payments deficit reaching record levels in 1956–57. Fianna Fáil tabled a no-confidence motion in the government in late January 1957, Costello dissolved the Dáil rather than risk defeat in the vote, and a general election was held on 5 March 1957. The new departure in Irish economic policy – involving closer integration into the European and world economies via foreign direct investment and export-led growth – about to be heralded by Lemass was prominent in his election speeches and policy documents. Fianna Fáil won a comfortable majority, Lemass resumed at Industry and Commerce (he would replace de Valera as Taoiseach in 1959) and T. K. Whitaker was already in place as a dynamic and outward-looking Secretary of the Department of Finance. The stage was set for Lemass to deliver on the commitment he made before he left office in 1954.

After three decades of plans, promises, false dawns and frustration, the 'prehistory' of Cork airport had finally come to an end; the history of Cork airport was about to begin.

THE 'FIRST CORK AIRPORT'

Cork Airways Company and the Farmer's Cross airfield, 1947–1960

All attempts to persuade the state authorities to develop an airport in Cork in the years after the end of the Second World War were continually frustrated, and even though meteorological observation stations had been set up at the proposed Farmer's Cross/Ballygarvan and Ahanesk sites in 1946, many despaired of ever seeing a Cork Airport. In 1947 two prominent Cork businessmen, George Heffernan and Dan Cullinane, joined forces and decided to form a company to establish a private airport to serve the needs of Cork. George Heffernan was a well-established shipping and travel agent and as early as August 1947 had organised a pilgrimage charter flight from Shannon to Lourdes. The potential for pilgrimage flights shown by Heffernan persuaded the French authorities to develop the former military airfield at Tarbes, a short distance from Lourdes, as the airport for the pilgrimage site. Dan Cullinane had a thriving stevedoring business in Cork and both men brought their many years of experience together when they formed the Cork Airways Company (CAC) in 1947. They acquired a twenty-five year lease on land at Farmer's Cross, opposite the present-day main entrance to Cork Airport, where the Cork Aero Club had been based from its inception in 1934 until it was wound up in 1942. The new company was granted an aerodrome licence in 1948 after the site was brought to the standard demanded by the Department of Industry and Commerce. A large number of trees had to be removed to clear the approach, and a grass runway of 860 yards in length and 260 yards in width, running from east to west, was prepared. The airfield was officially opened on Sunday 9 May 1948 by Liam Cosgrave TD, parliamentary secretary (junior minister) at the Department of Industry and Commerce, watched by a large crowd. Six planes had flown in to the airfield for the opening celebrations and 560 people were brought on pleasure flights over the city during that weekend.[60]

The principals of the CAC and the many campaigners for an airport in Cork were encouraged by the words of Liam Cosgrave in his opening address. It was government policy, he said, 'to encourage and assist private enterprise' and he was 'very pleased to see private enterprise and private flying fields play a major part in the development of civil aviation in this country'.[61] The new aviation company was optimistic that it would be permitted to run scheduled services from the new airfield even though its initial licence restricted it to non-scheduled flights in daylight hours only, which limited the commercial activity to private and small chartered passenger flights. The airfield had no permanent buildings or staff and was only manned when a flight was due to land or depart, or when air shows and pleasure flights were organised at weekends. From as early as 1949 Cambrian Air Services offered to operate a daily service between Farmer's Cross and Cardiff, using an eight-seater Rapide aircraft, having successfully used a similar aircraft for a number of chartered flights to Cork the previous summer. Other companies were also interested in operating cross-channel scheduled services from the Cork airfield. The CAC wanted to develop its airfield to take larger aircraft, but it was stymied in its wishes in that scheduled air traffic would be necessary to generate the profits for reinvesting in the upgrade work, something that would not be allowed on the airfield as it was. The company and local TDs lobbied government, especially Liam Cosgrave, in an effort to acquire a licence for scheduled services, but Cosgrave would not accede to the demands. Speaking in the Dáil on 22 February 1950 he explained why the licence was refused: the Anglo-Irish Air Agreement of 1946 'did not contemplate that airlines other than Aer Lingus should operate scheduled services between the two countries', and the airfield lacked the meteorological station necessary to satisfy international aviation requirements. In addition, the government felt that it could not justify the expenditure for a meteorological station at the airfield.[62]

George Heffernan thought that Cosgrave's explanation did not tell the full story, as he set out in a letter to a colleague, written in March 1950:

> If he [Cosgrave] could disconnect our application from the bug-bear of Aer Lingus losses, he may have a clearer vision of things. Our enterprise is a private one and if any loss is incurred the private concerns are prepared to bear same. There is of course the danger that a private concern might show a working profit and that would naturally reflect on State operated companies. Is the Minister afraid of this?[63]

Ted O'Sullivan, the present owner of the land, stands by the former runway of Farmer's Cross airfield. Cork Airport tower, about half a mile to the west, is visible to the right.

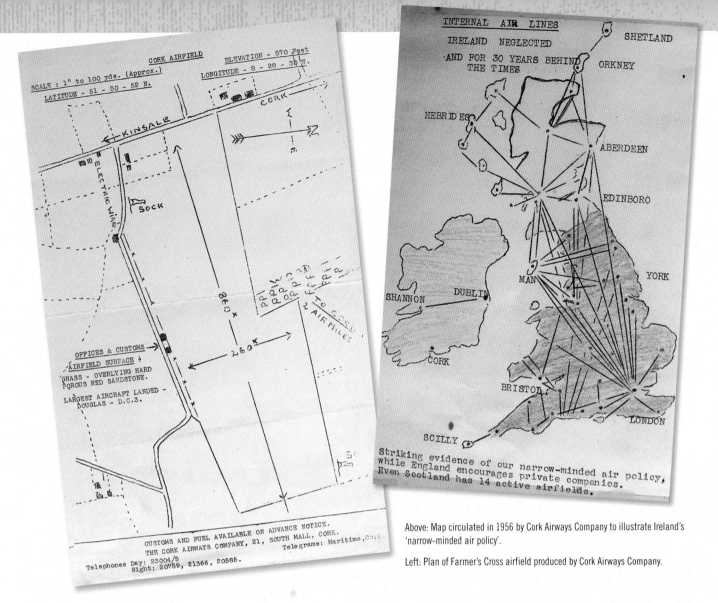

CORK AIRFIELD ELEVATION - 570 Feet
SCALE : 1" to 100 yds. (Approx.)
LONGITUDE - 8 - 28 - 30 W.
LATITUDE - 51 - 50 - 52 N.

KINSALE
CORK
ELECTRIC WIRE
SOCK
TO CORK
2 AIR MILES

OFFICES & CUSTOMS
AIRFIELD SURFACE
GRASS - OVERLYING HARD
POROUS RED SANDSTONE.
LARGEST AIRCRAFT LANDED -
DOUGLAS - D.C.3.

CUSTOMS AND FUEL AVAILABLE ON ADVANCE NOTICE.
THE CORK AIRWAYS COMPANY, 21, SOUTH MALL, CORK.
Telegrams: Maritime, Cork.
Telephones Day: 23004/5
Night: 20759, 21366, 20585.

INTERNAL AIR LINES
IRELAND NEGLECTED
AND FOR 30 YEARS BEHIND
THE TIMES
SHETLAND
ORKNEY
HEBRIDES
ABERDEEN
EDINBORO
SHANNON DUBLIN
MAN
YORK
CORK
BRISTOL
LONDON
SCILLY

Striking evidence of our narrow-minded air policy,
while England encourages private companies.
Even Scotland has 14 active airfields.

Above: Map circulated in 1956 by Cork Airways Company to illustrate Ireland's 'narrow-minded air policy'.

Left: Plan of Farmer's Cross airfield produced by Cork Airways Company.

Cork TDs Jack Lynch, Patrick McGrath, James Hickey and Patrick Lehane continued to lobby and speak in the Dáil on behalf of the CAC, but to no avail. In December 1950 Cosgrave again stated why Farmer's Cross could not be licensed for scheduled services: 'the facilities available at the airfield are not adequate and fall substantially below the internationally recognised standards for regular services. There has not been any relaxation in the international standards for safety.'[64] In 1951 a Fianna Fáil government took office, but there was no change in attitude. Seán Lemass, as Minister for Industry and Commerce, continued to repeat the line taken by his predecessors in refusing to grant a licence for scheduled flights. Patrick Lehane, an independent TD for the Cork South constituency (he had represented Clann na Talmhan in the 1948–1951 Dáil), made most of the running, speaking on numerous occasions between 1951 and 1954 in support of the CAC's demands. While the standard of facilities at Farmer's Cross was undoubtedly an issue, the position of Aer Lingus was also highly relevant, a point repeatedly made by

Lehane. On 28 November 1951 he pressed Lemass on the matter: 'Is the Minister not aware that Aer Lingus has adopted a dog in the manger attitude in respect to air services to Cork? They will not undertake them themselves and will not permit other companies or the Cork Airways Company to inaugurate their own services.' Lemass replied that the question of scheduled air services for Cork was being examined by Aer Rianta and he reaffirmed the primacy of Aer Lingus, saying, 'As far as I am concerned I want to be quite clear. As long as the present position continues I would wish to see all [scheduled] services in this country and with Great Britain operated by Aer Lingus.'[65]

While the campaign for scheduled services from the Farmer's Cross airfield continued, government thinking in relation to the provision of a 'proper' airport for Cork was changing and a decision in principle to give Cork such an airport was made in late 1952. It was not clear when or where the airport would be built, however, and in the meantime the airfield at Farmer's Cross provided Cork's only air link. Between 1948 and 1952 over 300 planes had

used the airfield and the owners felt that the Department of Industry and Commerce was being unreasonable in its refusal to allow scheduled flights.[66] The CAC also felt that an upgrading and expansion of its airfield would give Cork the airport it wanted at a fraction of the cost, estimated to be in the region of £1 million, of a newly built facility. In September 1952 the company circulated an illustrated booklet, *The Case for Cork Airfield*, outlining the history of the airfield and its claim for scheduled services.

The ongoing growth in commercial passenger aviation and the development of larger aircraft demanded increasingly larger and more sophisticated airports, and it was more and more unlikely that Farmer's Cross airfield would satisfy those needs, even in an upgraded and expanded state. A government report of 1953 shows that even then there was little or no possibility of the airfield becoming Cork's airport. The report on possible sites for an airport found that the airfield, sited on a hilltop plateau, did not have the necessary surrounding space for the construction of sufficiently

Bishop of Cork and Ross,
Cornelius Lucey (fourth from left) with the Papal Nuncio to Ireland,
Bishop Gerald O'Hara (sixth from left), at Farmer's Cross in the early 1950s. *IRISH EXAMINER*

long runways and that 'owing to the steep slopes downwards from the edges of the plateau, the installation of approach lighting and radio aids would be virtually impossible'. In January 1954 the decision was made to site the new Cork airport about half a mile west of Farmer's Cross and that effectively sealed the long-term fate of the airfield.[67]

Nevertheless, the CAC continued to function, maintained its demands for a licence for scheduled services, and retained a hope that its airfield would be upgraded as Cork's airport. In December 1955 the company once more wrote to the government and to the elected representatives of the Labour Party in Cork setting out again the reasons why the Farmer's Cross airfield could be developed as Cork's airport. 'The cost of developing Farmer's Cross would not amount to one-tenth the expense envisaged in starting a new airport only half a mile distance from ours'; the letter continued:

> We are responsible for the development of aviation in Cork over the past seven years and resent the fact that so many misleading statements on a Cork airport have been published within the past few years. We feel that our personal experience of Farmer's Cross, supported by outside surveyors, places us in a

much sounder position as to its possibilities than a few days survey by our Department officials, on which the Minister seems to rely solely... It is now a question of using the existing site at a nominal cost as compared with a grandiose scheme which must be borne by the ratepayers of this area and which cannot be made a paying proposition for many years ahead.[68]

In April 1956 Jean Davey, secretary of the company, wrote to the national newspapers accusing William Norton, Minister for Industry and Commerce, of 'political delaying tactics' in not finalising amendments to the 1946 Anglo-Irish Air Agreement that would allow airlines other than Aer Lingus to operate cross-channel flights. Such an amendment

would give the CAC an opportunity to expand as at least two British aviation companies wanted to run scheduled services from Farmer's Cross. Such services would, according to Davey, bring an extra 20,000 tourists into the Cork region. 'It is hard to understand,' she wrote, 'why a Government elected by the people of this country should go to such extremes in preventing a development which ... would be of considerable benefit to our nation'.[69] Later in 1956 she wrote in a letter to the press that Farmer's Cross could be enlarged 'at little cost' to enable it to handle up to 36-seater aircraft, a capacity deemed sufficient to satisfy demand on cross-channel routes.[70]

Also in 1956 Air Kruises (Ireland) Ltd was formed and in cooperation with the CAC announced plans to

Newspaper advertisement from 25 June 1956, part of the Cork Airways Company campaign for proper air services from Cork.

CORK AIRFIELD

Study Posters on Summer Hill and Southern Road

Irish Ratepayers give £420,000 for Shannon and Dublin
this year
NOTHING FOR CORK

Corkmen can help. Write to your T.D. about it

The Cork Airways Company
21 SOUTH MALL, CORK

TELEPHONE 24802

develop the Farmer's Cross airfield, involving the purchase of additional land, the laying of longer, better-surfaced runways, one of 1,100 yards and another of 930 yards, and the building of a small terminal. A flying club was also to be established on the site. By that time, upwards of 400 chartered flights had used the airfield and the plan was to operate an increased level of such services to Britain and Europe.[71] The development did not materialise, but the airfield continued to be used on an occasional basis for the following four years until Cork Airport opened in October 1961.

In an interview with the *Cork Examiner* on 5 January 1960, when the building of Cork Airport was under way, George Heffernan was adamant that the Farmer's Cross airfield could have been upgraded to fulfil the aviation needs of Cork – 'an airport suitable to the needs of the city could have been built at Farmer's Cross for £100,000', he said. He felt that the CAC had played a major part in getting Cork its new airport. 'The events during the past ten years have made the people of Cork air-minded,' he said, '… if this small airfield had not been going, there would have been no talk of a major airport today.'

Later the same year Heffernan appealed to the government for compensation for the loss of £3,900 his company had incurred in maintaining the airfield at Farmer's Cross for twelve years and facilitating over 500 charter flights. He felt that it was as a result of government restrictions that the airfield was never able to earn a profit and that his company's pioneering work was now to benefit the new airport: 'Had we not striven during these 12 years to direct attention to prospects in this area, we doubt if the new airport would receive the support which we are now satisfied that we can bring it.'[72] The request was refused, but Heffernan persisted. Three years later, at a time when the new airport was two years in service, his plea was still being made and still being refused. In a letter to the Taoiseach in September 1963 he detailed some of the expenditure his company incurred, which was, he claimed, of direct benefit to the new airport – the removal of trees that would have affected the approach from the east to Runway 07 at a cost of £600, for example. He also mentioned the promise of support he felt his company had been given by Liam Cosgrave in 1948, only to be disappointed: 'Now we are driven out of

business by the semi-state Aer Lingus which took over.' He asked, in vain, that an arbitration board be established to adjudicate on his claims.[73]

The request for compensation for losses aside, George Heffernan and the Cork Airways Company did have justification for some of their claims. There can be little doubt that they created an interest in and an awareness of aviation in Cork in the thirteen years from 1948 that worked to the advantage of the new airport. Tourism in the south benefited from the admittedly restricted chartered tourist flights that used Farmer's Cross and the general public of Cork had the opportunity of going to the airfield when pleasure flights or air shows were organised. The impact of even such a limited airfield on the attractions of aviation is illustrated by the memories of long-time Douglas resident Ogie O'Callaghan, in recalling her confirmation day in the spring of 1950. She remembers being given a choice of treats on her 'special day' – a meal in a city-centre hotel or a trip to the Farmer's Cross airfield in the hope of seeing a plane land or take off. She chose the latter.[74]

A group photographed at Farmer's Cross on 18 December 1955. (L–r:
Air Chief Marshal J. H. Edwards-Jones; D. A. Cullinane; Jean Davey (Secretary, Cork Airways Company); Dan Cullinane (Cork Airways Company);
Lady Jennifer Bernard; Air Marshal Sir Thomas Pike; J. R. Judge; Lord Bandon; A. F. Burke (Managing Director, de Havilland Engine Co.) *IRISH EXAMINER*

Construction gets under way at Cork Airport in 1960. *IRISH EXAMINER*

DELAYED ARRIVAL
CORK AIRPORT IS BORN
1958–61

SEÁN LEMASS, as Minister for Industry and Commerce, had proposals for an airport at Cork on his desk on numerous occasions since 1932. When the airport finally materialised, it coincided neatly with his ascent to Taoiseach and the new departure in Irish socio-economic life that he heralded. What more fitting symbol of Lemass's new, outward-looking, 'modern', internationalised Ireland than a new airport, which extended the internal air network and connected the south of the country to the wider world? At a practical level, the utility of an additional Irish airport at a time when exports were about to increase, multinational investment was being invited in, and tourist traffic was on the rise, was obvious.

Lemass was the guest speaker at the Cork Chamber of Commerce annual dinner in February 1958. He told the businessmen that Bord Fáilte, the tourism board, had estimated that the new airport would expand tourism income in the south by 25 per cent, making the expenditure on it 'a productive investment of the most important character'. The provision of an airport at Cork was, according to Lemass, a contribution to the region's long-term economic development, as well as being of immediate benefit to the tourist trade. He promised it would be of 'continental standard' and, like Dublin, service British and European traffic, as well as possibly linking up with Dublin and Shannon, although he added that air transport at that stage was not really competitive with land transport for distances under 200 miles.[1] A few days later the government announced that the planning of the new airport would be completed by the year's end: the land was being acquired and construction was due to start in early 1959, so that the airport would be ready in 1961.[2] The initial timetable envisaged completion of plans by October 1958, the issuing of contracts in early 1959 and completion of runways in February 1961. In late October 1958, due to engineering staff shortages and design difficulties related to the topography of the site, completion of plans was put back to February 1959, with knock-on delays meaning a provisional airport completion date of May 1961.[3]

Seán Lemass, Minister for Industry and Commerce, 1932–39, 1941–48, 1951–54 and 1957–59 and Taoiseach 1959–66, a crucial figure in the eventual decision to establish Cork Airport.

Dan Crowley, 107 acres of whose land were compulsorily acquired to facilitate the building of the airport.
IRISH EXAMINER

Left: Winifred Cottrell, whose farm made up much of the land now occupied by Cork Airport.
IRISH EXAMINER

Below: Winifred Cottrell's house, which lay to the south of the present airport access road.
IRISH EXAMINER

'The Steppes of Russia came to mind': land acquisition and surveys

Sufficient land was required not just for terminal buildings, runways, and so on, but for potential expansion and development in the future. Almost 500 acres were acquired by the Land Commission at a cost of over £40,000 (the estimated total cost of the airport was £1 million), consisting of three major holdings of 186, 129 and 107 acres respectively, four smaller holdings of 5 to 26 acres, and three 1-acre Cork County Council plots with cottages. Engineers Edwin McCarthy and Brendan Clancy began a survey of the site in March 1958, led by Pat Hackett, who remembered the 'amazing sight' that greeted them on first visiting the site – 'wheat to the right, left and as far as the eye could see in all directions. The Steppes of Russia came to mind.'[4] Headquarters were established at a central location in an outhouse in the former farmyard of the Cottrell family (the largest of the original landowners) in Lehanaghmore, and a team of workers, twenty at its peak, was recruited through the Employment Exchange, providing the first tangible economic benefit of the airport to the broader Cork community. The men were paid the agricultural labourer rate of £8 per week. Pat Hackett recalled that after about three months, bad weather had slowed progress and reinforcements, in the shape of two additional engineers, were required. At least three of the original survey work crew went on to find employment at the airport: Ger Kelleher, later employed in ground maintenance; Barry Cullinane, who went on to work in the electrical section; and D. D. O'Leary, who later became maintenance supervisor for Aer Rianta at the airport.[5]

In July 1959 the government put out the call for tenders for the construction of runways, taxiways, apron and approach road, and in October the contract was awarded to John Paul &

Cork Airport Delayed By Weather

At question time in the Dail yesterday, the Minister for Transport and Power, Mr. Childers, told Deputies A. A. Healy (F.F.) and Sean Casey (Lab) that owing to the very adverse weather conditions since work started on the

Weather held up work on Cork Airport

THE report of the council to be presented to the Cork Chamber of Commerce at its 141st annual general meeting to-morrow states that due to the abnormal amount

January Rainfall Second Highest Since Records Began

Fall Of 9-14 Inches Recorded

THE rainfall for January, officials at the Meteorology Section

Another Night Of Gales

Wettest November For Almost 20 Years

Vessels Take Shelter

Co. of Dublin; the contract completion date was 31 July 1961.[6] In early November 1959 heavy machinery and fuel tanks were moved onto the site, and work began under the overall supervision of T. L. Hogan, Chief Airports Engineer at the Department of Transport and Power, a new department established in July 1959 by Lemass following his appointment as Taoiseach. The first Minister for Transport and Power, who now had responsibility for the airport project, was Erskine Childers, later President of Ireland. There was widespread welcome in Cork for the news that work on the airport was finally beginning. Seamus Fitzgerald, a long-time champion of the cause, hailed the 'very excellent news', pointing to the incentive to industrialists an airport would provide, and referring to Cork having suffered because of its lack of one. J. M. Sutton of the Chamber of Commerce mentioned the advantages for Cork business people, who would now be able to make day-trips to London, as opposed to the three-day journey it hitherto involved. Referring to tourism, he said he had often met transatlantic liner passengers who would have stayed in Cork had air facilities direct from Cork been available to them.[7]

The Irish weather is rarely a selling point in Irish tourism, and that notorious creature was the main culprit in causing delays in the project over the coming year, rousing Cork ire and complaint yet again.

More delays

The year following the beginning of construction was the wettest of the century to that point. In the twelve months following the onset of work in November 1959, there were 183 wet days, during which 57 inches of rain fell. There was 39 per cent more rain than average between January and October 1960, and 70 per cent above normal in the July to October period.[8] According to the senior engineers who oversaw the project, 'weather conditions greatly affected progress with the excavation and filling'. Filling could not commence until April 1960, and had to be suspended again in October, not to be resumed until the spring of 1961.[9] While the weather was blamed by the engineers and the government for the delays, some in Cork saw it as just another excuse in the sorry saga that had been dragging on for three decades. The mood was captured by the *Cork Examiner* in March 1960, following the news that the airport was running behind schedule and the more likely completion date was August 1961, which would mean missing the summer season:

The entire project of Cork Airport has been dogged by delays and disappointments since it was first put forward nearly thirty years ago. It is difficult, indeed, to refrain from expressing resentment at the dilatory fashion in which it

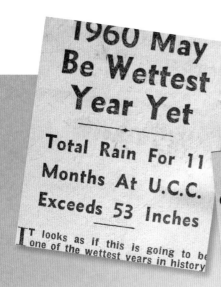

has been handled by the authorities in Dublin. There were innumerable postponements before it was finally conceded that Cork had an unanswerable case for an airport of its own. Then came prolonged investigations in to possible sites before at last Ballygarvan was selected ... three more years followed before land for the airport was acquired [followed by] ... another two years of planning and speculation ... if only the authorities in Dublin had some of the vision and faith in the future that Cork businessmen had, this city would have had a flourishing airport long before now.

The leader-writer urged Cork's public representatives to 'urge on the Minister for Transport and Power by every means at their disposal the urgency of having this work completed in time ... Cork has waited too long already for its airport; the public should not tolerate any more delays.'[10]

Progress was slow but steady. The ESB removed 10 miles of electricity lines and re-erected them clear of the airport site. About 11 miles of banks, hedges and walls and approximately 500 trees were removed and several houses demolished. It was necessary to strip and replace 170,000 cubic yards of topsoil and excavate and place infill of 820,000 cubic yards of earth and rock.[11] By June 1960, a major portion of the approach road had been constructed, preliminary drainage and fencing work was completed, and construction of the runways, taxiways and apron was under way. The Minister told the Dáil that he was 'doing everything possible' to see that the target of July 1961 was achieved: 'Every contractor has been made aware that every day saved adds to the value of the first year's aircraft movements, but inclement weather is an unpredictable factor'.[12] A week later tragedy struck when a 28-year-old worker on the site, Michael Joseph O'Connor from Enniskeane, died when the tipper of his lorry came into contact with an overhead electric cable.[13] At that stage over 150 men were employed on the site, a majority of whom had been previously on the dole.[14]

In July 1960 the £300,000 contract for constructing the main buildings (terminal, control tower, boiler house, freight building) was awarded to another Dublin-based firm (though its three directors were from County Cork), John Jones Ltd, the contract for the structural steelwork having already been awarded to a Carlow firm, Thomas Thompson Ltd.[15] In August 1960 Cambrian Airways of Wales received British government approval for its proposed links between Cork and London, Bristol, Swansea and Cardiff.[16] The Cork Examiner reported in September that progress on the airport was 'tedious and undramatic' but steady, and in October Aer Lingus published its proposed air fares from Cork, covering Barcelona, Birmingham,

Aerial view of the two runways and terminal buildings under construction, from the northeast, October 1960. *IRISH EXAMINER*

Blackpool, Bristol, Cardiff, Edinburgh, Glasgow, Isle of Man, Jersey, Leeds, Lisbon, Liverpool, London, Lourdes, Manchester and Paris.[17] All plans were thrown into turmoil when, a week later, Erskine Childers announced in the Dáil that: 'Owing to the very adverse weather conditions experienced in the Cork area since work commenced at the Airport site last November it will not be possible to have the constructional work completed by the contract completion date of the end of July.'[18] A statement from his department in early November put the completion date as 'about the end of 1961', with limited services commencing on 1 September 1961.[19]

'A race against time'

The year 1960 had been the wettest in Cork for seventy-six years.[20] The rain continued to fall in January 1961, and the *Evening Echo* reported that there had been only one rainless week in Cork

Aerial view of the two runways and terminal buildings under construction, from the west, October 1960. *IRISH EXAMINER*

since the previous July. Work continued, however, and in January Cork Corporation and the County Council began work on the approach roads. Newspapers carried the first advertisements for farms and houses that indicated their distance from Cork Airport, and Aer Lingus declared 1961 as 'Cork's year'. The company announced its initial services, to begin on 1 September. These were: a daily Viscount service between Cork and London; a twice-weekly Cork–Bristol–Cardiff service; a Cork–Paris service on weekdays, and a

Cork–Dublin service four days a week. The British routes would be operated in a pool with Cambrian Airways.[21] In February the first appointment proper of the new airport was made when Cork man Jack McGrath, who had been employed in the aviation radio section at Dublin Airport, became officer-in-charge of communications, including radio navigation and landing aids, and began overseeing the installation of as much equipment as possible, seeing as many of the main buildings, such as the control tower, were not yet

Tower and terminal building under construction, from the west, June 1961. CORK AIRPORT

complete. The rain poured down in record quantities again in April 1961 as the government confirmed that the airport in Cork would be managed by the Department of Transport and Power, which also ran Shannon – Dublin alone at this stage was managed by Aer Rianta – and named the airport's first manager, Vincent Fanning (aged thirty-nine), a senior civil servant in the civil aviation division of the department.[22]

Vincent Fanning, Airport Manager 1961–67.

'Men at work' on Cork Airport construction, 1960–61. *IRISH EXAMINER*

'Men at work' on Cork Airport construction, 1960–61. CORK AIRPORT

Crisis Point Nears In Cement Strike

Opening Of Cork Airport May Be Delayed

arge Scale Lay Off Of Men Seems Likely

RISIS point will be reached in a matter of a week or so in the cement strike position which has already caused unemployment thousands of building workers and is holding up construction work l over the country.

ports from building contractors ended. Already the firm has had to men affected in Cork City as a resu ork indicate that to keep workers lay

---

Cork Airport

Should Be Operational In Time For 1961 Tourist Season

Cork's New Airport Is Rapidly Taking Shape

CONSIDERABLE progress has been made on Cork's new airport, which is planned to come into operation in

total cost of the whole scheme will be £95,000. Five houses will have to be demolished to make way for the new road and telephones lines will also have to be

---

Cork's airport reaches the halfway mark

MORE than 150 men—many of them from Cork's unemployed — have now worked their way through nearly half of the £2,000,000 Cork Airport, scheduled to open next year.

Cork airport operations to begin on Oct. 16

IRISH PRESS Reporter

"WE will start operations as scheduled on October 16," was the confident prediction of youthful Jerry Houlihan, Assistant Manager at Cork Airport yesterday. He was watching, from his office in an old farmhouse on the site, an army of 350 men aided by heavy machinery shatter the stillness of the Cork hills in their race against time.

route with Aer Lingus but the other companies have not disclosed details of their services yet.

MORE BUSINESS

Initially it is expected that 30,000 travellers a year will pass through the airport but within five years this number may well be sixty thousand.

THE CORK EXAMINER WEDNESDAY, MAY 10, 1961

Cement Strike Hits Building Trade

Labour Court Investigates Claim By 650 Workers

WHILE the building trade through

strongly supported by the fact that there was an equal willingness both parties to reach a negotia solution.

Mr. Cuffe said that the compa felt that the present conflict shou have been avoided. They had go very far during the protract negotiations to achieve agreement It was, in the company's opini only fair that their workers shou

---

CORK AIRPORT RACE AGAINST TIME

Services may start on October 16th

Irish Times Reporter

ALTHOUGH Aer Lingus and Cambrian Airways are planning to start services from the new Cork airport on October 16th,

One step forward was, as ever with Cork Airport, followed rapidly by two steps back when, on 29 April, the delivery of cement to the site ceased due to a nationwide strike by workers at the cement factories. As there was no significant stock in reserve, all construction work involving the use of cement practically halted for the next five weeks. Huge quantities of cement were required for the construction of the runways, taxi-strips and aircraft parking aprons, as well as the new road to the airport. The total paving area was over 220,000 square yards and the runway concrete was a foot thick, requiring the placing of 62,260 cubic yards of concrete.[23] The 1 September deadline could not now be met, and following the end of the strike and resumption of supplies in early June, which coincided with the arrival – finally – of good weather, the government announced a new opening date for restricted services of 16 October 1961.[24]

Among those whose plans were thrown into disarray by this most recent setback were the organisers of the Sixth Cork Film Festival, which was to run from 27 September to 4 October. The festival had planned to capitalise on its first opportunity to fly attendees directly to Cork, and had advertised package tours incorporating season tickets, accommodation and flights. Over 40,000 leaflets were distributed in the UK, mainly via the film societies there.[25] The festival, which had been running since 1956, had been hampered in its efforts to attract overseas guests and audiences by the lack of a local airport; 'just when the problem appeared to be solved,' wrote 'Stephen' in the *Cork Examiner*, 'along comes the Department to wreck their plans.'[26] About a dozen packages had been sold when the announcement was made that forced the festival to abandon the air travel aspect (there was also a cheaper ferry option in the offer). Following lobbying of the Minister by festival director Der Breen, Aer Lingus agreed to fly those who had already booked to Dublin, and transfer them to Cork by train at no extra cost.[27]

Tadg Lynch, first Aer Lingus Station Manager at Cork Airport. *IRISH EXAMINER*

In July Aer Lingus announced the appointment of Tadg Lynch as its station superintendent at Cork, with responsibility for all the company's functions at the airport, including equipment, maintenance and traffic. Lynch was a native of

Kinsale and had been a senior duty officer with Aer Lingus at Shannon.[28] Meanwhile, a team of 250 workers was working around the clock, in what the media described as 'a race against time', to meet the deadline of 16 October. By the end of July the 6,000-foot, north–south main runway was complete and the 4,300-foot, east–west second runway was nearly ready. The apron and taxiway were progressing, and the 80-foot-high, six-storey control building was nearing completion, as was the new roadway from the city.[29]

One of the new Airport Manager's first meetings was with Cornelius Lucey, Catholic Bishop of Cork and Ross. Lucey requested that an oratory be provided in the terminal building as, according to Fanning, 'he felt that many people would like to say a last-minute prayer before embarking on a flight'. He was told that it was not possible to alter the design at this stage, but was offered a site for a chapel. The bishop rejected the offer, as the proposed site was outside the terminal building and 'passengers might not be disposed to visit it, lest they might miss their flight'. Lucey then asked about flights to Lourdes, which the manager explained was a matter for Aer Lingus, and that he would raise it with them.[30]

Dark clouds

Just one month before the airport was due to open a storm of hurricane-force winds struck Ireland on Friday and Saturday, 15 and 16 September 1961. Fifteen people were killed across the country in storm-related incidents and two trawlers were lost off the southwest coast. The almost completed buildings at Cork Airport did not escape damage – a 60-foot-high steel crane was blown over and it collapsed onto the roof of the main terminal building, badly damaging the roof of the observation lounge. Nobody was injured, but the already tight schedule for the completion of works

During a storm on the night of 15–16 September 1961, a crane was toppled by high winds, damaging part of the almost completed terminal roof. CORK AIRPORT

came under great pressure as a further delay to the airport's opening could not be countenanced.

The Irish public's confidence in the safety of air travel was severely dented in the weeks before the airport's opening. In the early hours of 10 September an American DC-6 airliner crashed into the estuary of the River Shannon shortly after take-off from Shannon Airport, killing the eighty-three passengers and crew on board. The plane belonged to President Airlines and was en route

Wreckage of the President Airlines DC-6 that crashed at Shannon on 10 September 1961, killing all eighty-three people on board. *IRISH EXAMINER*

from Dusseldorf in Germany to its eventual destination of Chicago. It had stopped at Shannon for refuelling. This was the biggest loss of life in a single aircrash in 1961, a year in which 1,196 people lost their lives in twenty-six fatal passenger aircraft losses. Only nine days later, on 19 September, a Starways DC-4 airliner crashed onto the Dublin–Belfast road after it left the runway, having landed at Dublin Airport. There were sixty-nine passengers and crew on the chartered plane that was returning with pilgrims from Lourdes. There were no fatalities in the incident. In the previous year, on 26 February 1960, thirty-four people lost their lives when an Alitalia plane crashed shortly after taking off from Shannon. These incidents were widely covered in the press and fuelled a fear that many had of travelling by air. It was unfortunate that Cork Airport was being built during the worst two-year period for air crashes in Irish aviation history. However, the

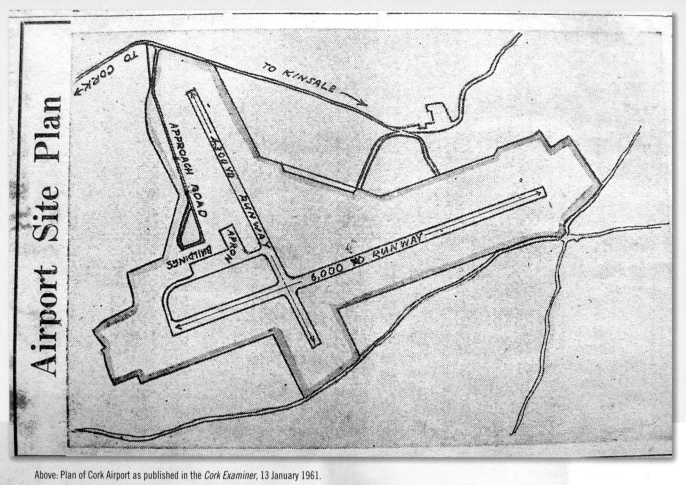

Above: Plan of Cork Airport as published in the *Cork Examiner*, 13 January 1961.

Below: Architect's drawing of the tower and terminal buildings at Cork Airport.

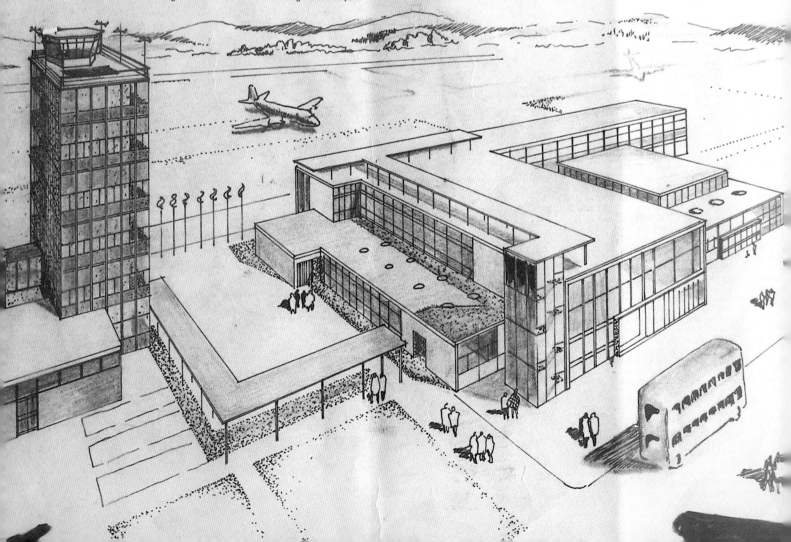

much-publicised advances in space travel at the time created a sense that exploration and adventure were very much alive: in April 1961 Yuri Gagarin became the first person in space, and the following month Alan B. Shepard became the first US astronaut. In Ireland air travel was only beginning to become accessible to the mass of the population and for many aviation still had the allure of adventure and celebrity about it.

The Cork Airport team takes shape

In August, Gerard Holohan, a Cork man who had been based at Shannon, was appointed assistant manager of Cork Airport. He was followed by a raft of other appointments: resident engineer, Gerard Murphy, seconded from the civil works department of the ESB; his deputy, Brendan Clancy, an engineer attached to the Department of Transport and Power; Robert Howley, who had served at both Shannon and Dublin, was made officer-in-charge of air traffic control; Mick Murtagh from Crosshaven was transferred from Shannon to take charge of the meteorological office.[31] Murtagh had carried out the original meteorological survey at Ballygarvan in 1946. He recalled the bedlam that greeted him when he arrived in 1961, with builders and rubble and

temporary premises: 'Things were chaotic, but we got by.' He was assisted by Brendan Smith from Dublin headquarters in the installation work, and later two assistants, Sean McAuliffe and Denis Cahill.[32] Gerry Tracey was appointed head of the fire, rescue and security service, and his initial team of eleven, which included future Airport Manager Barry Roche, was gradually assembled. A former fireman in Limerick, Tracey recalled his first impressions of the fire station, which were 'not good': the fire appliance bays were too small, there were no gates and the interior was incomplete.

Despite all the teething problems, the various elements of the airport took shape in September. As the primary operator, Aer Lingus assembled its own team to join station superintendent Tadg Lynch, including: Thomas Foley, aircraft maintenance engineer; Brendan Cannon, station engineer; Charles Brennan, sales promotion manager; Michael Verling, reservations and passenger bookings office supervisor; and J. P .G. Fitzgerald, district sales manager. On 13 September Aer Lingus and Cambrian Airways announced in the press that 'from October 16th, Cork is only minutes away from the main British cities.'[33]

On 12 October Aer Lingus and Cambrian Airways ran proving flights to Cork airport. The

An Aer Lingus Fokker 27 Friendship lands at Cork on a proving flight from Dublin, 12 October 1961. GABRIEL DESMOND

Aer Lingus F27 Friendship 40-seater named *St Fiachra* flew from Dublin with Aer Lingus officials and journalists. The captain, William J. Martin, declared it 'a very pleasant surprise to see the airport and find it so good as it is. It is excellent from any point of view.' The *St Fiachra* was followed by Cambrian's Dakota DC-3 from Wales.[34] Both flights proved successful, and the way was clear for the grand opening of Cork Airport four days later, on 16 October 1961.

The Aer Lingus Fokker 27 Friendship on the apron at Cork Airport, 12 October 1961. *IRISH EXAMINER*

Cornelius Lucey, Bishop of Cork and Ross, blessing the airport on the morning of 16 October 1961. *IRISH EXAMINER*

Official opening, 16 October 1961

'Now, Ireland has marched a step further in the world of aviation in possessing in Cork the most modern airport in the world.'[35]

O God, who, directing all things to Thyself, hast destined all in this universe for human use, bless, we beseech Thee, this airport, its runways and equipment; so that they may minister to Thy honour and glory and, without accident, loss or peril lead to greater expedition in human affairs and foster in the minds of all the faithful who use them a longing for heavenly things ... Pour forth, we beseech Thee, Thy blessing on this airport; so that those who fly from it ... may arrive happily at their destination and return safely to their own ... O God, graciously send an angel from heaven as companion for Thy servants travelling by air and praying for thy assistance; so that they may be protected by him in all their journeyings and brought safely to their destination.[36]

With these words Bishop Cornelius Lucey accompanied by other diocesan clergy, Minister for Transport and Power Erskine Childers, and airport officials, blessed the airport facilities early on Monday morning, 16 October 1961, the day Cork Airport was officially opened. In a fateful twist, Father Edward Hegarty, one of the group attending the bishop, was to die in March 1968 in the Tuskar air crash.

Following the blessing, an Aer Lingus Viscount from Dublin landed just before 10 a.m., carrying a number of dignitaries for the official opening ceremony. The first to disembark was Taoiseach Seán Lemass; he was greeted by the Lord Mayor of Cork, Anthony Barry, accompanied by Erskine Childers, and the Airport Manager, Vincent Fanning. Also on the plane were Minister for Industry and Commerce Jack Lynch, Lord Mayor

(L–r) Kathleen Lemass, Taoiseach Seán Lemass, Lord Mayor of Cork Anthony Barry TD and Erskine Childers, Minister for Transport and Power, make their way to the terminal building for the opening ceremony, 16 October 1961. *IRISH EXAMINER*

of Dublin Robert Briscoe, a party from the Dublin Junior Chamber of Commerce, members of Aer Lingus senior management and representatives of Messrs W. & R. Jacob and Co. Ltd, the biscuit manufacturers. The dignitaries were led inside the new terminal building and up to the first floor balcony. From this vantage point overlooking the crowded concourse below, the Lord Mayor and other speakers addressed the assembly. Fianna Fáil had recently triumphed in the general election held on 4 October, and having been elected Taoiseach one week later, Seán Lemass had appointed his

government ministers, including local TD Jack Lynch as Minister for Industry and Commerce. The Lord Mayor, an opposition Fine Gael TD, was magnanimous in his words of praise for Lemass: 'it is particularly appropriate for the head of government to attend because we all realise, no matter which way we are pigeon-holed politically, that he is the particular architect of our eminence in the air.' The Lord Mayor reflected the attitude of most Cork people to their city's belated direct connection to international air travel: 'Cork is now moving with giant strides into the contemporary

Erskine Childers TD, Minister for Transport and Power, speaking at the official opening of the airport from the balcony over the concourse, 16 October 1961. *IRISH EXAMINER*

world. We are facing a great period of expansion and the airport is an intrinsic adjunct to this progress'.[37]

Erskine Childers spoke next and outlined the necessity of an airport to Cork's growing significance as a commercial and industrial centre. He also saw it as a potential catalyst for growth in the southern region, especially in the area of tourism: 'There is no better way of assisting farmers, big and small, than by bringing tourists to consume Cork's unrivalled agricultural produce close at hand to the farmers' fields,' he remarked, highlighting the importance and potential attraction of the local producer that is such a key part of food marketing and promotion today, especially in the Cork region. As the guests left the

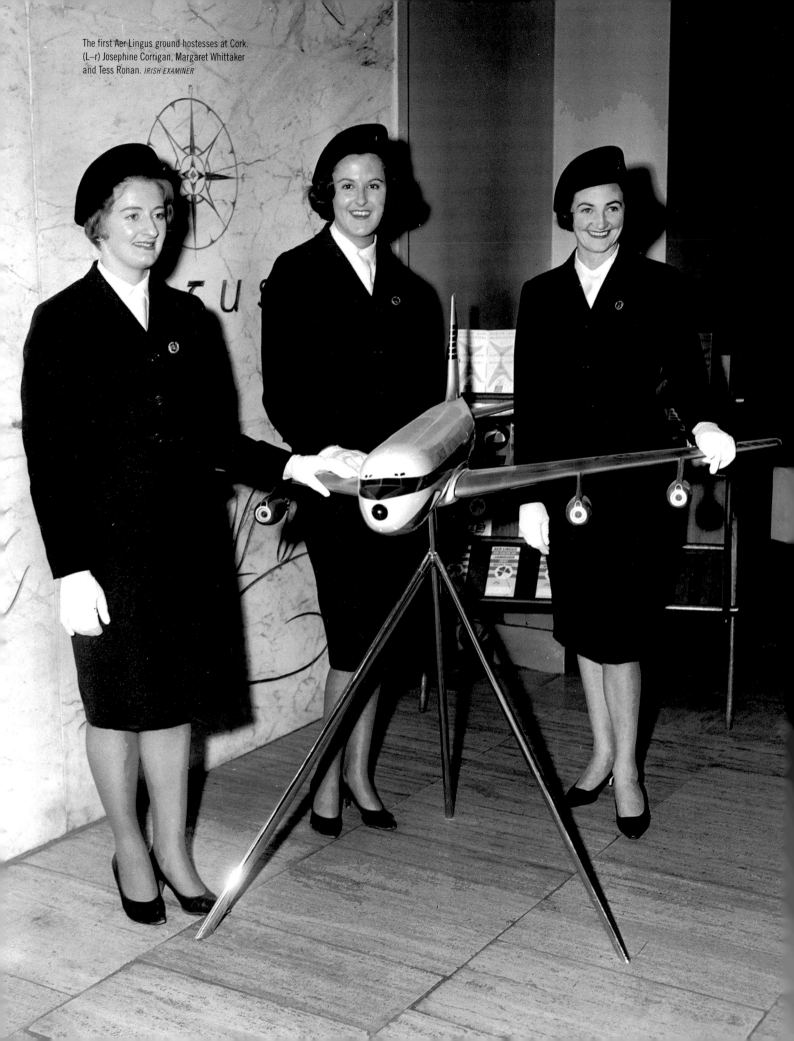

The first Aer Lingus ground hostesses at Cork. (L–r) Josephine Corrigan, Margaret Whittaker and Tess Ronan. *IRISH EXAMINER*

A group of Aer Lingus loaders at Cork Airport some days before the official opening. (L–r): Donie Ford, John O'Shea, Eddie Mullins, Mick Hayes (back), Jimmy Keane (front), Jim Forde and Eddie Hegarty. *IRISH EXAMINER*

airport the No. 2 Army Band played them out with 'The Mountains of Pomeroy', prompting 'Quidnunc' of *The Irish Times* to wonder why the great Cork sea shanty 'The Holy Ground' had not been played! The Cork Junior Chamber of Commerce later hosted a luncheon at the Imperial Hotel in the city centre and in his address to the guests, Stephen Barrett TD, who was deputising for the Lord Mayor, spoke with great humour about the importance of the new airport:

> Apart from today being a great occasion for us in Cork, it is also a great occasion for London, Cardiff, Bristol and other overseas settlements – since it is the first time that they have been brought in immediate contact with the true centre of modern civilisation.[38]

Later that evening the Taoiseach spoke at a celebratory dinner held at the same hotel. He saw the new airport as symbolising the progress and purpose of the increasingly modern Irish economy. Lemass's objective for Ireland was admission to

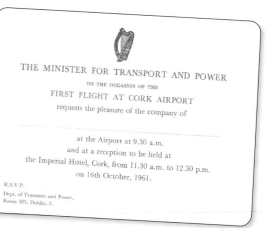

THE MINISTER FOR TRANSPORT AND POWER
ON THE OCCASION OF THE
FIRST FLIGHT AT CORK AIRPORT
requests the pleasure of the company of

at the Airport at 9.30 a.m.
and at a reception to be held at
the Imperial Hotel, Cork, from 11.30 a.m. to 12.30 p.m.
on 16th October, 1961.

R.S.V.P.
Dept. of Transport and Power,
Room 505, Dublin, 2.

Above: Invitation to the official opening of Cork Airport and reception at the Imperial Hotel, 16 October 1961. NATIONAL ARCHIVES OF IRELAND

Left: Seán Lemass with the group taking the first flight from Cork Airport to London. *IRISH EXAMINER*

the European Economic Community and the new airport was part of the country's progress in that direction. The airport, he said, 'will help us in our desire to have the world see us as a modern progressive state, coming rapidly and fully into line with all others in modern equipment and facilities'. He was fully confident about the prospects for Cork Airport and added presciently that 'it will not be many years before the facilities at Cork Airport will prove insufficient and will have to be enlarged'.

'Fasten seat belts . . . and extinguish cigarettes': first flights

At 11 a.m. that morning the first passenger-carrying flight to leave Cork Airport was a Dublin-bound Aer Lingus Fokker Friendship, the *St Fiachra*, piloted by Captain Aidan Quigley, assisted by his co-pilot Tom Evans. This plane was chartered by Jacobs and amongst the passengers were a number of people who had won tickets for this historic flight in a competition promoted by a radio programme called *Come Fly With Me*, sponsored by the biscuit manufacturers, as well as representatives of the retailers whose customers had won. Also on board was a group of well-known sports personalities – rugby internationals Tony O'Reilly and Jim McCarthy; GAA stars Christy Ring, Jim 'Tough' Barry and Eddie Coughlan (Cork minor football captain); swimmers Philomena Darcy and Jack Cantillon; and Cork's best-known road bowler, Mick Barry. A reporter from the *Cork Examiner* also travelled and described the trip for the following day's edition. It is a measure of the novelty of air travel at the time and of the excitement generated by the opening of the airport that such a detailed account of the flight would be published. Indeed, for many of the passengers, including, possibly, the reporter, it was their first experience of air travel:

St. Fiachra climbed swiftly into and through the cloud layer, so that, apart from brief glimpses through gaps in the fleecy cloud, little was seen by those on board of the city and surrounding countryside. It seemed only seconds later, actually it was about seven or eight minutes, when the voice of Capt. Aidan Quigley informed us that we were travelling at a height of 7,000 feet, at a speed of 295 m.p.h., and that we would shortly be passing over Kilkenny.

Indeed, so swift was our flight that hostesses Ursula Crotty and Anne McAuley barely had time to collect empty cups and trays before the order came to 'fasten seat belts' and 'extinguish cigarettes'.

During the flight, compere Harry Thullier, himself a leading figure in the world of sport, was busy interviewing the prizewinners and sporting personalities, and he too found himself nearly caught for time as we came in to land at Dublin …

In Dublin we went straight to Jacob's factory, where, after a reception, we were entertained to a lavish lunch. Then came a tour of the factory, at once informative and eye-opening; afterwards a bus tour of part of Phoenix Park and then back to Collinstown.

While in Dublin the party was joined by another well-known figure in the world of sport – Rugby International Andrew Mulligan. It was quite a sight to see Messrs. McCarthy, Mulligan and O'Reilly in animated discussion, frequently hilarious, with Messrs. Ring and Barry …

For the return journey Friendship St. Finbarr was pressed into service (Capt. Paul Bowe, Co-Pilot Jack O'Neill and Hostesses Joan Lee and Liz Canavan), and about 6 p.m. we touched down, ever so lightly, at Cork's new airport once again.[39]

The second flight to depart the airport took off at 12.43 p.m., an Aer Lingus Viscount, *St Aodhán*, bound for Heathrow. This was Cork's first scheduled flight and was captained by Joseph Barrett of Youghal, assisted by First Officer P. W. Kennedy from Kildare. The passengers included the Lord Mayor, Jack Lynch, Bishop Cornelius Lucey, representatives of a number of business and development organisations, journalists and travel agents, whose objective was the promotion of Cork and the southern region as a destination for tourism and business. Again the *Cork Examiner* published a full account of the journey, the reporter savouring every detail of the adventure:

Watched by a big crowd of spectators, St. Aodhán went from the tarmac to the south-eastern extremity of the main runway, and, without the usual halt and revving up of engines, she turned around and the throttles of the four Rolls Royce turbo engines were opened up. Within 35 seconds – before the terminal buildings were abeam on the starboard hand – the plane was airborne and winging her way over the western suburbs of the city. The time was 12.43 p.m.

Looking down, she seemed to pass over the University College buildings, Patrick's Bridge and then Glanmire, with Lough Mahon beyond. The northern side of Great Island showed up conspicuously, and next the whole of Cork Harbour with its group of islands and the sun-speckled sea beyond ...

A passenger information sheet revealed that the plane's speed over St. George's Channel as she sped towards the Strumble Head marker was 345 m.p.h., and dead on the scheduled time the slight banking as she altered course for London could be felt as she reached the Welsh coast ... [40]

Unfortunately, one of the main runways at Heathrow was blocked for a number of hours after an airliner burst three tyres on landing. The Cork flight had to circle and was forty minutes late in landing. The passengers were met by the London-based Aer Lingus management personnel and the Lord Mayor had a meeting with his London counterpart. There were eleven aircraft movements in all on that first day, six arrivals and five departures. Cambrian Airways, a subsidiary of British European Airways, operated two cross-channel flights, using DC-3s, one of which remained overnight at Cork, and Aer Lingus operated the rest.

Catering facilities at the new airport were not available to passengers until early 1962, after which the airport became a popular venue for wedding receptions. On the airport's second day of operation, however, its first bit of nuptial history was made. Patrick Dowling and Breda Shortt of Fermoy were the first honeymoon couple to fly from the airport. Their wedding had been organised to coincide with the airport's opening and they had had to postpone their plans to tie in with the delayed opening date of 16 October. The event was reported in the local press, along with two other 'firsts': the bride's five-month-old niece became the youngest person to visit the airport, while another member of the wedding party, 84-year-old Nora Geary, became the first great-grandmother to visit.

THE FIRST FLIGHT FROM CORK AIRPORT
Mary Blyth remembers

'How can I travel on a plane when I'm expecting a baby?' Mary Blyth remembers asking when she heard that she had won a pair of tickets for the first flight from Cork Airport on 16 October 1961. Mary did not know anyone at that time who had travelled by air and she was worried for her expected baby's well-being. Eventually she paid a visit to her doctor, who advised her that she had nothing to worry about. Mary had been married to Robert since 1950 and they had five children at the time. Although she had been reassured about the safety of her unborn baby, she worried about her children being left orphaned in the event of their plane crashing. Robert had an answer

that eased her concerns: 'If we come home the children will be as poor as ever, but if we don't come home they'll be rich!'

Jacob's Biscuits, as the firm of W. & R. Jacob & Co. Ltd was better known, sponsored an afternoon radio programme, hosted by Frankie Byrne, called *Come Fly With Me*, a title inspired by the song made famous by Frank Sinatra. To coincide with the official opening of Cork Airport the programme ran a competition for its listeners, with prizes of two return tickets to Dublin for each of five winners and two further tickets for each of their nominated retailers.

Mary recalls that to enter she had to rank six different brands of Jacob's

Mary Blyth

biscuits in order of their popularity and also submit a number of empty biscuit packets. 'That was no problem to me because with five children there were always biscuits in the house,' she remarks. When she heard that she was a prizewinner she was 'gobsmacked'. Excitement was growing in Cork as the date of the opening of the airport approached and the people of the city, Mary and her friends and neighbours included, felt that at long last Cork was

about to take a leap forward and become a modern, well-connected city.

On the morning of 16 October a limousine arrived at Mary's home in Iona Park, Mayfield, to take her and her husband Robert to the airport. Family and neighbours gathered at the roadside to wish them well. Mary wore a light-coloured coat, a black skirt and a colourful top, 'to hide my news', and black shoes, gloves and hat. Mary was a little taken aback with her first view of the airport – 'It was still like a building site' – but the glamour and commotion inside the terminal building quickly dissipated that sense of disappointment. The Jacob's representatives gathered the prizewinners and the special guests who were to accompany them and a formal photograph was taken on the tarmac by the Aer Lingus Fokker Friendship *St Fiachra*, before they embarked. Like Mary and her husband Robert, most of those on board had never flown before and Mary remembers a palpable nervousness in the cabin as the plane accelerated down the runway. Safely in the air, Harry Thullier, a well-known radio personality, moved between the passengers recording their stories for later broadcast on the *Come Fly With Me* programme.

In Dublin a bus brought the guests to the Jacob's factory on Bishop Street in the city centre. 'The factory was all done up for the visit and the walls were covered in curtains for the occasion. You'd imagine it was into a palace you were going and not into a factory,' Mary recalls. After lunch the group was brought on a tour of the factory and Mary remembers being amazed to see women trimming and icing biscuits by hand. A bus tour of Dublin followed and Jacob's entertained the guests to afternoon tea before they departed for the airport. Tony O'Reilly, then a famous rugby international, was in the party as a guest of the sponsors and Mary remembers him speaking on behalf of the guests in formally thanking their hosts. 'He was a brilliant orator. I was surprised that he could be so humorous and outspoken and still stay within the rules. He was brilliant.' When the party boarded the bus for the return journey to Collinstown, now Dublin Airport, a tin of Jacob's biscuits awaited every guest on their seat. 'There was a picture of Killarney on the cover,' Mary says, 'and I still have that tin. I knit for my great-grandchildren now and I keep my knitting in it.'

It was dark as the return flight approached Cork that evening and Mary's fears were rekindled as the plane circled the airport a number of times before landing: 'When we were lined up for landing, I remember the runway lights coming up on both sides to meet us. It was a wonderful sight.'

***

Mary Blyth is now in her mid-eighties and is widowed. She reared nine children and is a great-grandmother, the matriarch of a large and extended family. When her youngest children started school, Mary turned her hand to poetry and has been widely published. She writes under the nom de plume of Yvonne O'Connor (Yvonne and Connor being the names of her two youngest children). She lives within sight of the lights of Cork Airport and she had a second, though tragic, connection with airport history when her friend and next-door neighbour, Hannah Burke, died in the Tuskar air crash of 1968, as did Hannah's mother, Bridget O'Callaghan.

Winners of the Jacobs' *Come Fly With Me* competition prior to departure on the first commercial flight from Cork on 16 October 1961. Mary Blyth is fifth from the left and her husband, Robert, stands behind her right shoulder. *IRISH EXAMINER*

16 OCTOBER 1961

'Next day, suddenly, it was the real thing'

G. F. AHERN

It was the best of times and the most challenging of times. Just a few weeks before Cork Airport was due to open in 1961, there was a problem – it was nowhere near ready; it was still a building site! All appeared to have been going to plan until events intervened. Adverse weather and a cement strike meant that the opening day deadline of 16 October was looking less and less likely to be met. There had been such optimism around Cork too. Even an 'outsider' like me could sense the thrusting momentum around the place. Ford and Dunlops were thriving. Whitegate Oil Refinery and Verolme Cork Dockyard were establishing themselves. In this climate of optimism and economic expansion, a new airport for Cork seemed entirely appropriate.

As the date for the opening of the airport loomed, colossal earthmovers lumbered about, mechanical dinosaurs scooping up 20-ton loads. High-grade concrete was still being poured on runways and taxiways. Frenetic activity continued around the terminal area. Dust was everywhere, befogging the new plate-glass expanses of the terminal building. When rain fell there was an abundance of muck. Apart from more visible work, much infrastructure, vital for the commencement of flights, was being painstakingly put in place. Communications and navigational aids (checked by the American Federal Aviation Agency), a telecommunication network, a local radio communications system, external and internal telephone systems, along with necessary cabling, were being installed and tested.

The airport would operate under the overall aegis of the Department of Transport and Power. Staff for the various agencies had been arriving in dribs and drabs. These included Airport Management, Air Traffic Control, Air Radio, Fire and Security, Meteorological Office, Customs and Excise, Department of Post and Telegraphs, Deptartment of Agriculture, Aer Lingus and Shell-BP Oil. A considerable degree of 'getting to know you' between groups ensued, along with a little wariness and 'territorial' niggles. The majority were already experienced in their fields and some had worked together in Shannon or Dublin. In time, the strangers turned out (in most cases) to be 'just friends who had not yet met' and an overall airport team spirit began to evolve.

Approval of the airport by the International Civil Aviation Organisation was essential. First, Air Traffic Control, Meteorological and Radio services, along with the Airport Police/Fire and Rescue Service, had to be operational. Members of the latter service, however, had only just been recruited and only began to arrive on site in mid-September. Apart from the officer-in-charge, all were new to the job in which they needed to be 'ICAO-standard' by opening day. In these circumstances, great faith, or perhaps, some suspension of disbelief was required. With or (mostly) without the necessary equipment, for the next month those recruits did little else but train.

As 16 October loomed, it was a case of all shoulders to the wheel, as all groups made do with quite primitive facilities in which to work, eat, etc. Some wondered would it always be like this; the experienced ones knew better. By early October, the countdown was on. Lots of technical terms floated about, such as 'VOR', 'VHF' and 'ATC'. It became clear that '17/35' was not clocking-off time (nor even the time when a fancied horse was running) but the orientation and official designation of the main runway. Daily conversation might include reference to 'AFTN', 'ILS', 'stand-pipes', 'anemometer', 'ceilometer' and 'foam tender'. Some of us who had never touched a plane, never mind been inside one, would soon get our chance to do both.

Four days before opening day, two 'proving' flights landed. Collectively, many breaths were held but all went well. The Aer Lingus Friendship, in national green livery, glided in like the most graceful of morning birds, its silver belly shining beneath its overhead wingspan. The distinctive ringing whine of its twin turbo-prop engines heralded its approach to the terminal. The passengers, made up of airline staff and press, disembarked. Later, the piston-engined DC-3s of Cambrian Airways trundled in, stubby, chunkier, not as modern as 'our' Friendship. Like the Friendship, it made an instrument landing. The day before opening, a Sunday, Cork people came in their droves to see the new airport.

Next day, suddenly, it was the real thing. The best face possible was to be shown to all, VIPs and public alike (but especially the former). Everything that could be spruced up had been, including, miraculously, the previously dusty plate-glass windows of the terminal building. There was an invigorating sense of excitement. Now, the runway lights were on, an 'easy' had been issued by the tower to the fire-crew, putting it on stand-by. The first commercial flight at Cork was inbound, an Aer Lingus Viscount. This plane had been considered so avant-garde that lounge bars had actually been named after it! The tarmac was crowded with airline and airport executives, some of the latter attending on the Lord Mayor and Bishop Lucey. The passengers disembarked and the formalities and speeches ensued indoors. The concourse had as yet no catering facilities, but what matter? Jack Lynch was there, as Minister of Industry [and Commerce], amongst his own, on a proud day in his native place. Taoiseach Seán Lemass, newly re-elected, and Minister for Transport and Power Erskine Childers were there too, up on the balcony. They all had nice words to say, congratulatory and optimistic.

Inwardly, I think, all of us on duty felt a restrained pride and gave a silent cheer. The rest, as they say, is history.

Evening Echo, 3 January 2011

4

Terminal building, April 1962. GABRIEL DESMOND

AIRBORNE

1961–69

FOLLOWING THE GRAND OPENING of October 1961, structural work at the still incomplete airport continued and a skeleton timetable was operated. Cork finally had its airport, but frustration continued about issues such as airfares, the limitations of the Cork–Dublin connection, and flight diversions due to fog. Gradually, however, the airport took shape and the number of flights and passengers outstripped expectations. Meanwhile, Cork people took the airport to their hearts, holding weddings, parties and other gatherings there, visiting in large numbers to see off or greet family and friends or just watch planes landing and taking off, and in the hope of spotting a visiting celebrity. In many ways, the airport served as a gateway and window to a more glamorous, exciting world beyond the still relatively parochial city of Cork. On the negative side, there was tragedy in the shape of a private plane crash in 1964 and the loss of the *St Phelim*, en route from Cork to London, near Tuskar Rock in 1968. By the end of the 1960s, questions were being asked about the airport's continued viability, and whether it was proving to be an expensive 'white elephant'.

Encroachments!

Cork Airport's winter schedule would see the airport closed on Sundays from 1 November for the following five months. On 29 October, the last Sunday before the winter closures, the weather was unseasonably fine and thousands of people came to visit the new facility 'by bus, car and even on foot'. So many cars had been parked on the approach road that one airport bus could not reach the terminal building and its passengers had to walk several hundred metres carrying their luggage. Other difficulties arose later when the excitement created by the imminent departure of an aircraft drew a large number of spectators on

Newspaper advertisement, 9 September 1961.

to the apron on west side of the terminal. The *Cork Examiner* reported: 'By 5.30 in the afternoon when a plane was taxiing for take-off, the crowds had moved on to the apron to such an extent that officials, purely as a safety measure, created a barrier by playing the fire hoses in front of the huge throng'.[1]

An encroachment of a different type occurred ten days later during a South Union fox hunt when a fox was being pursued from near Fivemilebridge, south of the airport:

He finally emerged near Liss Cross and turned east to the airport chain-link fence. The wily animal raced half a mile before finding a gap into the airport. The hounds took a little time to find the same entrance; the mounted members of the hunt had to detour; and while this was going on the fox raced along the runways.

The first car park opened in August 1962. Prior to that it was permitted to park cars on the south ramp.
GABRIEL DESMOND

The terminal, tower and fire station, from the ramp, August 1963.
GABRIEL DESMOND

Terminal building, December 1963.
GABRIEL DESMOND

He gained a lot of valuable time, and although chased for another few miles, finally made good his escape'.[2]

What's in a name?

In the weeks after the opening of the airport a debate was engaged in the letters page of the *Cork Examiner* as to the proper Irish language translation of 'airport'. Road signs had been erected in the city and on approaches to the airport with *aerphort* as the Irish version, but in his letter Diarmuid Ó Murchú pointed out that official government publications on standardised spelling in Irish and the most recent English–Irish dictionary gave *aerfort* as the correct version.[3] James O'Connor pointed to the potential for confusion to non-Irish speakers in the use of *aerphort*: 'An Englishman who was driving to the airport on Wednesday for the first time saw the sign "Aerphort" and asked is the airport far from the village, thinking that the signpost was indication [sic] of the next town or village. In fact his pronunciation was phonetically arep-hort'.[4] Another correspondent preferred *eitillport*, while Eoghan Ó Faircheallaigh argued for *eiteall-phort*, as suggested to him thirty years earlier by Gaelic scholars 'who would now be over 100 years old'. Exasperated by the ongoing argument and pedantry J. R. H. James offered a solution: '... while the Gaelic scholars battle it out over an acceptable translation ... a sign without lettering depicting pictorially an aeroplane would be more than adequate.'[5]

Schedules and passenger numbers

Two weeks after its official opening, Cork Airport's first winter timetable came into operation and Aer Lingus and Cambrian Airways were the sole operators of scheduled services until the spring of 1962.[6] London, Bristol, Cardiff, Paris and Dublin were the destinations initially served, but on a quite limited basis. One direct return flight to London was available on Monday, Thursday, Friday and Saturday, while on other days and at some other times flights to London were by way of Bristol or Cardiff. The flight to Paris operated only on Mondays. When the airport opened the cheapest return fare available on the Cork–London route was £15.6.0, and the equivalent fares to Bristol and Cardiff were £10.18.0 and £10 respectively. The cheapest return fare to Dublin was £4 and an excursion return ticket to Paris was £20. With the introduction of the winter timetable on 1 November fares rose by 5 per cent, bringing the lowest London fare, for example, to £16.2.0. (At that time an assistant in air traffic control at the airport would have had a starting weekly wage of £6.10.0).

It had been anticipated that the Cork–Dublin air service would cater for the demand, from business people in particular, for a day-return service between the two cities. Many expected a morning and evening return flight on at least some working days that would enable people from either city to transact business in the other and return home the same day. Business people and others were disappointed in the Dublin service provided, as there was no morning flight from Cork and consequently no possibility of a day return service to the capital. Passengers from Dublin fared slightly better because a round trip was possible twice a week, allowing a stay of four hours in Cork. When Aer Lingus had published its proposed timetable for Cork early in 1961, a letter-writer to the *Cork Examiner*, 'Cork Commercial', captured the disappointment of many in the south:

Since the original concept of the airport was to cater for the South it is not too much to expect

A Jersey Airlines DC-3 at Cork. This airline operated a summer service to Exeter from 1962. GABRIEL DESMOND

that the majority of the flights would permit of this one-day journey, particularly as it was due to the persistent efforts of our businessmen that the project was not shelved indefinitely ... Where the ex-Cork traveller is concerned, he leaves in the late afternoon, arrives in Dublin when all business premises are closed, has the additional expense of over-night stay, and must leave the city for the latest flight home at 11 a.m. approximately. This gives him a maximum of two hours (9 a.m. to 11 a.m.) for business at a cost around £7/10.[7]

Business interests in Cork campaigned for a better service. In September 1964 Vincent Fanning, manager of Cork Airport, made a detailed submission to the Civil Aviation Division of the Department of Transport and Power on the matter, pointing out that, with the exception of the Saturday flights to and from Dublin, all others were 'merely positioning flights for other services from Cork'. Fanning wrote that until a proper service was provided by Aer Lingus or some other operator, the needs of Cork people were not being

met. Aer Lingus claimed that there was a lack of space to park planes overnight in Cork.[8] It was felt by some, with justification, that Aer Lingus, the national airline, was not giving Cork the service it was due. That sense of grievance had grown in the two decades before the airport was built, as many in Cork believed that reluctance on the part of the airline to commit to serving the city fully had delayed the decision to construct Cork Airport. However, the attitude of CIÉ, the national rail and road transport operator, was also a factor in refusing or delaying a full commuter service between Cork and Dublin. In May 1961 CIÉ had objected to the Aer Lingus proposed fare on the Cork–Dublin route, as it felt it would give the airline a competitive advantage. Negotiations followed and in December of that year Erskine Childers, Minister for Transport and Power, directed Aer Lingus to set the fare at a level that would 'remove the competitive element of the service vis-à-vis the surface transport'. Aer Lingus complied under protest.[9] By late 1965 some additional capacity had been provided on the route, but the demand for daily services, morning

Douglas DC-4s were not used on scheduled services to Cork, but this Trans-Meridian DC-4 was chartered by Ford workers from Cork for their annual visit home from Dagenham. GABRIEL DESMOND

and evening, was still not met. Fanning and others continued to petition and lobby but their efforts were not to bear fruit until the end of the decade.[10]

Prior to the opening of the airport, Aer Lingus predicted that total passenger traffic at Cork would be about 30,000 annually in the first two to three years, rising to about 60,000 after five or six years.[11] By the end of 1961, after a little over two months in operation, it was clear that these predictions would be exceeded, as 10,257 passengers had used the airport in ten weeks. The annual figure was 77,649 for 1962 and by 1966 this had grown to 160,443, more than two-and-a-half times greater than initially expected. While Cork continued to run a deficit in these early years, the steady growth in passenger numbers suggested a profitable future for the airport. With the onset of the 1962 tourist season new routes were added to the Cork schedule and there was also an increase in frequency and capacity on existing routes. On 6 April Aer Lingus began a Birmingham service and on 5 May a Lourdes/Barcelona route was added. In June Aer Lingus began a service to Jersey; Jersey Airlines opened a summer service to the Channel Islands by way of Exeter, while Starways began its Liverpool service.

A number of charter companies also began to use the airport.

As the 1960s advanced so too did the number of airlines operating out of Cork and a wider choice of destinations became available, especially in the summer months. Derby Airways (later to become British Midland) flew to Birmingham, British Eagle took over from Starways on the Liverpool route and operated until 1968, and British United Airways flew to Exeter in the summer months from 1965 to 1967. Cambrian expanded its routes and served Liverpool and Manchester for different periods during the mid and later 1960s. Aer Lingus began a service to Manchester in May 1965. Inclusive tour charters into Cork began in the mid-1960s, with Martinair operating a weekly flight from Amsterdam and later in the decade Transavia operated charter flights into Cork on behalf of Dutch tour operators. Trans-Meridian, an airline based in Southend in England, flew charter flights to Cork at holiday times in the 1960s. These carried Ford workers from the company's Dagenham plant where many people from Cork were employed and workers from the Cork Ford plant travelled as a 'back load' on the return flight to holiday in Britain.

Above: A Cambrian DC-3 in December 1963. These planes were used by Cambrian on services to London, Cardiff and Bristol up to 1969. GABRIEL DESMOND

Below: Passengers board an Air Links Handley Page Hermes in August 1964. GABRIEL DESMOND

The first jet to land at Cork was a BOAC Comet. BOAC operated a London flight for Aer Lingus on 31 July 1964. GABRIEL DESMOND

Aer Lingus Carvair EI-AMR, St Gaul, at Cork, April 1963. GABRIEL DESMOND

Early aircraft

Aer Lingus generally used Fokker 27 Friendships on Cork services while Cambrian generally used DC-3s in their first years at the airport. Seating capacity was limited on these aircraft, the Friendship having forty-eight seats and the DC-3 only thirty-two, and both airlines soon began to use Viscounts, which could carry sixty-nine passengers, on the busier routes. Cambrian used Viscounts to London from 1963, but continued with the smaller capacity DC-3 to Bristol and Cardiff. By 1966 Aer Lingus was using Viscounts on all its cross-channel routes and had standardised its fleet, buying nine Viscount V-803s from Dutch airline KLM in that year. Its fleet of seven Friendships was disposed of. The first jet to land in Cork was a BOAC Comet 4, which operated a London flight on behalf of Aer Lingus. It landed on 31 July 1964 watched by a large group of enthusiasts. The arrival of Cork's first jet had been publicised in advance and crowds came to the airport, parking cars along the approach road and cramming the viewing balconies. The steep climb of the Comet as it took off and the novelty of the roar of jet engines thrilled the spectators.

Increasing passenger numbers and the attractions of jet aircraft led Aer Lingus to acquire four BAC 1-11 jets in March 1965. They each carried seventy-nine passengers and were initially used on European routes. An Aer Lingus BAC 1-11 made its first visit to Cork in May 1965 when a group of invited guests was brought on a thirty-

The first BAC 1-11 to visit Cork in May 1965. Aer Lingus purchased four of these jets in 1965 to serve its European routes. GABRIEL DESMOND

Aer Lingus Carvair ready for loading, summer 1965. *IRISH EXAMINER*

minute promotional flight over west Cork. The airline took delivery of its first Boeing 737, with a seating capacity of 119, in 1969 and by 1971 a decision was made to change to an all-jet fleet. Cambrian Airways began to use the BAC 1-11 on its London route in 1970, having discontinued flights to Bristol and Cardiff by then.

Air car-ferry services, 1963–66

As early as 1960 interest was being expressed by a British company in running an air car-ferry service between Cork and Britain. In September of that year the British Ministry of Aviation granted conditional approval to East Anglian Flying Services to operate such a service between Bristol and Cork, but approval would also have to come from the Irish government before it could become

a reality.[12] Later, in response to a licence granted to Channel Airways by the British authorities to operate a car-ferry service, Aer Lingus acquired its first two ATL-98 Carvair car-ferry aircraft in February 1963, with a third delivered later.[13] The Aer Lingus service began operating in May 1963 and the routes were Dublin–Liverpool, Dublin–Bristol, Dublin–Cherbourg and Cork–Bristol. The first flight from Cork was on 5 May when four vintage cars were flown to Bristol to take part in the annual London-to-Brighton car rally. Scheduled services began one week later and initially operated twice weekly, later rising to four times per week during the peak of the holiday season. The Cork–Bristol service carried 660 cars and 66 bicycles during the summer of 1963.[14] The Carvair was a development of the DC-4 and could carry five cars and twenty-two passengers, or four cars with thirty-four passengers. Cars were loaded

Vintage car being loaded at Cork using the Hylo scissors lift. JOHN BUCKLEY

through a nose door using a Hylo scissors lift. On the Cork–Bristol route the rate for a small car was £12.10.0, and £29 for a longer vehicle, with accompanying passengers paying the normal passenger rates. While there were lower rates for mid-week travel, the service was quite expensive and was never going to cater for large-scale traffic, especially given the limitations on capacity.

The reliability of the Carvair was poor, resulting in frequent delays, and turnarounds were slow. Despite relatively high loads on the services, it was not possible to make them profitable and Aer Lingus ceased their operation in 1966. The introduction of sea-borne car ferries on the Irish Sea was another factor in hastening the decision as shipping companies began to operate large capacity roll-on roll-off services at rates that airlines could never meet. It took Aer Lingus two years to sell the three idle Carvairs.

Teething problems

When the airport opened in October 1961 much of the building work had not been completed and for the following nine months or so work continued both inside and outside the terminal. The second shorter east–west runway, Runway 07/25, was not ready until December 1961 and the ILS (Instrument Landing System) Glide Path navigation aid was not operational until April 1962. Without the full range of planned ancillary services for passengers, conditions were somewhat spartan until the summer of 1962. No catering facilities had been available to the public until the bar and restaurant were opened in May 1962, Great Southern Hotels having won the concession for their operation. Harrington's took over the concession in 1964 and held it until 1992. In August 1962 the first bank and shop were opened and in that month also the car park first became available, a great ease to flight operations as for

the previous nine months the travelling public had been permitted to park vehicles on the south ramp.

In September 1962 Colonel K. G. F. Chavesse of Cappagh House in County Waterford fell foul of the new parking arrangements and wrote a letter of complaint to Erskine Childers, the Minister for Transport and Power. He had been dropping 'a distinguished general and his wife' at Cork Airport and had parked his car outside the terminal. As he made to leave he was stopped by the airport police who thought he had been in the car park and was leaving without paying. A stand-off ensued and after Vincent Fanning, the Airport Manager, was called to the scene, the enraged Chavesse was allowed to leave. 'I have never been treated by a policeman in any country in which I have served or travelled as I was by this man. It seemed more like Nazi Germany than Ireland … this man seemed to have an exalted idea of his own importance,' he wrote. Chavesse felt his grievance was all the more valid as his wife told him she had been treated similarly on another occasion.[15]

The previous month Elizabeth McGillycuddy ('of the Reeks'), from Beaufort in County Kerry, who described herself as a 'constant user' of the airport, wrote to the manager detailing her complaints about the airport and its facilities. Her first complaint was 'certainly essential for female well-being', she wrote. In the ladies' cloakroom the mirrors were positioned at a low level and two armchairs were provided so that it was 'possible to powder one's nose sitting down'. However, most women did not have the time or inclination to use the armchairs, according to McGillycuddy, and she suggested raising the level of the mirrors. She also suggested that spare cartons of lavatory paper should always be available in the lavatories. The condition of the ornamental pool located below the outdoor viewing balcony also disappointed her. It was full of 'every conceivable refuse and dirt … it will I am sure always be used as a litter bin and look too sordid for words'. The restaurant did not meet Ms McGillycuddy's expectations either. She found the food not up to the standard suggested by the prices, the staff not properly trained, and her table grubby. 'The only thing that came promptly was the bill', she wrote, adding that 'it seems a great pity to me that the first impression to be gained by travellers at Cork should be one of inefficiency and tattiness'. The manager acted on her complaints and reported to the Department of Transport and Power on the actions taken. Ms McGillycuddy was pleased with the follow-up actions as she wrote again three months later expressing her delight at the improvements.[16]

John Alley from Inniscarra near Cork suggested in August 1962, ten months after the airport began operating, that a flight information board be erected in the terminal as 'it was impossible to hear the announcements over the loudspeaker when the motor lawn mower was operating in the vicinity of the outside balcony'. The manager replied promptly and explained that the airport was still not completed and that an arrivals board was planned for the terminal concourse.[17] A board was erected later and flight details were handwritten by airport police, an arrangement that lasted for a number of years until electronic boards were installed.

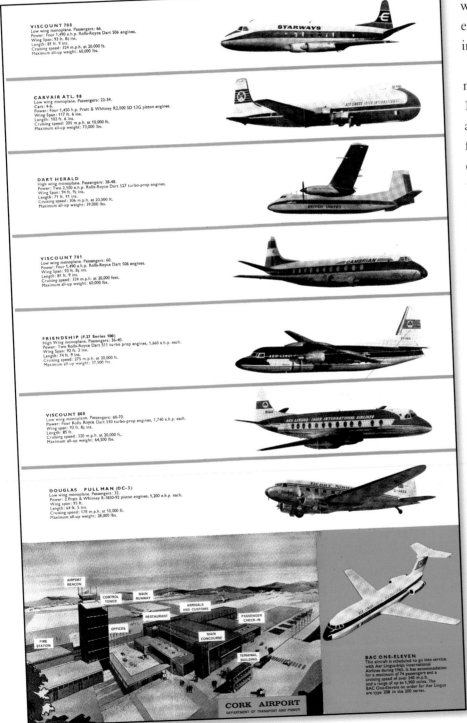

1964 brochure promoting Cork Airport.
NATIONAL ARCHIVES OF IRELAND

Above: Passengers check in for a flight to London Heathrow, March 1963. GABRIEL DESMOND

Below: For a number of years before electronic information screens were erected, security personnel had the task of writing flight information on a large board in the terminal concourse. GABRIEL DESMOND

Cork Airport

Cork Airport was opened to traffic on October 16th, 1961. Simultaneously, the province of Munster and Ireland's southern Capital entered fully into the Air Age. Through direct links with Dublin, the West of England, London and Paris, the great, globe-spanning trunk routes were now accessible.

Modern airports are not created overnight. In this regard, Cork Airport is no exception. Much careful surveying of many possible sites was necessary before the best location was decided on. Freedom of approach for aircraft, as well as dependable meteorological conditions were prerequisites if safety and reliability of operations were to be ensured.

The site occupies 500 acres, ample space to accommodate runways, buildings and other installations.

There are two runways. The longer measures 6,000 feet and is capable of taking jet transports, if required. The subsidiary runway is 4,300 feet in length.

The Control Tower dominates the airport, not only because it is the tallest building (it is over 80 feet high), but also because it houses the Air Traffic Control centre, where the latest electronic aids act as the eyes and ears of the officials who regulate the movement of every aircraft that lands or takes off.

Apart from the Control Tower, the airport has two other main buildings, viz. the passenger and freight terminals. The former's accommodation includes a customs hall, concourse, restaurant and viewing terrace. In the single-storey freight building, provision has been made for import and export stores as well as the accommodation of customs staff.

The airport buildings have been designed to allow maximum flexibility in catering for future expansion while ensuring that such alterations will be not aesthetically unpleasing.

It was estimated that Cork Airport would serve 30,000 passengers in its first year of operation and that this figure would be doubled at the end of five years. In fact, 77,000 passengers used the airport during the first twelve months of its existence, when upwards of 400 tons of freight were also handled—in the year ended December 31st, 1963, these figures increased to 95,466 passengers and over 900 tons of freight.

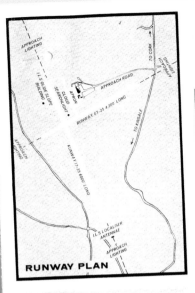

RUNWAY PLAN

KEEP YOUR AIRPORT

PUBLISHED BY AER RIANTA EDUCATIONAL SERVICE
INFORMATION LEAFLET NO. 3—64
Printed in the Republic of Ireland by Wood Printing Works Ltd., Dublin 1.

CORK
AIRPORT

1964 brochure promoting Cork Airport.

NATIONAL ARCHIVES OF IRELAND

Aer Lingus Irish International Airlines

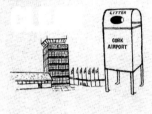

Aer Lingus and Aerlinte Eireann, the two Irish airlines, combine their services under the single marketing name, "Aer Lingus—Irish International Airlines".

Founded in 1936, Aer Lingus had its original headquarters at Baldonnel military aerodrome. The Company's fleet then comprised one five-seater D. H. "Dragon"; the staff totalled twelve persons and, it is recorded, there were just enough spare parts to fill a biscuit tin!

On May 27th of that year, the newly formed airline opened its first route from Baldonnel to Bristol, a distance of 232 miles. The aircraft carried a full load—five passengers. A few months later, this route was extended to London and a service to Liverpool was inaugurated.

The Company continued to expand until the outbreak of war in 1939, when all services were suspended. The service to Liverpool was reintroduced shortly afterwards and, sometimes using Manchester as the terminus, was maintained throughout the difficult years that followed.

Post-war expansion began in 1946 and Aer Lingus has grown steadily since then. From a one-route, one-aircraft undertaking that carried less than 900 passengers in its first year of operations, the Company has become an important international airline with a modern fleet of turbo-prop Vickers Viscounts and Fokker Friendships serving points in Great Britain, France, Spain, Italy, Germany, Switzerland, Holland, Belgium and Denmark, as well as three airports within Ireland.

In the year ended December 31st, 1963, Aer Lingus carried 838,040 passengers and over 17,000 tons of freight and mail.

Aerlinte Eireann, the sister-company of Aer Lingus, was formed in 1947, to operate a transatlantic service. Operations, however, were postponed until 1958 when routes linking Dublin and Shannon with New York and Boston were inaugurated. Boeing Shamrock Jetliners now operate these services.

Added to the 83,062 passengers and 1,175 tons of freight carried by Aer Linte Eireann during 1963, the Aer Lingus figure brings the Irish Air Companies' totals to 921,102 and 18,175 respectively.

CAMBRIAN AIRWAYS

Cambrian Airways, Britain's oldest independent airline operator, has developed scheduled services linking Cardiff and Bristol with Paris, Dinard, Dublin, Jersey, Belfast, Liverpool, Manchester, Glasgow, Bournemouth, Southampton and in association with Aer Lingus, has linked Cork with Bristol, Cardiff and London.

In April, 1963, Cambrian's jet-prop Viscounts went into service on the London-Cork route.

Cambrian also operate a network over London, the Isle of Man, Liverpool, Manchester and Belfast.

BKS AIR TRANSPORT LIMITED

BKS is the largest British domestic independent airline operating scheduled services. Its services emanate from London, Leeds/Bradford and Newcastle to Ireland, the Channel Isles and numerous destinations on the Continent. The Fleet comprises Britannias, Avro 748s, Elizabethans, DC-3s and Bristol Freighters. BKS have ordered five of the new Turbo-prop Avro 748s, two of which have already been delivered and operating regularly into Dublin Airport. The letters BKS represent the names of the original three Directors. The Company is now owned solely by Mr. C. J. Stevens.

BRITISH UNITED C. I. AIRWAYS

British United C. I. Airways (formerly Jersey Airlines, Silver City Airways, and Manx Airlines Ltd.) link the Channel Islands with London (Gatwick), Bournemouth, Southampton, Manchester, Blackpool, Dublin, Cork, Glasgow, Edinburgh, Coventry, Exeter and Plymouth, the Isle of Man with Belfast, Birmingham, Blackpool, Glasgow, Edinburgh, Carlisle, Newcastle and Leeds; and Blackpool with Newcastle, Leeds, Dublin and Belfast. Continental services connect the Channel Islands with Paris, Dinard, St. Brieuc, Quimper and Granville, London (Gatwick) with Brittany / Exeter with Paris, Bournemouth and Southampton with Brittany and Paris, and Newcastle with Amsterdam and Dusseldorf.

The British United C. I. Airways fleet includes 6 jet-prop Dart Heralds, 14 DC-3s and 2 Herons, and the Company forms part of the British United Airways Group together with such concerns as British United Air Ferries, Morton Air Services, Airwork International, etc.

STARWAYS LIMITED

Starways Limited is a wholly owned subsidiary of British Eagle International Airlines. Starways Limited was founded in 1947 and acquired by British Eagle on the 1st January, 1964. They originated Air Pilgrimages on regular flights to Lourdes. Scheduled services include a network of Cornwall and Devon flights. Other services include London, Glasgow, Cork, Blackpool, Ostend, Chester as well as many inclusive holiday flights to Spain, Italy, France, etc.

DERBY AIRWAYS

Derby Airways is one of a group of companies, based at Derby Airport, which first entered the field of civil aviation in 1938. The present fleet consists of three 75 seater pressurised Rolls-Royce Argonauts and seven Pullman Douglas DC-3s. Its extensive network includes services from Derby to Dublin, Cork, Belfast, Isle of Man, Glasgow, Channel Islands, Rotterdam, Ostend, Newcastle. Channel Islands services are also operated from several other provincial airports. Services to Amsterdam, Barcelona, Majorca, Genoa, Valencia and Ostend are operated from Cardiff and Bristol, and Rotterdam, Ostend, Isle of Wight, Channel Islands and Newcastle from Birmingham.

Novelty

While some complained about the lack of a proper commuter service between Cork and Dublin and others had occasional difficulties as outlined above, passengers and the general public were generally well pleased with the airport. Passenger numbers grew steadily through the 1960s, apart from 1968, when a 2.8 per cent fall was recorded.

(This fall was due in the main to the outbreak of foot-and-mouth disease in Britain in the winter of 1967/68, which resulted in restrictions on travel between that country and Ireland, but the crash of an Aer Lingus Viscount, en route from Cork to London, off the County Wexford coast on 24 March 1968 also had a negative impact.)

The airport attracted large numbers of visitors, especially at weekends, even though the number

The open balcony was a popular vantage point for airport visitors. *IRISH EXAMINER*

Above: An Aer Lingus Fokker Friendship watched by enthusiastic spectators. In its early years the airport was a great novelty and crowds walked to the airport from the city in summer to watch the aircraft. GABRIEL DESMOND

Below: Summer 1966. Aer Lingus was using the BAC 1-11 jet on continental routes and the Viscounts on domestic and British services. The balcony was very popular with spectators who often threw coins into the pool below, visible to the left. GABRIEL DESMOND

of flight movements was relatively small. On such days the open-air balcony overlooking the apron was crowded as family, friends and the general public waved to arriving and departing passengers. Children and adults would gather there to look at a parked aircraft or to await the arrival of a flight, often hours away. The sound of an aircraft passing over the city and suburbs of Cork in the 1960s was still enough of a novelty to have many people, young and old alike, pause and look skywards. The airport restaurant was a popular venue and was especially busy at lunchtime on Sundays. This was also a favoured location for wedding receptions and dinner dances as it could seat 250 guests and had a dance floor.

The airport also attracted a number of people with a more serious interest in aircraft and aviation. Gabriel Desmond [p. 190], Geoffrey Farrar, Ray Shanahan and the Frost brothers, Gabriel, Paul and the late Noel, have been photographing aircraft at Cork Airport since it opened in 1961 and they have created an unrivalled photographic record of regular and unusual aircraft that have visited the aiport over the past fifty years.

The airport was Cork's gateway to a wider world, often a connection to the world of celebrity and fame. Stars of film, pop music and sport were photographed on their arrival at the airport when coming to holiday, to play or to do business. A number of these people purchased houses in the region, especially in west Cork, as the airport made access from cities like London and Paris much easier.

Santa Claus and a group of Cork children at the airport, Christmas 1963.
IRISH EXAMINER

A Cambrian
Airways DC-3
arrives at Cork,
16 October 1961.
IRISH EXAMINER

A party of pilgrims on the first charter to Lourdes, 23 October 1961.
IRISH EXAMINER

The O'Sullivan sisters from Athea, County Limerick, are seen off on their return to Nigeria. They were the first missionaries to fly from Cork Airport, 24 October 1961. *IRISH EXAMINER*

Pilgrims progress … by air

The Cork–Lourdes route for scheduled and chartered services proved to be one of the more successful from the new airport. George Heffernan of the Cork Airways Company had pioneered chartered flights to the pilgrimage centre in southern France in the 1940s and the Cork travel agency that bears his family name still organises such flights. The first pilgrimage charter from Cork was on 23 October 1961 when a group of forty, organised by the Heffernan travel agency, flew to Lourdes.

The Cork-to-Lourdes scheduled service began on 5 May 1962 when a party of travel agents, journalists, Aer Lingus officials and clergy, led by the Lord Mayor of Cork, Anthony Barry TD, flew to Tarbes on the inaugural flight. The party was entertained at a reception at the airport on arrival in France, hosted by the civic, religious and commercial dignitaries of Lourdes. Later that evening the Irish group were guests at a banquet held in their honour. The historic links between the two countries were mentioned frequently in the speeches and particular recognition was given to Ireland, and to Aer Lingus in particular, for fostering a continuing interest in the Marian shrine at Lourdes. Aer Lingus had begun scheduled flights to Lourdes from Dublin in 1954 and had carried over 40,000 pilgrims from Ireland in 1958 for the centenary celebrations at the shrine. So significant was the route, and more especially the location of Lourdes, that Aer Lingus used it as a virtual hub. In 1955 it extended its Lourdes route to Barcelona, and in 1958 an extension to Rome was inaugurated. In 1958 also, a year of great Marian devotion, the airline opened an extension to Lisbon in Portugal, to serve pilgrims wishing to visit the shrine at Fatima. The Cork–Lourdes–Barcelona service operated once weekly and was very well supported. As the correspondent of the *Kerryman* newspaper, who travelled on the inaugural flight, noted:

With the opening of Cork Airport the provision of a service from the southern capital to Lourdes was a logical development. A high proportion of the Irish pilgrim traffic originates in the southern counties and indeed it is on record that the first Aer Lingus charter from Ireland to Lourdes was organised by a Cork group.[18]

Tragedies

September 1962: plane crash in North Atlantic

Less than one year after Cork Airport opened, its staff were confronted for the first time with the grimmer side of air travel when the airport was involved with the rescue of survivors from a plane crash in the Atlantic. On 23 September 1962 a Super Constellation of the Flying Tiger airline, en route from McGuire US Air Force airbase in New Jersey to Frankfurt in Germany, ditched in the North Atlantic about 500 miles from the Irish coast following the failure of three of its four engines. Twenty-eight of the seventy-six people on board died. Fifty-one survivors, many of whom were injured, took to the only life raft of five that could be reached and spent six hours adrift before the freighter *Celerina*, bound for Antwerp, arrived on the scene at dawn following day, 24 September. By then three more of life raft's occupants had died. The ship took forty-four survivors on board and proceeded at speed towards the south coast of Ireland. The remaining four survivors and the bodies of the three dead on the life raft were taken by the Canadian aircraft carrier HMCS *Bonaventure* and brought to the coast near Shannon Airport from where they were brought ashore. Cork Airport was put on alert and two RAF Westland Whirlwind rescue helicopters flew to the airport on the morning of 26 September to refuel before flying to a rendezvous with the

This RAF Shackleton, refuelling at Cork, directed two RAF Westland Whirlwind rescue helicopters, which winched seventeen survivors of the Super Constellation crash from the freighter *Celerina*, September 1962. BILLY JESTIN

The wreckage of the Piper-24 Comanche, which crashed shortly after take-off from Cork on 8 August 1964, killing all four on board. *IRISH EXAMINER*

Celerina off the Galley Head on the Cork coast, guided by an RAF maritime patrol Shackleton. Seventeen injured survivors were brought to Cork Airport where a team of doctors and nurses was on stand-by, and after initial assessment ambulances brought them to hospital in the city. The *Celerina* continued on her voyage to Antwerp with the remaining survivors.[19]

AUGUST 1964: FOUR KILLED IN PLANE CRASH AT CORK AIRPORT

On Saturday 8 August 1964 a privately owned Piper PA-24 Comanche aircraft crashed shortly after take-off from Cork Airport, killing all four on board. The pilot was James Coupe from England who had flown the plane from Southampton to Cork the previous day for a weekend trip, accompanied by three passengers. One of those passengers was 25-year-old Brian Gaule, whose family lived in County Cork, and the pilot offered to take the Gaule family on a sightseeing flight from Cork Airport. Brian Gaule's father, Patrick, who was a bank manager in Youghal, declined to go but Brian, his mother Maureen and twelve-year-old brother John joined James Coupe for the flight. Patrick Gaule watched from the airport viewing balcony as the plane took off northwards from the main runway at 4.45 p.m. As it climbed, black smoke was seen to pour from the aircraft and the pilot then appeared to attempt a left-hand turn in a possible effort to regain the runway. Unfortunately, the plane stalled and crashed into a field just outside the perimeter fence of the airport. All of this was seen by Patrick Gaule, three of whose family were on board, and as rescue vehicles rushed to the scene he descended from the balcony in a distressed state and 'dashed wildly across the runway, across the fields to the scene of the crash'.[20] He was restrained by airport personnel and brought back to the terminal building.

This was the first crash at the airport. A less serious incident had occurred on the evening of 24 March 1963 when an Aer Lingus Viscount left the runway, having landed after a flight from London. Nobody was injured in the incident and the plane was undamaged. Indeed, many on board were unaware that anything untoward had happened.

MARCH 1968: THE CRASH OF AER LINGUS VISCOUNT, *ST PHELIM*, NEAR TUSKAR ROCK

At 11.32 a.m. on Sunday 24 March 1968 Flight EI 712, an Aer Lingus Viscount 803 EI-AOM named *St Phelim*, with fifty-seven passengers and four crew on board, took off from Cork Airport bound for London Heathrow. About forty minutes later the plane crashed into the sea near Tuskar Rock, off the County Wexford coast, killing all those on board. It has not been possible to explain the cause of the crash definitively, and the consequent uncertainty has added to the sense of loss and tragedy, while different theories, some quite sensational, as to what happened have been able to gain currency in the information vacuum left. Regardless of the precise cause, the loss of the aircraft and those on board traumatised relatives and friends, shocked all who worked at the airport, and dented the sometimes fragile confidence of the public in air travel. Most of the passengers were Irish and, as thirty-six of those were from the Cork area, the crash had a profound local impact, captured in an editorial in the *Cork Examiner*:

It is here in Cork that the sense of loss will be greatest. By the standards of great cities ours is a very small community and a majority of the victims was widely known in its intimate circle. Inevitably, this has created a sense of personal sorrow which will be reflected here today in an atmosphere of mourning seldom experienced before.[21]

The last message from the plane was just after 11.58 a.m. when the pilot radioed: 'Five thousand feet, descending, spinning rapidly.' It quickly became clear that the plane had crashed into the sea. A full alert was called and while there was initial hope that some had survived, by early afternoon the full gravity of the situation was becoming known. As soon as the news broke many anxious relatives of passengers made their way to Cork Airport, fearing the worst but hoping for some positive news. Many were in quite a distressed state and Aer Lingus officials and airport personnel, themselves traumatised by the tragedy, struggled to comfort those relatives as confirmation of the scale of the loss came through. A number of clergymen came to the airport to help bereaved relatives, and public representatives, led by the Lord Mayor of Cork Pearse Wyse, also came and offered condolences. Local, national and international media personnel gathered as a local tragedy became an international news story.

The pilot of the Viscount was Captain Bernard O'Beirne, aged thirty-five. He was a very experienced pilot and had over 6,000 hours' flying time, 1,679 of which were flown on Viscounts. The co-pilot was First Officer Paul Heffernan, aged twenty-two, from Ballintemple in Cork. He had 1,139 hours of flying time, 900 on Viscounts. Shortly before the crash he had received news that he was being granted his senior commercial pilot's licence. Paul Heffernan had been scheduled to fly on a different flight but, in a fateful twist, had changed places with another first officer. The two cabin crew were Mary Coughlan and Anne Kelly. Mary Coughlan had been flying for only one month and, like Paul Heffernan, had changed shifts with a colleague who had requested the day off. Anne Kelly's body was the first of only fourteen recovered after the crash.

As the names of the passengers were released, the media began to piece together the details of those who had perished. Amongst them was

Father Edward Hegarty, a curate in the parish of Ballyphehane and Catholic chaplain to Cork Airport. He had assisted the Bishop of Cork at the blessing of the airport on the day of its official opening in 1961 and had given the last rites to the four people killed when a private plane crashed at the airport in August 1964. He was travelling with some of his parishoners to London to attend a function organised by Ballyphehane emigrants. Hannah Burke was manageress of the cafeteria at the airport and was travelling with her mother, Bridget O'Callaghan. They had intended travelling the previous day, but had changed their booking to the Sunday morning. Three employees of the Norwich Union insurance company – Rory Delaney, Barney O'Rourke and Kevin O'Callaghan, all from Cork – were heading to a training course at their company's head office in England. Both Rory Delaney and Barney O'Rourke were due to be married within a short time. Michael Cowhig, John Nyhan and Tom Dwane also died in the crash. They worked at the Moorepark agricultural research centre near Fermoy and were on their way to deliver papers at a conference in Reading. A group of nine Swiss anglers who had spent a holiday in County Kerry died, as did a party of five Belgian anglers who had been fishing in the Fermoy area.[22]

Many stories were told about passengers who had missed the fatal flight or who had changed their booking to another day. Three Germans who were in Ireland researching a series of travel articles for a newspaper were speeding from Barley Cove in west Cork towards the airport on that Sunday morning to catch flight EI 712 to London. They were delayed when their car broke down and they eventually arrived half an hour after the plane had left. May O'Leary, a ground hostess with Aer Lingus, had been due to fly on the plane also, but had changed her flight to the following day to enable her attend a Station Mass at the home of a neighbour near Bantry.[23]

Left: An Aer Lingus Viscount 800 at Cork. By the mid-1960s Aer Lingus was using Viscounts on all its cross-channel services. GABRIEL DESMOND

Below: 30 March 1968. The remains of one of the victims of the Tuskar air crash of 24 March 1968 are brought ashore. IRISH EXAMINER

As the search for wreckage and for the bodies of the victims got under way, the Lord Mayor of Cork called for a day of mourning in the shocked city and asked businesses to close for one hour at noon on Tuesday 26 March as a mark of respect to those who had died and to enable employees attend religious services. Bishop Lucey of Cork celebrated a requiem Mass in the North Cathedral attended by Taoiseach Jack Lynch, Lord Mayor Pearse Wyse, representatives from the Swiss and Belgian embassies, a host of representatives from public, business, sporting and academic bodies and over 200 relatives of those who had died. A memorial service was also held at St Fin Barre's Cathedral, presided over by the Church of Ireland Bishop Perdue, and Erskine Childers, Minister for Transport and Power, led the dignitaries attending that service.

In all only fourteen bodies were recovered after the crash and in the region of two thirds, by weight, of the Viscount's wreckage. Neither the tailplanes (the smaller 'wings' at the rear of the aircraft) nor the elevators (the hinged flaps on the tailplanes that help control ascent and descent) were found, apart from a portion of the elevator spring tab from the port (left-hand) elevator that was recovered from a beach about 7 miles west of the crash location and a portion of trim tab from the starboard (right-hand) elevator found with the main wreckage. Flight recorders were not carried and the first investigations into the crash, by Aer Lingus and the Aeronautical Section of the Department of Transport and Power, relied principally on the plane wreckage, which was partially reconstructed at Casement Aerodrome, Baldonnel, witness statements and the transcripts of radio communications with the St Phelim. The Department of Transport and Power report into the accident, published in 1970, did little to offer an explanation as to the cause of the disaster and certain speculation in the report added to the more sensational theories that had been circulating since

the aircraft's loss.[24] The last of the twelve conclusions to the report states:

There is evidence which could be construed as indicative of the possible presence of another aircraft or airborne object in the vicinity which, by reason of collision, or by its proximity causing an evasive manoeuvre to be made, or by its wake turbulence, might have been the initiating cause of an upsetting manoeuvre resulting in the Viscount entering a spin or spiral dive. There is no substantiating evidence of such a possibility, but it cannot be excluded for it is compatible with all of the presently available evidence.[25]

This conclusion gave credence to the rumours that had been circulating since the accident that an RAF missile, drone or manned aircraft had caused the loss of the Viscount. Although there was 'no substantiating evidence of such a possibility', as the report itself states, much discussion of the accident over the past four decades has been coloured by this suggestion.

The thirtieth anniversary in 1998 led to renewed questioning and speculation on the events surrounding the accident. In a response to public demand Mary O'Rourke, Minister for Public Enterprise, ordered a review of all files held in Ireland and Britain relating to the accident, with a view to allaying disquiet and providing more definite conclusions as to the cause of the crash. This report was published in 2000.[26] It concluded that the 1970 report was inadequate in a number of ways, especially in that a cause 'other than a collision or near collision with another airborne object' was not adequately investigated.[27] The 2000 report also noted a number of other issues it considered pertinent to the debate. The recovered wreckage of the Viscount that had been held at Casement Aerodrome was disposed of 'without adequate notice to interested parties who may have wished to examine same'.[28] The report also raised a number of points in relation to the maintenance history of the Viscount – paperwork relating to the maintenance of the plane was missing, there were 'serious errors' in the Aer Lingus maintenance operating plan of the *St Phelim*, and the Department of Transport and Power had failed in its role of approving and auditing that plan. While there was no evidence that any of these items had a bearing on the cause of the accident, the report noted that the omissions from the 1970 Report were 'difficult to comprehend'.[29] The report also raised an issue that posed a potential conflict of interest and could potentially give rise to conspiracy theories. R. W. O'Sullivan, Inspector of Accidents at the Air Accident Investigation Unit, headed the 1968–70 investigation and was accordingly the author of the 1970 report. It was he who had approved the Certificate of Airworthiness for the *St Phelim*, an approval that was given in spite of the unavailability of the required complete maintenance history of the aircraft.

A further investigation into the accident was ordered in 2000, again by Mary O'Rourke. This was undertaken by an experienced independent international team of three aeronautical investigators, Yves Lemercier, Manuel Pech and Colin Torkington. Their report was published in 2002 and runs to over 150 pages.[30] At the outset of their work the team called for any witnesses to the accident who had not previously come forward to contact them. This elicited some new information. Their investigation did not have access to the plane wreckage nor to the taped radio communications between the *St Phelim* and Shannon Air Traffic Control (ATC). A transcript of the latter was available, but the original recordings had been disposed of or had been taped over around 1976. The 2002 report is the most exhaustive study of the material relating to the accident and gives the most plausible reconstruction of the plane's flight path and the most convincing explanation of the probable causes of the crash. It rejects all theories relating to a second aircraft or drone or missile being involved in the accident. It points out inconsistencies in the transcripts of the radio communications between Shannon ATC and the *St Phelim*. These transcripts and the recorded timing of the various communications formed the basis for the reconstruction of the flight path, or route, of the aircraft in the 1970 report. Where eyewitness evidence contradicted this reconstruction it was either ignored or used to support the suggestion of the involvement of a second aircraft. The 2002 report details the inconsistencies in the Shannon ATC transcripts and points to failings in procedures rather than in personnel as being the cause of those inconsistencies. Those inconsistencies contributed in no way to the cause of the accident, but formed the basis for the original reconstruction of the aircraft's flight path, a flight path rejected in the 2002 report. Forty-six eyewitness accounts were considered by the 2002 team and their statements provide a complete and plausible reconstruction of the route taken by the plane and allow a technically logical description of the process that led to its loss.

The *St Phelim* took off from Cork at 11.32 a.m. and headed eastwards while climbing steadily. Between ten and twelve minutes into the flight there was a loss of control and the plane dived suddenly over the Old Parish area on the coast of County Waterford. This event was precipitated by damage to the port tailplane by a bird strike, metal fatigue, corrosion or some other cause. The pilot and first officer regained a measure of control and probably decided to head back towards Cork Airport, but were unable to bring the aircraft about. The plane was increasingly difficult to manoeuvre as the initial damage resulted in severe vibrations in the tail area, leading to further damage or degradation, which in turn caused further loss of control. Struggling with the controls the cockpit crew flew eastwards, low over the sea, crossing Tramore Bay and Brownstown Head before the plane turned left and headed inland in a northerly direction. About fourteen or fifteen minutes after the first dive the plane dived a second time in the area of the Kennedy Arboretum in County Wexford at around 11.58 a.m. The crew again regained some control and flew at a very low altitude in a southwesterly direction towards the church in Ballykelly, where witnesses saw the plane, clearly identifiable as a Viscount, head towards the church steeple only to veer left at the last moment. It continued towards Fethard-on-Sea where it made a number of right-hand turns before heading eastwards again over the sea in the direction of Tuskar Rock. At this stage the tail of the plane was degrading rapidly and the complete port tailplane or its elevator became detached and fell into the sea. Witnesses reported hearing or seeing a large splash, while others reported seeing something floating on the surface of the sea east of Fethard-on-Sea that afternoon. A portion of the elevator spring tab from the port tailplane was recovered from a beach in this area, an item that could not have floated there from the crash site 7 miles to the east. A short time later the plane became impossible to control and crashed into the sea near the Tuskar Rock at about 12.15 p.m.

This scenario, as outlined, means that the crew managed to fly the plane for about thirty-two minutes after the first loss of control and dive, and succeeded in regaining control a second time after a further potentially catastrophic dive some fifteen minutes later. The authors of the 2002 report are very clear in their praise for the crew for their efforts to keep the plane airborne, given the process of degradation in the tail area following the initial upset, and suggest that their feat of airmanship should be properly acknowledged.

Aer Lingus had earlier lost two other Viscounts in crashes – on 22 June 1967 EI-AOF, called *St Cathal*, crashed near Ashbourne in County Meath while on a training flight, killing the three crew on board. On 21 November 1967 EI-AKK *St Aidan* crashed while attempting to land in poor conditions at Lulsgate Airport near Bristol, injuring one hostess and a number of passengers.

'A White Elephant'?

Following spectacular growth in its first seven years of operation Cork Airport saw its first fall in passenger numbers in 1968, from 167,701 to 163,048, a drop of 2.8 per cent. Although passenger numbers jumped to 173,333 the following year, that fall raised the question of the long-term viability of the airport. The airport had also operated at a loss through those years, the deficit being £38,000 for 1968 and £24,423 the following year. (Cork Airport did not record its first operating surplus until 1985, twenty-four years after it opened.) On 1 April 1969 Aer Rianta took over the management of Cork and Shannon airports from the Department of Transport and Power and immediately began an investigation as to why the growth at Cork had slowed.

In January 1969 the president of the Irish Airline Pilots' Association, Captain Alan Bowes, speaking at a function in Dublin, had some harsh words of criticism for the airport at Cork. He felt that it should not have been built on the Ballygarvan site, given the frequency of low cloud and fog resulting in a high diversion rate, especially in winter. He said that Cork Airport was 'an example of the ship of aviation being spoiled for a ha'pworth of tar – or should I say for a gallon of runway centre-line paint'. A statement from the Government Information Bureau repeated that the site was the most suitable of those examined and added: 'The diversion rate at Cork Airport

An aerial view of the ramp and terminal buildings from the southwest, September 1969. GABRIEL DESMOND

averages 2½% per annum and is well within the standard laid out by the International Civil Aviation Organisation for airports.'[31] While the diversion rate may have been within the accepted international standard, Cork had a higher diversion rate than the other Irish airports, and this continued to be the case until 1989 when improvements in navigational aids and landing technology led to the airport achieving a Category II status, bringing diversions down to a below-average rate.

In August 1969 the *Irish Independent* reported on the concerns being expressed about Cork Airport's viability: the article described the airport as being 'like a ghost installation in winter time' and claimed there was 'a growing school of

thought that the airport is losing the aviation battle and may soon become a costly white elephant'. R. C. O'Connor, the general manager of Aer Rianta which had recently taken over the management of the airport, put some of the blame on travel agents in the south who did not route their air charter business through Cork. Others felt that Aer Lingus should be operating more services out of Cork, while Bord Fáilte was said not to be doing enough to promote tourism through the airport. The *Irish Independent* writer pointed the finger of blame more generally – at the people of Cork:

> What it all amounts to is that Cork looked for the facilities and are now not using them in sufficient numbers to justify the huge capital

cost and the heavy expenditure on maintenance ... A smug community must be made to realise, also, that it must get up, shake off its obvious complacency and set about working to preserve what is a precious asset.[32]

The honeymoon was over, and some turbulent years lay ahead for the 'smug community' and its 'precious asset'.

A John Hinde postcard of Cork Airport, late 1960s.
JOHN HINDE STUDIO

Photo: E. Nägele, John Hinde Studios.

The Terminal Building, Cork Airport, Ireland.

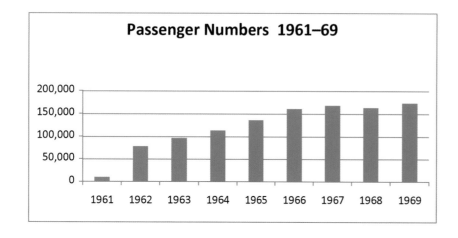

Passenger Numbers 1961–69

Charlie Chaplin with his wife Oona, 3 April 1964. IRISH EXAMINER

President of Ireland Éamon de Valera waves to onlookers as he leaves the terminal building to board a helicopter, 24 July 1966. GABRIEL DESMOND

President of Ireland Patrick Hillery (right) with President Karstens of the Federal Republic of Germany, to his right, at Cork Airport, 1 May 1980. GABRIEL DESMOND

Fred Astaire and Aer Lingus ground hostess Margaret Kelly, July 1969.
IRISH EXAMINER

Rory Gallagher, 26 June 1978. IRISH EXAMINER

Actor Howard Keel (right) with Denis Maher. CORK AIRPORT

Actor Richard Harris and family, 2 January 1965.
IRISH EXAMINER

Actress Jayne Mansfield, 24 April 1967. IRISH EXAMINER

Paul and Linda McCartney with children Heather and Mary, 20 August 1971. IRISH EXAMINER

Jack Doyle, the 'Gorgeous Gael (right), is welcomed back to Cork by Pat Twomey of the Country Club Hotel, 20 November 1972. IRISH EXAMINER

The Bee Gees arrive in Cork, 1967. IRISH EXAMINER

George Best with some airport personnel in the manager's office. CORK AIRPORT

Keith Floyd, celebrity chef, 'bon viveur' and occasional west Cork resident, who described Cork Airport as 'the pub with a runway'. CORK AIRPORT

King Karl Gustav of Sweden inspects a guard of honour prior to his departure from Cork Airport on 9 September 1992. GABRIEL DESMOND

A pilgrimage group about to depart for Lourdes in 1970. BARRY MURPHY

TURBULENCE

1970–84

THE 1970s AND EARLY 1980s were turbulent times for Ireland and Cork, and Ireland's newest airport often struggled to negotiate its way through the stormy conditions. The perpetual fog problem resulted in a high rate of diversions; there was a perceived lack of commitment to the smallest of Aer Rianta's three airports from the management body itself, Aer Lingus and central government; the troubles in Northern Ireland hit tourist numbers, especially from Britain, and economic recession, particularly Cork's own black days in the early 1980s, had serious knock-on effects for the airport. Despite all the obstacles, the airport held tough, gradually improving its facilities and increasing its passenger numbers. Cooperation between staff and management, together with a major marketing drive, would see the airport poised to make an operating profit for the first time in the mid-1980s, heralding a bright new era in its history.

Seeing through the fog

Aer Rianta noted in its annual report for 1970 that 'the company continues to encourage local interests to assist in the development of the airport and the co-operation it has received, together with the favourable trend in 1969–70 results, augurs well for the future of Cork Airport'. Cork was still being subsidised heavily, however. Its revenue for 1969–70 was £94,811 (4 per cent of the total income from the three airports), while expenditure was £119,234 (9 per cent of the total amount spent on airports).[1]

Two landmark events occurred in August 1970: on Sunday 2 August the airport had its busiest day since it opened, when 2,500 passengers passed through. The main reason was the cancellation of flights the previous day due to fog. Then, on 27 August, jumbo jets landed in Cork for the first time when three transatlantic Aer Lingus Boeings

Cork Airport is very prone to fog and in the years prior to its upgrade to Category II status in 1989 the diversion rate at Cork was relatively high. This photograph shows a C-160 Transall of the French Air Force forced to stay overnight at the airport in heavy fog. GABRIEL DESMOND

were diverted due to heavy fog in Shannon. A key problem, which was receiving increased attention, was that Cork's main runway was not long enough to accommodate larger jets, and as a result the airport was losing out on important charter traffic. One travel agent who planned to operate a Cork–Spain direct charter had to cancel the plans for this reason in 1970 and run instead from Shannon and Dublin.[2] Depending on the length of the journey, large planes like Boeing 707s could take off from Cork, but rarely with full loads. An Aer Rianta survey indicated that only an additional 500 feet of runway were required, but the terrain made the work extremely costly. According to the Department:

> The limitations of the present main runway may from time to time impose economic penalties on individual aircraft operations but such penalties would be negligible compared to the cost of extending the runway; and there is as yet no evidence that the development of traffic at the airport is being inhibited by the present runway lengths.[3]

Aer Rianta intended a full survey of the airport, on foot of a pilot study by researchers at University College Cork that suggested that it was operating not nearly at its full potential. While passenger figures increased by nearly 20 per cent in the first six months of 1970, the overall annual total of 73,321 was considered relatively small, considering that Cork was the second city in the state, the largest county, and the gateway to Ireland's most popular tourist region.[4]

A major problem for Cork was the prohibitively high cost of airline tickets. A midweek flight from Cork to London cost £14, compared to £11 18s from Dublin, because the Cork route was longer. This tempted some to travel to Dublin and fly from there. Travel agents argued that airlines should fix uniform rates for all flights to and from the State's three airports to give Cork a more competitive position. In October 1970 the government surprised Aer Lingus when it refused it permission to increase prices on its UK flights from Cork, while allowing a 7½ per cent hike to equivalent prices on flights to the UK from Dublin and Shannon. Days later Aer Lingus announced that it was considering withdrawing the Cork–Lourdes–Barcelona service from the following year's schedule due to heavy losses. This bad news was partly offset by the announcement soon after by Heffernan's Travel that it was going to begin weekly charter flights from Cork to Malaga, beginning the following June. A special working party with representatives from Ivernia (the Cork–Kerry tourism organisation), local hoteliers, travel agents and Aer Rianta personnel was established in 1970 to promote tourism. As part of this promotional drive, an Aer Rianta delegation attended the Association of British Travel Agents conference in Cannes the following year to create awareness of Cork Airport as a natural gateway to the south of Ireland.[5] Speaking on the occasion of the airport's tenth anniversary ceremonies in October 1971, when a tribute plaque to Seán Lemass, who had died earlier in the year, by Cork sculptor Seamus Murphy was unveiled, Minister for Transport and Power Brian Lenihan referred to the growing interest of the travel industry in the facilities at Cork. He said that the growth of the inclusive tour business in and out of Cork was most satisfactory, and that this reflected the travel industry's interest in utilising the many facilities the airport had to offer: 'near immediate access to the sea-angling centres such as Ballycotton, Cobh and Kinsale, and access within an hour or two to the incomparable scenery and hospitality of west Cork and Kerry.'[6]

The recurrent fog problem – which led to the diversion of over 4 per cent of flights annually in the early years, though the annual average for the 1960s was 2.5 per cent (the number would have

A snowy morning at Cork, January 1977. Work on a new extension to the terminal is under way. GABRIEL DESMOND

been much higher but for the fact that there was less traffic from November to March) – was eased slightly in 1970 when a new radar unit was added to the existing instrument landing system. Other improvements in 1970 included the completion of new stores and an engineering building; a new communications centre, combining an airport duty office, telephone exchange and information desk was opened in May; and Marathon Oil Company built a new hangar at the airport for housing helicopters used in servicing its offshore drilling operations. Meanwhile, in the passenger terminal building, Bank of Ireland replaced Ulster Bank, which had held the banking concession since the airport first opened. In 1970–71, airport revenue increased to £113,492 (£7,135 of which came from rents and concessions), but expenditure also

increased, to £160,000, mainly as a result of increased maintenance costs. Highlighting Cork's Cinderella status in comparison to its two sister airports, Dublin returned an operating surplus of just under £1 million in that same year, while Shannon's profits were almost £1.5 million. Passenger numbers were up 10 per cent at Cork, with no seasonal peaking, which was regarded as a positive sign indicating increasing business activity, illustrated by the increase in freight traffic of almost 100 per cent between late 1969 and late 1971 and the opening of two new air freight company offices at the airport. A Visual Approach Slope Indicator (VASI) system on the main runway was completed in 1971, as part of an ongoing programme to improve operating efficiency and safety at the airport.

Two Lockheed C-141A Starlifters of the US Air Force at Cork Airport during an operation to recover a midget submarine, *Pisces III*, with two crew on board, which had sunk off Mizen Head in August 1973. The mission was successful. GABRIEL DESMOND

Troubles and strife

By 1972 Cork was serving five cities with scheduled services: Dublin, London, Manchester, Birmingham and Paris. There were also weekly summer charters to Amsterdam and Spanish sun destinations. Continental traffic was up by 40 per cent across the year and in September a new duty-free shop was opened in the terminal building in what one newspaper described as 'a further effort to narrow the amenity gap between it and the bigger rival ports at Dublin and Shannon'.[7] Basic infrastructural improvements continued, with the installation of a new water reservoir and piping. Many in Cork continued to express frustration at what they saw as the Dublin-centric policies of Aer Lingus. In November 1972 the company was

heavily criticised by Denis Murphy, president of the Cork Chamber of Commerce, for reducing its Dublin–London fares. He described the decision as 'a typical example of centralised bureaucracy looking no further than the boundary of Dublin when making decisions', and asked whether the time had not come for another airline to take over the main business at Cork Airport.[8]

In 1972–73, passenger numbers fell for the second time since the opening of the airport, reflecting a general pattern – passenger numbers at the three airports dropped by 5 per cent, while Cork lost over 4 per cent. A common explanatory factor was the worsening conflict in Northern Ireland, which was deterring British visitors in particular, the main source of tourism. An indication of the atmosphere was the refusal of both the Scotland and Wales rugby union teams to travel to play Ireland in the 1972 Five Nations championship; this followed the burning of the British Embassy in Dublin in the aftermath of the Bloody Sunday massacre of civilians by the British army in Derry. Revenue fell and Cork's deficit more than doubled in 1972–73. The revenue drop was exacerbated by the decision of the Department of Transport and Power to reduce domestic landing charges in January 1973, which hit Cork particularly badly as landing charges had not increased there since the airport opened in 1961. Increased expenditure on security was also necessary; hijacking of planes was a growing phenomenon worldwide, and fears that it would spread to Ireland were real, especially given the

worsening troubles in the North. Ireland's entry to the EEC in January 1973 opened up an avenue of hope for increased passenger and goods traffic with the continent. The Cork Harbour region was also developing into Ireland's centre for multinational pharmaceutical and chemical industries. In July 1973, Gerard Holohan, assistant manager since the airport opened, was appointed manager, replacing Paddy O'Grady, who moved to Dublin as international affairs manager at Aer Rianta head office.[9]

The oil crisis of 1973–74 increased fuel costs and contributed to a general economic downturn worldwide. The year 1974 began badly when the 'big wind' on 11 and 12 January, with gusts of up to 112 mph, inflicted major damage at Cork

Gerry Holohan (Airport Manager 1973–84) left, makes a presentation to his predecessor, Paddy O'Grady (Airport Manager 1967–73) on the occasion of his transfer to Dublin Airport in September 1973.

Spectators on the balcony viewing an Aer Lingus Boeing 737-200, 1 August 1977. GABRIEL DESMOND

Airport; several planes were destroyed, as was the Joyce Aviation hangar.[10] Passenger numbers at Cork increased slightly by 3 per cent in 1974. The fire station was finally extended to provide better accommodation for staff and equipment, and a total of eighty-three workers were now employed, out of Aer Rianta's total workforce of 1,708. The operating deficit remained at over £100,000, however, and Aer Rianta initiated a long-term strategy to stimulate the development of the airport. Plans were developed to extend the passenger terminal and the freight buildings, and Aer Rianta invited interested organisations to participate in a Cork Airport Consultative Committee, to enable local interests to participate in and be informed about promotion and development. A commercial development officer for the airport, Barry Roche, was appointed in September 1974 and in October the Consultative Committee held its first meeting, attended by representatives of local authorities, trade unions, airlines, and commercial, tourism and travel organisations.

Hopeful developments

Tourism numbers improved considerably in 1975, and the intensification of oil and gas exploration off the southwest coast also contributed to the 8 per cent increase in traffic through Cork. This, together with increased landing and passenger charges introduced in the summer of 1974, led to a 42 per cent increase in revenue. However, costs, such as pay and security, also increased, resulting in a net deficit of £193,000 in 1975. The Airport Consultative Committee met regularly, and Barry Roche, the commercial development officer, continued to work with local tourism interests as well as forging links in the UK. This resulted in a new regular scheduled service to Plymouth using ten-seater Islanders, operated by the British company Brymon Airways, which commenced in June 1975 and lasted until 1977, and a number of other contracts in the following years. The freight buildings were extended in 1975, and plans for a 4,500 square foot extension to the passenger terminal were well advanced. The extension,

The inaugural Dan Air flight on the Cork–Bristol–Cardiff route, 6 April 1977. *IRISH EXAMINER*

which would enable 200 arriving and 200 departing passengers to be handled simultaneously each hour at peak times, was seen as essential if the airport was to advance towards profitability at last – something that would require an estimated half a million passengers a year, representing a more than doubling of the numbers. British Airways took over the scheduled service to London run previously by Cambrian (which it had absorbed) in April 1976, increasing the airport's London capacity by 46 per cent. This ran until 1991. Security fears in its early days saw British Airways' checked baggage on the ramp beside the aircraft with passengers having to identify their own bags as they boarded the plane, after which it was loaded.[11] Travellers to and from Britain represented 80 per cent of the traffic at Cork, and Aer Rianta continued to pressurise the Revenue Commissioners to allow duty-free sales for these passengers. The existing duty-free shop had an annual turnover of £40,000; extending it to UK passengers would increase the turnover to an estimated £200,000.[12]

In October 1976 work began on the expansion and remodelling of the terminal building, which would be undertaken on a phased basis over two

An Taoiseach Jack Lynch cuts the tape to officially open the new terminal extension, 29 June 1978. *IRISH EXAMINER*

years by John Sisk and Son of Cork. The original terminal was designed to deal with smaller planes such as 28-seater DC-3s and 40-seater Friendships. With the steady growth in passenger numbers and the shift to larger carriers, like the modern 113-seater Boeing 737s and 123-seater Tridents, the upgrade and extension was essential. As well as an additional 4,500 square feet of space, the project involved major alterations within the existing building aimed at rationalising the traffic flow and improving the baggage-handling facilities, including new green and red channel systems for customs clearance. According to manager Gerry Holohan: 'This will help to make the airport more attractive, both to the traveller and the airlines, by improving such basic services as passenger reception, baggage-handling facilities and public accommodation generally, including a better self-service restaurant.' A variety of larger offices and working areas was also included, and larger shop spaces, including a trebling of the size of the duty-

free shop.[13] Improvements completed in 1976 included an automatic car-park system, new office accommodation for British Airways, and the installation of a weather radar surveillance station.

April 1977 saw the inauguration of a new, year-round Cork–Bristol–Cardiff service, operated by the UK-based Dan Air company, and a weekly summer schedule to the Breton cities of Rennes and St Nazaire provided by the French airline, Touraine Air Transport.[14] Passenger numbers rose by 9 per cent, and there was a great increase in non-scheduled aircraft movement due to the extra helicopter and fixed-wing traffic generated by the construction of the first gas production platform in the Kinsale gas field. Despite a revenue increase of 24 per cent to over £500,000, Cork's deficit increased by 16 per cent because of increasing costs. The introduction of cross-channel duty-free facilities in March 1978 was a huge boost, a new, extended duty-free shop having opened in preparation in December 1977. The new terminal

A KLM Sikorsky S-61 on lease to Irish Helicopters is refuelled on the south ramp as a Bell 212 lifts off, August 1976. Irish Helicopters opened its own hangar and offices at the airport five years later in June 1981. GABRIEL DESMOND

building was officially opened on 29 June 1978 by Taoiseach Jack Lynch, although 20 per cent of the work remained to be completed. One factor in the delays was the strike by clerical staff in a pay dispute with Aer Lingus, which caused major disruption at the airport between March and May. Despite the strike, passenger numbers were up 15 per cent. A Cork–Amsterdam year-round service was introduced in May, a seasonal Cork–Jersey service began in June and there was continued growth in non-scheduled air movements due to the intensification of work schedules at the Kinsale gas field. The total amount spent on Cork Airport by the end of 1978 was £2.648 million, incorporating the £632,000 that the 1977–78 improvements eventually cost.

Continuing difficulties

The year 1979 began with Cork Airport at the centre of the search-and-rescue efforts following the Whiddy Island disaster. In the early hours of 8 January the French oil tanker *Betelgeuse* exploded near the oil terminal at Whiddy in Bantry Bay. The explosion and huge fire killed fifty people; a Dutch diver died during the salvage operation. The air-based search-and-rescue operation was centred on Cork Airport, where the Irish Air Corps, Irish Helicopters and the Royal Navy helicopters refuelled. There was a more general growth in helicopter movements through the airport as the year progressed, with the continuing intensification of oil and gas exploration off the Cork coast. A decision was taken to construct a specialised helicopter base, and work on this project began towards the end of the year. In the summer Touraine Air Transport began a weekly service to Paris and Aer Lingus started a summer service to Zurich. The new extension facilitated more efficient traffic handling and passenger numbers were up 4 per cent to 348,538. This was less than expected, and a number of factors contributed. A protracted postal strike impacted heavily on tourism numbers. Added to this were rumours of a petrol shortage in the country, and the killing of Lord Mountbatten and eighteen British soldiers by the IRA on 27 August 1979, which deterred many potential British tourists.

Liaison between Cork Airport management and persistent critics of the airport, the Cork Chamber of Commerce, led to the formation of a Cork Airport Users' Committee, which met regularly throughout the year. In February 1979 a new tax-free shop opened ('duty free' means free of excise charges, while 'tax free' refers to VAT), which generated £30,000 profits to add to the £250,000 profits from the duty-free shop. An unofficial lightning strike by craftsmen in March created serious disruption for twenty-four hours; more serious was the disruption caused by a twenty-day strike by the airport police and firemen.

Despite the many problems posed by the turbulent 1970s, Cork Airport finished the decade in a much healthier state than it had begun in terms of passenger numbers, aircraft movements and facilities, but continued to suffer increasing losses. Passenger numbers rose steadily, from 198,585 in 1970 to a peak of 348,538 in 1979 (a high not surpassed until 1985), but the improvements made over the decade meant that the airport could handle double the number of aircraft. Revenue had risen from £156,000 to £862,000 over the decade, but expenditure rose even more, from £160,000 to £1,395,000. Manager Gerry Holohan believed that an additional 70–80,000 passengers per year would allow the airport to go into profit for the first time.[15] Stimulating that growth was the aim as Cork Airport entered the new decade.

Stormy conditions

The airport management's planned drive to increase passenger numbers hit stormy conditions in 1980 as the international recession affected both tourist and business traveller numbers. These general problems were exacerbated by a number of other, specific problems, which combined to produce a reduction of 10 per cent in passenger numbers and 3 per cent in aircraft movements. A strike at Aer Lingus in June and July 1980 – which reduced normal scheduled services to one (the Cork–London flight) – resulted in a loss of approximately 11,000 potential passengers, while another 7,000 were lost to Cork when seventy charter flights to Lourdes, Malaga and Parma were transferred to Dublin at the last minute on the instructions of the Department of Transport, causing much consternation and anger, and prompting the Lord Mayor of Cork to condemn the decision as 'a seemingly national policy to centralise an increasing amount of activity in Dublin to the detriment of major growth centres such as Cork'.[16] Senator John A. Murphy voiced the anger of many in the Cork area in the Seanad, where he stated that 'the decision to cancel a large number of the charters brings into question the whole development of Cork Airport … It is difficult admittedly at the moment to make convincing economic arguments in favour of a 24-hour airport in Cork, but the whole credibility of the airport's future is called into question if reasonable arrangements are not made for its functioning during the summer season.' He questioned Minister for Transport Pádraig Flynn about the reasons for the failure to extend opening hours at the airport and if it had to do with difficulties with the air traffic controllers.[17] Flynn denied there were any problems with the controllers, or any policy to downgrade Cork. He claimed the problem centred on safety considerations, which precluded the possibility of air traffic control staff working excessive hours. Spare staff were not available for transfer from elsewhere, and in general, he argued:

It is not an economic proposition to staff the airport all night for periodic openings for a very simple reason: if we were to take on extra staff, if we had them and if they could be deployed

Illustrations from Aer Rianta Annual Report 1979

Above: From *Aer Rianta Annual report*, 1972

Left: From *Aer Rianta Annual report*, 1971

A Bell 212 and a Sikorsky S-61 helicopter on lease to Irish Helicopters during a busy season of oil and gas exploration off the south coast in the summer of 1978. GABRIEL DESMOND

from anywhere else, we are talking about keeping staff there all night, a large part of it for one flight per night. I do not think that in any economic circumstances that is possible. However, seven all-night openings have been accommodated since April of this year and the Department have told the interested parties, both the tour operators and the airlines involved, that the maximum number that can be accommodated in safety is between four and five per month. If the airlines and the tour operators could be persuaded to reschedule their flights to take advantage of the services that have been provided by the Government in Cork during its opening hours [7.30 a.m. – midnight, Sunday to Friday and 7.30 a.m. – 10.30 p.m., on Saturdays], a lot of this tension and a lot of the strong feelings that have been referred to could be removed. If there is a shortage of aircraft in the national airline to accommodate themselves in this way then the opportunity is always there for them to hire out aircraft, but they have the opportunities and they have the wherewithal to accommodate all who wish to use this airport.[18]

There was also a steep decline in non-scheduled aircraft movements with the drop-off in the oil exploration off Kinsale. A rare boost came with the commencement of a twice-weekly flight to Morlaix in Brittany, operated by Britair, in June 1980, while a new hangar and operations base for Irish Helicopters was completed and opened in December. In the meantime, a team of consultants was commissioned to examine the airport's general suitability for expansion while Aer Rianta and Bord Fáilte combined to promote the airport as a tourist gateway, targeting the French, Dutch, Belgian and Swiss markets in particular. The freight business at the airport had all but ceased, unable to compete with the frequency, convenience and economy of roll-on roll-off ferry services out of Cork Harbour; only occasional services, with freight and passenger space split 50 : 50, operated from the airport.[19]

On 5 April 1981 the *Sunday Tribune* ran an article claiming that passengers at Cork might be in danger due to poor facilities and lack of government funds. It said that the main runway was too short, planes sometimes took off with less than full loads because of this, that the radar system had been rejected by other Irish airports and was outdated, and that Dublin and Shannon were being promoted at the expense of Cork. Aer Rianta hit back immediately, denying the claims and calling the article 'misleading and warped'. Karl O'Sugrue, Aer Rianta public relations manager, pointed out that the government had earmarked £500,000 to develop Cork, including a runway extension. He denied that the runway was too short and that planes had to take off with empty seats, and also rejected the radar claims and those regarding discrimination.[20] In 1981 there was a reversal in the severe traffic decline of the previous year, and the airport recorded a 2 per cent rise in passenger numbers. UK traffic remained low (down 4 per cent), but European figures were up 14 per cent. Work continued on the airport development plan, geared towards catering for the projected increase in traffic in the years ahead. Work began on the installation of new apron floodlighting and preparatory work on the extension of the main apron, aimed at increasing the number of aircraft parking positions and improving safety with regard to aircraft manoeuvring. A new telephone system was also installed. Duty-free and tax-free sales were up 20 per cent, and profits from these helped to reduce the deficit levels by 18 per cent in comparison to 1980. Promotional work continued in the UK and European markets, and a specially commissioned film was produced to aid in the tourism promotion drive. A new Dan Air thrice-weekly Cork–Gatwick service was inaugurated, and Britair extended its Cork–Morlaix service to include Quimper in Brittany.[21]

Clouds (and silver linings)

The airport celebrated its twenty-first birthday in 1982. Eight men and two women who were born on 16 October 1961, and so were celebrating their big birthday along with the airport, were entertained, and one of them won a prize of two Aer Lingus return tickets on any of its routes.[22] Cork man Dick Hogan of *The Irish Times*, reflecting back on the opening, noted that 'many of us in school at the time were more than glad to see the thing opened because at least it put an end to all those essays on how the airport would change our lives'.[23] A series of events was held to mark the anniversary, including a photographic exhibition at the airport, which recalled its early days. The year 1982 was a difficult one for civil aviation generally, in Ireland and internationally. Two airlines – Laker and Braniff – failed and the three Irish airports suffered from the cutbacks many airlines imposed as part of cost-cutting programmes. While aircraft movements were up at Cork, passenger numbers fell by 1 per cent, which turned out to be the only dip in the steady increase in passenger numbers throughout the decade. The British market continued to flounder, European traffic also declined, but domestic numbers increased by over a quarter, due to the introduction of a new Cork–Dublin commuter service by Avair, using 33-seater Shorts 330 planes, which proved immensely popular. Increased profits in duty-free and tax-free sales helped to reduce the overall deficit by another 10 per cent. Gradual infrastructural improvements continued with the completion of the apron extension, and the installation of an electricity-generating stand-by plant and a new communications system for the security personnel.[24] In August Barry Roche, who had begun as part of the original fire and security team in 1961, and had been commercial development officer since 1974, was appointed deputy general manager. He succeeded Gerry Holohan as the airport's general manager on the latter's retirement in 1984.

The following year, 1983, saw Cork in the novel position of being the only Irish airport to record an increase in passenger traffic. While

Above: In 1982 Avair began commuter services between Cork and Dublin using 33-seater Shorts 330s. The aircraft also bears the Aer Lingus logo as the two airlines had a marketing agreement for a period. GABRIEL DESMOND

Below: An Aer Lingus Commuter 35-seater Shorts 360, December 1984. GABRIEL DESMOND

Dublin and Shannon both suffered a 5 per cent decline, Cork's numbers were up by over 8,000. This represented a 2.7 per cent increase overall, and was attributable to the dramatic success of Avair's Dublin service, which contributed to a rise of 35 per cent in domestic passenger numbers. International numbers were down again, however, by 7 per cent, or over 17,000 in total. Slow international traffic hit the profits of the commercial sector, which were down 16 per cent, contributing to a significantly increased overall deficit of £728,000.[25] These figures prompted Aer Rianta to ask staff to discuss the elimination of wasteful expenditure, including 'unjustifiable payroll costs'. Chief Executive Martin Dully declared that 'continuing losses of this nature are not acceptable' and warned of 'drastic' measures, though he denied a rumoured plan to impose redundancies to reduce staffing levels by 25 per cent. Cork's Lord Mayor Hugh Coveney admitted in April 1983 that 'storm clouds' were hovering over the airport, but assured Corkonians that there was a keen awareness in government 'that people down here won't tolerate a serious or permanent downgrading of Cork'. As part of a recovery plan, negotiations began to eliminate overtime, while further cost-cutting measures considered by management during 1983 included closing the airport at 6 p.m. in the winter months.[26]

The airport's problems reflected the broader economic downturn in the country as a whole, and Cork in particular. Two of the city's major industrial employers, Dunlop's tyre factory and Ford's car plant, closed in 1983 and 1984 respectively, adding substantially to the city's growing unemployment figures, while Verolme Dockyard in the harbour shut in 1984 also. Many smaller businesses were closing down and emigration was on the rise, resulting in what one journalist called 'a grim city whose lifeblood had systematically drained away'.[27] A group called the Cork Forum, with representatives from the

Barry Roche, Airport Manager 1984–98. JOHN O'REGAN

corporation, county council, the Industrial Development Authority and the Harbour Commissioners, which had been established in 1982 to fight for the industrial development of the region, saw the upgrading of the airport as a central plank in any regeneration drive.

Cooperation between staff and management had resulted in significant savings in 1984, and Aer Rianta began a major drive to promote and develop the airport. In March it announced the establishment of Cork Airport Marketing, a subsidiary of Aer Rianta, headed by Tom Haughey, with an annual budget of £250,000 over

Location:	
Lat. 515027N, Long. 082920W.	
Elevation:	502 ft. AMSL
Designation:	07/25 Length 1310 metres
	Width 45 metres
	Surface: concrete
	17/35 Length 1829 metres
	Width 45 metres
	Surface: concrete
Refuelling:	Normal refuelling facilities available.
Operational Hours:	07.15 – 24.00 hrs. (local time) April – October (inclusive).
	07.15 – 23.00 hrs. (local time) November – March (inclusive).
Postal Address:	Cork Airport, Cork, Ireland.
Telegraphic Address:	Aerrianta, Cork.
Telephone No.:	(021) 965388
Telex No.:	75085

From *Aer Rianta Annual Report*, 1983

the following four years. The goal was a 33 per cent increase in passenger numbers over five years. Aer Rianta Chief Executive Martin Dully said that if existing airlines did not upgrade their services out of Cork (Aer Lingus had abandoned its year-round services to Birmingham and Manchester, and reduced the Paris and Amsterdam services), 'then we will have to go out and find airlines who would be interested'.[28] A combination of improved marketing, agreed cost-cutting and better commercial sales figures resulted in the airport's trading loss being reduced from £728,000 in 1983 to £72,000 in 1984. Domestic traffic suffered a 5 per cent dip due to Avair's decision to wind up its services from the airport. International passenger numbers recovered significantly, contributing to an overall increase of almost 10,000 and freight traffic increased by 29 per cent. The gloom of the previous three years was replaced by a feeling of confidence, as Aer Rianta announced that it was budgeting for a surplus at Cork for the first time ever in 1985: 'the achievement of that objective would give a major boost to an operation which, for too long, has had to accept the "poor relation" status in comparison with the other two State airports.'[29] Airport manager Barry Roche was equally confident, if slightly less optimistic, predicting a break-even year in 1985, followed by a profitable 1986.[30] Cork Airport had turned a corner; the worst of the turbulence had been negotiated, the fog was clearing and it seemed as if the only way was up.

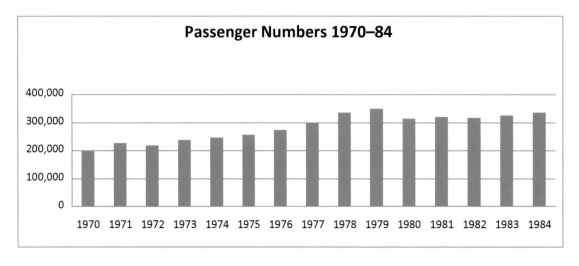

Watercolour of tower and terminal building at Cork, 1985.

THE ONLY WAY IS UP!

1985–99

THE 1980s was a decade of two halves for Cork Airport. The early 1980s were dark years economically in the Cork region, and the airport reflected the gloom, not only as one of the exit points for the dramatically increasing numbers of young emigrants, but also in its own growing financial problems. The airport was dogged by bad publicity and in 1983 laboured under rumours of forced redundancies and even closure. However, by the middle of the decade matters had improved considerably, and as the airport prepared to celebrate its silver jubilee, it announced an annual profit for the first time in its history. A new marketing division, new low-cost flights to England and better domestic services, as well as the gradual improvement of facilities and Cork's general economic health, all contributed to the ascent in fortunes in the second half of the decade. Passenger numbers grew impressively each year, and the airport expanded in response; the main runway was extended in 1989 and in 1991 a new terminal building was opened. Traffic subsequently increased far ahead of expectations, so that by the end of the century, plans for further expansion were already in place.

Cover of the programme for the Air Spectacular, scheduled to take place at Cork Airport on 18 August 1985 as part of the celebrations for Cork 800. Dense fog caused the event to be cancelled, much to the disappointment of the over 50,000 spectators expected to attend.

Cork 800

Cork 800 was the title given to the 1985 events and celebrations organised to mark the 800th anniversary of the granting of a royal charter to the city, aimed at boosting tourism, the economy and morale in the depressed southern capital. Aer Lingus, which had been the subject of persistent criticism for its perceived lack of commitment to Cork, announced early in the year that it was inaugurating new services from Cork to Rennes (with which Cork was 'twinned') and Jersey in the summer, additional services on the Dublin and London routes to cater for the expected increase in traffic, and a direct summer service to Zurich.

The airline also announced that it would promote European tourist programmes and conference travel to the city during Cork 800. It renamed one of its commuter aircraft on the Cork–Dublin route (which it took over following Avair's departure in 1984) the *St Finbarr* and changed the designation of the 6 p.m. Dublin flight to EI 800.[1]

One of the main events of Cork 800 and the centrepiece of the airport's participation in the year's celebrations was the 'Cork Air Spectacular', billed as the greatest air show ever to take place in Ireland and scheduled for 18 August 1985. An expected crowd of 50,000 was to be treated to displays from Freece Tricolori, the Italian aerobatics team, air force teams from the US, Germany and France, and the Irish Air Corps. However, as the day dawned, the organisers' worst nightmare became apparent: Cork Airport was enveloped in thick, low-hanging fog and the show had to be cancelled, with no hope of rescheduling owing to the massive logistical issues involved.[2] Fog, Cork Airport's nemesis since the beginning, had struck again. 1985 also saw Cork Airport host its first wide-body aircraft (large planes with two passenger aisles), an Airbus 300, brought in by TEA of Belgium. With the media assembled, the Airbus burst two tyres near the end of its landing run, but thankfully taxied on with no further problems. Air Liberté would later run Friday charters from Paris to Cork in the early summer using Airbus 300s.[3]

The good news, however, was that in 1985 Cork Airport recorded a surplus (of £71,000) for the first time in its history. This represented an almost 200 per cent improvement on 1984. Operational revenues were up 18 per cent and commercial profits increased by 11 per cent. European traffic was down, in line with national trends (probably as a result of the poor summer weather), but the key UK market was up 10 per cent, resulting in an overall increase of 2 per cent in passenger numbers. The total of 342,418 passengers was the second highest on record to that date (surpassed only in the peak year of 1979).[4] In the Dáil the government outlined planned expenditure on the airport: over £1.3 million in total, covering the replacement of the instrument landing system at the main runway, extension of the terminal building and additional floodlighting and ground equipment. However, Cork TDs continued to argue for more, including the long-promised runway extension, as part of their campaign to get the government to take Cork's economic woes more seriously.[5] Ned O'Keefe of the opposition Fianna Fáil party told the Dáil in May 1985 that:

the lack of a ferry and the failure of the Government to develop Cork Airport are major constraints in the industrial development of that region. We have been told that Cork has only a 6,000 feet runway and that they need one in the region of 8,000 feet to 10,000 feet. I am aware, from meeting business people, that because of the lack of other facilities at Cork Airport it takes three days to go from Cork to Hamburg whereas, if you live in Dublin, you can do it in a day. The Government must examine that whole area and see that Cork Airport is developed to its full status if we are to get the maximum from the region and the county.[6]

Loss of Air India Flight 182

Shortly after 8 a.m. local time on Sunday 23 June 1985, Air India Flight 182 was destroyed off the south coast of Ireland following an explosion on board while flying at a height of 30,000 feet. The Boeing 747 had begun its journey in Toronto and had flown on to Montreal before beginning the transatlantic leg of the flight. It was due to stop over at London and then fly to Delhi and Bombay. All 329 passengers and crew were killed when a small bomb detonated and the aircraft disintegrated. The Marine Rescue Centre at Shannon raised the alarm when the plane disappeared from the radar and a search-and-rescue operation was begun. Shipping was alerted and a cargo ship, the *Laurentian Forest*, was first on the scene and discovered wreckage and bodies in the water, confirming the loss of the plane.

Cork Airport became the centre of the recovery effort and the RAF sent four Sea Kings and three Chinooks to join the operation, and an eighth helicopter came from a US Air Force base in Britain. The Irish Air Corps and Irish Helicopters, based at Cork Airport, also supported the

A victim of the Air India disaster is carried from an RAF rescue helicopter at Cork Airport, 23 June 1985. *IRISH EXAMINER*

operation. Irish naval vessels and a host of other ships and aircraft also took part in the search and recovery, which lasted several days. By 3 p.m. that Sunday afternoon the first bodies were landed at Cork and in all 131 bodies of the 329 who perished were recovered. The airport had never experienced such activity with the constant arrival and departure of helicopters and other aircraft, while the normal scheduled operations had also to be accommodated. When a helicopter landed teams of army medics carried the recovered bodies on stretchers to the waiting ambulances amid the roar of aircraft engines, while a growing band of photographers and other media personnel crowded every vantage point. Armed guards patrolled the ramp, and the scene reminded many of a war zone. The passenger cafeteria was converted into a media centre and Bord Telecom,

the national telephone company, installed scores of telephone and telex lines to facilitate the growing number of reporters from around the world who were converging on the airport, while RTÉ, the national broadcaster, provided facilities for television and radio communications. Catering and other facilities had also to be organised. Regular media briefings were held through the following days. In addition to the media, Irish air accident investigators as well as their Canadian and Indian counterparts also came to Cork Airport as it was chosen as the base for the preliminary investigations into the loss of the plane. Recovered wreckage was brought to the airport also. Relatives of many of those lost in the tragedy came to Cork in the days after the crash and over fifty local families offered accommodation and other help to ease the trauma of their situation.

In the days and weeks after the loss of Air India 182, the facilities and staff at Cork Airport were stretched to their limit in dealing with unprecedented levels of activity in all areas of operation. Airport staff in all departments worked in cooperation with the civil and military authorities as well as with the myriad airline and investigation personnel who were involved in the aftermath of the tragedy, ensuring as smooth an operation as possible in such terrible circumstances. The airport authorities and the people of Cork were widely praised and received messages of thanks and appreciation from the Canadian and Indian governments, as well as from media organisations, airlines and the air forces who had come to Cork to take part in the search and recovery.

Nearly twenty-five years of investigation and speculation have followed this tragedy. It has been established beyond doubt that a bomb caused the loss of the aircraft but only one person has been convicted for involvement, having pleaded guilty to manslaughter in a Canadian court in 2003 after admitting to making the bomb. The most recent investigation into the events surrounding the crash was conducted by a retired Canadian Supreme Court Justice, John Major. His report was published in 2010 and concluded that errors, omissions and delays on the part of the Canadian government, the Canadian intelligence services and the Royal Canadian Mounted Police enabled those responsible for the bombing to succeed in their plot.[7]

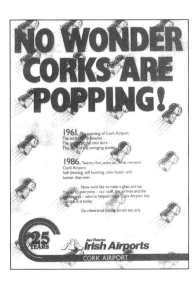

Above and right: Advertisements in the *Cork Examiner*, 16 October 1986.

Below: Invitation to Cork Airport 25th Anniversary Dinner.

'No wonder corks are popping!'

The clouds that had hung over the subdued twenty-first anniversary celebrations in 1982 seemed to have blown away by the time the airport marked its silver jubilee in 1986. A surplus was recorded for the second year running – a modest but satisfying £117,000 – and the largest number of passengers in its history – 357,710 – used the airport, an increase of 4 per cent. Almost all of the growth occurred in the second half of the year when lower fares on the Cork–London route were introduced. The increased traffic led to profits of over £500,000 from duty- and tax-free sales.[8] The celebrations were soured, however, by the government's failure to mark the anniversary with an announcement approving the extension to the main runway. Peter Barry, Cork TD and Minister for Foreign Affairs, was widely expected to make

A Colt hot-air balloon at Cork Airport for Open Day, 16 October 1986. GABRIEL DESMOND

the announcement at the 'Open Day' celebrations at the airport on 16 October, but it never happened. Thousands flocked to the airport on the day, including many school groups, to watch flying displays, including a spectacular routine by Captain Fergus O'Connor in an Irish Helicopters' Sikorsky S-61, which also gave pleasure trips around the city. There were displays by the Air Corps, parachutists and by UK aerobatic champion Richard Goode in a tiny Pitts Special biplane. Aer Lingus was celebrating its fiftieth anniversary in 1986, and the restored *Iolar*, its first plane, was flown to Cork for the day and brought the Lord Mayor and other dignitaries on circuits of the city.[9]

There was bad news in December 1986 when the chief executive of the new Irish low-cost airline Ryanair, Eugene O'Neill, announced that unless it received a licence (applied for six months

previously), it would not be in a position to offer the planned daily Cork–Luton service, a route that represented 'the biggest single growth opportunity for Cork Airport for many years', according to the Cork Airport Marketing's Tom Haughey. Ryanair's proposed flat return fare of £99 from April (rising to £119 in June), which compared favourably to the existing unrestricted Cork–London fare of £240 from Aer Lingus, British Airways and Dan Air, was expected to increase traffic from Cork by 15 per cent, adding a badly needed 76,000 passengers a year (based on the increases experienced by Dublin following the introduction of Ryanair's low-price London service).

The new year brought some good news. The Dáil was dissolved on 20 January 1987 and the following week the Minister for Communications, Jim Mitchell of Fine Gael, gave the go-ahead for

Aer Lingus began flying in 1936 with a de Havilland DH84 Dragon called *Iolar*, which was destroyed during the Second World War. To celebrate the airline's 50th anniversary another Dragon, pictured here, was restored and given the original plane's registration and name. Here it visits Cork to mark the airport's 25th anniversary in 1986. GABRIEL DESMOND

the long-awaited 1,000-foot extension to the main runway. The volte-face, according to the opposition Fianna Fáil party, was the result of panic on the part of the government following the publication of poor opinion poll results for the government parties in the Cork area. Work on the £4 million package (which included the installation of an instrument landing system, the upgrading of navigational aids and centre-line lighting) was scheduled for completion in 1989. The news was met with delight in Cork, where any misgivings about political strokes were outweighed by the advantages of what was seen as an overdue decision. Airport manager Barry Roche said the improvements would upgrade the airport to Category II status, reduce the diversion rate and allow the introduction of aircraft such as the

Airbus and the Boeing 767 jet. Holidays in the sun, Roche said, would no longer require Cork passengers to meet connecting flights in Dublin if they wanted to travel to countries other than Spain and Portugal.[10] The general election saw the return of Fianna Fáil to power, and the new Minister (of the newly created Department of Tourism and Transport), John Wilson, announced the granting of a licence to Ryanair for its Cork–Luton service, which began in June 1987. Until the end of the year Ryanair's Luton flight had to touch down in Dublin on both legs until its direct licence was granted by the UK authorities. A new development for Cork heralded by Ryanair was that it self-handled its passengers. They were followed in this by British Airways in December.[11]

A group of employees with over 425 years of combined service at Cork Airport, photographed on 1 November 1994. Back row (l–r): M. McAuliffe, T. Russell, P. Dempsey, S. Mac Suibhne, J. Milner, D. Maher, T. Kerrigan, W. O'Keeffe, B. Roche. Front row (l–r): M. Healy, J. O'Brien, D. McSweeney, M. Staunton, P. Gallagher, D. Harris, B. Clancy, K. Farrell. RAY SHANAHAN

A group of long-serving airport employees October 1986, photographed with Martin Dully, Aer Rianta chief executive. Back row (l–r): D. Maher, W. O'Keeffe, T. Kerrigan, P. Dempsey, J. Riordan. Middle row (l–r): M. Healy, J. O'Brien, T. Russell, S. Mac Suibhne, D. Harris, J. Milner, D. McSweeney, M. McAuliffe. Front row (l–r): B. Roche, K. Farrell, M. Dully, P. Gallagher.
RAY SHANAHAN

Ryanair's first route was between Waterford and Luton, using a 19-seater Bandeirante and later this 36-seater HS 748, seen here at Cork following a diversion from Waterford, 18 March 1988. GABRIEL DESMOND

A Brymon Airways DHC-6 Twin Otter from Plymouth, with the tower and fire station behind, 13 April 1986. GABRIEL DESMOND

A record high in passenger numbers was recorded for the second year running in 1987, with 441,336 using the airport, attributable mainly to the cheaper fares on cross-channel routes, although European and domestic numbers also showed a healthy increase. New charters included a Club Travel pilgrimage flight to Medjugorje in Yugoslavia. Tax- and duty-free turnover was up 21.8 per cent, yielding a record profit of £1.8 million and contributing to an overall surplus of £284,000. Preliminary earth-moving for the runway extension began in September, followed by work on the first phase of the terminal building extension, which was intended to incorporate the relocation of the airport bar and the provision of much-needed additional public viewing and dining areas.[12]

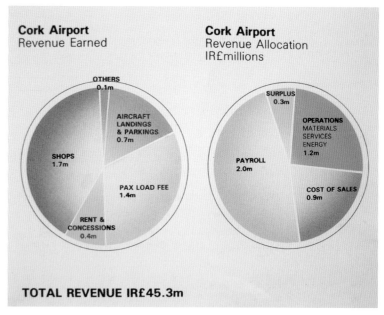

From *Aer Rianta Annual Report*, 1987

In May 1986 TAT began a Paris–Cork service on behalf of Air France. GABRIEL DESMOND

J. J. Walsh (legendary editor of the *Munster Express*), the 500,000th passenger through Cork Airport in October 1987, is presented with a gift by Joe O'Connor, then Assistant Airport Manager. (L–r): M. Ahern, K. Carroll, J. O'Connor, J. J. Walsh, M. Walsh, L. Horne, S. Power. RAY SHANAHAN

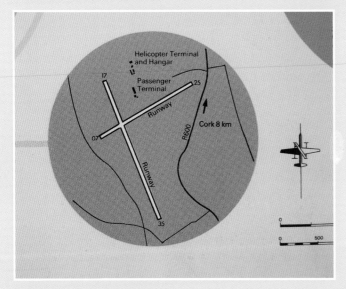

From *Aer Rianta Annual Report*, 1986

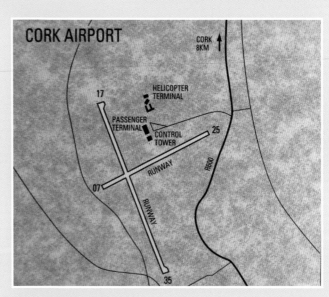

From *Aer Rianta Annual Report*, 1991

Official opening of the 1,000-foot extension to the main runway, 5 July 1989. The ribbon is being cut by John Wilson, Minister for Tourism and Transport. GABRIEL DESMOND

Ascent continues

The omens were good for 1988 when Aer Rianta announced in April that passenger numbers through Cork were up 41 per cent on the same period for 1987. The trend continued, and for the fourth successive year all previous records for both passenger numbers and profitability were broken. Over half a million passengers passed through (an increase of 24 per cent), with the London route being the best performing, as both Aer Lingus and Ryanair operated extra flights throughout the summer. Domestic traffic also increased, by almost one third. The marketing drive also showed dividends, with increased numbers of holiday charters.[13] The results would have been even better

were it not for the severe weather in October. Low cloud cover combined with the temporary unavailability of the instrument landing system and high intensity lighting, which were withdrawn from service due to works in connection with the extension of the runway, led to the diversion of a large number of flights.[14] An era ended in 1988 when Cork and Dublin airports ceased to be forecast offices for Met Eireann, and aviation forecasting for the three airports was centralised at Shannon.

Sales were up in all departments in 1989 and the annual trading surplus was just under £1 million. The 1000-foot extension to the northern end of the main runway was completed, as was the construction of a new southern wing to the

Two RAF Sea King rescue helicopters from Brawdy in Wales on the ramp at Cork Airport, 4 April 1994. GABRIEL DESMOND

terminal building, incorporating a new bar. However, the surge in passenger traffic created congestion at peak periods and plans were prepared for a major extension to the terminal.

The new runway extension was officially opened on 5 July 1989 by the Minister, John Wilson, marking Cork's upgrade to Category II status.[15] Aer Lingus flew a Boeing 747 into Cork for the occasion, the largest aircraft ever to land at the airport.[16] Several new charter services from France during the summer of 1989 indicated the continuing success of the marketing division, and the general trend since 1985 continued with a 16 per cent overall increase in passenger numbers to 627,032. UK traffic was up 13 per cent, despite Dan Air discontinuing its Gatwick service in

March, and domestic numbers increased by 32 per cent for the second year in succession. Shop sales were also the best ever, showing profits of £2.5 million. The good news continued at the year's end with the opening of a new flight training school at the airport, the European College of Aeronautics, which ran one-year training courses for commercial pilots. Iona Airways had already begun pilot training there earlier in the year.[17]

The 1980s, which began in the doldrums for Cork Airport, ended on a high. Its expansion, development and profitability reflected, and contributed to, increasing confidence and an economic upturn in the broader Cork region. In a reflection on the city's fortunes at the end of the 1980s, Cork journalist Mary Leland noted that nobody wanted to be too optimistic, yet, about Cork's reassertion of progress, but 'the indicators are there: the thriving festivals, the success of Kinsale as a gourmet centre and the ripple-effect improvement in Cork's hotels and restaurants, the housing and the prices paid for it, the roads, the airport, the docks, the new small industries, the lively sense of something happening'.[18] Would the airport, and the region it served, continue its ascent in the new decade?

Blip

The new decade began where the previous one had ended for the airport, as it continued its upward trajectory. The year 1990 set new records, with UK traffic up 7 per cent, 14 per cent more domestic travellers, and an overall total of over 700,000 passengers, up over 80,000 on 1989. The growth in traffic was, as usual, reflected in increased operational revenue and commercial profits, which were up 10 per cent. The two flight training schools, which had been established in 1989, expanded their operations. The airport's navigational aids were upgraded again, confirming its status as a designated Category II airfield, while the control tower was refurbished and all equipment was upgraded to state-of-the-art standards.[19]

In February 1991 the first phase of the major terminal extension and development was opened by Taoiseach Charles Haughey. It included a new baggage hall, departure hall, check-in desks, lifts and escalators, departure gates and duty-free shop, as well as a plush new executive lounge, a tropical fish aquarium and a number of 'homely' natural gas fires. He also inaugurated a new Access Control security system, developed by Aer Rianta in association with Nixflu Ireland.[20] Cork was the first Irish airport to have this system, which was subsequently sold to numerous other

organisations. In his speech, Haughey referred to the spectacular 60 per cent increase in traffic over the previous four years, but warned that the Gulf War, which followed the US-led attack on Iraq in August 1990, with its severe impact on Atlantic traffic, along with the downturn in the UK economy and commercial decisions taken by operators, were all impacting negatively on air travel, in Cork as elsewhere.[21]

The half-yearly figures released in July 1991 confirmed the worst, with an 11 per cent drop in passenger numbers at Cork compared to the first six months of 1990.[22] While matters improved slightly in the second half of 1991, an overall drop in passenger numbers of 8.9 per cent was recorded at the year's end, the first 'blip' since 1982. The extended duty-free shop led to another record year, however, with a £2.8 million turnover. Work continued on the next phase of the extension and upgrading of navigational equipment. The impact of the Category II approach equipment was shown in the drop in the diversion rate due to fog from 2.5 per cent to 0.6 per cent in 1991, an all-time low for Cork. Two new scheduled services were inaugurated in 1991 – Birmingham European from Birmingham and KLM from Amsterdam – while there was a substantial increase in the French charter market.[23] On the downside, the newly privatised British Airways announced in January 1991 that it was dropping all its services to the Republic of Ireland.[24]

A new joint-venture catering company was established by Aer Rianta and Campbell Bewley, and its first venture was its takeover (commencing in January 1992) of the catering and bar facilities at Cork Airport, improvements to which were carried out in 1991 at a cost of £1 million.[25] In all, between 1987 and 1991, the government and Aer Rianta had spent approximately £16 million on Cork Airport – £6 million by the government on the provision of radar and navigational equipment, and £10 million by Aer Rianta on the

A new passenger bar and restaurant at the airport was opened in January 1992.

extension to the terminal building and runway.[26] An important factor in increased capital expenditure was the availability of structural funds from the European Union. Between 1992 and 1996 it would receive £2.436 million in EU grant funding.[27]

'Utterly charming Cork Airport': from Cinderella to poster child

In July 1992 Minister for Tourism, Transport and Communications (the department having undergone yet another name change) Máire Geoghegan-Quinn officially opened the extended duty- and tax-free shop and the new Aer Rianta/Bewley's restaurant. A month later a major art exhibition opened at the airport as part of the Aer Rianta Homecoming Festival. Organised by Norah Norton, in conjunction with the Crawford Municipal Gallery and the National Sculpture Factory, it featured paintings and sculpture by twenty artists and was universally well received. 'An Irishman's Diary' in *The Irish Times* declared that the main concourse in 'the utterly charming Cork Airport' was 'almost designed as an exhibition space' and that the exhibition was

worth a trip to the airport, even if one did not have a plane to catch.[28] (Appropriately, in March 2011, the by-then abandoned terminal building became just that – an exhibition space – when it hosted the 'Terminal Convention' art event (see Chapter 7).)

The reaction of passengers and the public to the new expansive terminal was equally positive. The reversal of the blip began, with passenger numbers up almost 50,000, or 7 per cent. This reflected a general upturn in airline traffic following the end of the most active phase of the Gulf War. A new charter service commenced from Zurich to Cork, and the French charter market continued to perform well. Manx Airlines, a member of the British Midland Group, started a Manchester–Cork route, introducing the Jetstream 41 to Cork. The so-called 'sun charter' business was also on the up. The new, improved navigational systems yielded results for the second year running; the diversion rate due to weather was down to 0.4 per cent, which was on a par with the international airport average. Capital investment continued, with the installation of additional approach lighting and new navigational systems on the main runway.[29] Bad news came with the closure in July of the European College of Aeronautics, which had been training pilots at the airport since 1989.

The year ended on a positive note, however, with the announcement in December of plans for a 'Euro Park' development at the airport, a joint venture between Aer Rianta and a UK property development firm, incorporating a hotel, leisure and conference centre, and industrial and business units. Planning permission was sought, and was granted in January 1994. This would eventually take shape as the Cork Airport Business Park, involving Aer Rianta with different partners, which opened in 1999.

Cork Airport recorded its highest ever number of passengers in 1993, when 723,242 people passed through it, an increase of 4.5 per cent on the previous year, more than double the number of a decade previously and over three times more than in 1973. Aer Lingus inaugurated a new daily service to Paris and a scheduled service to Exeter and Newquay in Cornwall was commenced by Newquay Air. The charter business continued to prosper, with two new destinations, Turkey and Tunisia. The airport's reliability record was further enhanced, with a diversion rate of only 0.3 per cent in 1993. The final phase of the terminal expansion programme began, and construction started on a new warehouse for freight and cargo. The tax- and duty-free shop continued to flourish, with sales up 9 per cent to £3.4 million, and the airport declared a profit of over £1 million for the fifth year running.[30]

In January 1994, Cork TD Gerry O'Sullivan, Minister of State at the Department of the Marine, hosted a reception at Cork Airport for the Royal Air Force Search and Rescue Squadron based at Brawdy, South Wales, to mark their contribution to search-and-rescue operations off the Irish coast over many years. The final phase of the new passenger terminal building was completed in 1994, and Aer Rianta proudly declared that 'Cork Airport can now boast of having a terminal comparable with any airport of its size in the world'. Cork's transition from the Cinderella of the Irish airport business to its state-of-the-art poster child was reflected again in the installation of a new 'smart' wiring system, for telecommunications, fax, computers and flight information. It was the first airport in Europe to have this system. The new freight terminal building was also completed. Passenger numbers continued to rise, with the 800,000 mark passed for the first time. New services inaugurated in 1994 included a revived Aer Lingus link to Birmingham and a Manx Airlines service to Manchester, while the latter's Birmingham service began to utilise larger aircraft. Ski charters to Salzburg and Toulouse commenced, as did services to Stockholm, Billund and Copenhagen. July 1994 was the busiest month in the history of the airport, with 100,000 passengers.[31]

A special marketing fund for Cork Airport of £500,000 was announced early in the year, and a marketing task force, chaired by Airport Manager Barry Roche and comprised of representatives of airport management and local commercial interests, was established, promoting Cork with the rather cheesy motto, 'The small airport with the big heart'.[32] Arising from this, a special promotional supplement was published in *The Irish Times* on 26 October, containing features on all aspects of the airport, past and present, and provides a useful snapshot of its operations in the mid-1990s. Anne Cahill reported on the work of the Aviation Authority, a recently created semi-state body that employed thirty-five full-time staff at Cork, operating the air traffic control facilities. Headed up by John Casey, the team had at its disposal one of the most up-to-date air navigation systems in Europe. The meteorological service, under John Collins, had thirteen employees at the time, providing a 24-hour service to all aircraft. In an interview, manager Barry Roche pointed out the danger of Cork Airport becoming a victim of its own success, 'in that State aid is not as freely available to us as it is to other airports'. This was the argument put forward by the lobby group CASE (Cork Airport Seeks Equality), which maintained that Shannon, Dublin and even privately operated airports such as Farranfore in Kerry were better treated than Cork when it came to exchequer funding.

Although the new, expanded and improved passenger terminal had only been completed in 1994, within a year Aer Rianta had appointed a task force to examine further expansion due to the rapidly increasing passenger numbers. These were up again in 1995, by 21.1 per cent, to 971,319, helped by new additions such as Cityflyer's Gatwick service. Continuing marketing initiatives yielded dividends with increased French charter traffic and a series of charter flights from Sweden and Iceland. The Spanish and Canary Islands markets also grew significantly. The new freight terminal was officially opened in November 1995. It comprised 7,000 square feet of warehousing and 2,500 square feet of office space. Because it had its own taxiway and aircraft parking area, the airport now had a stand-alone freight operation for the first time, which boded well for the future of this aspect of the business. Other capital works in 1995 included an extension to the airport's long-term car park and a new ESB substation. Duty- and tax-free sales were up 23.5 per cent, with sales exceeding £5 million.[33]

'A major resource for the local economy'

A study of the airport's economic value to Cork and surrounding counties was commissioned by Aer Rianta and carried out in 1995 by a team of researchers from University College Cork's Department of Economics. The study (published in 2001) confirmed the broader contribution that the airport was making to the Cork, Kerry, Waterford and south Tipperary region, which was identified as its catchment area, concluding that it was 'a major resource for the local economy which it serves'.[34] In terms of its direct contribution, the airport and the businesses located or directly associated with it (see table):

- employed 521 full- and part-time workers, paying £9.73 million annually in wages and salaries.

- accounted for purchases of £6.14 million worth of goods and services, of which half were produced in the catchment area, and £2.5 million worth of goods for resale in the duty- and tax-free shops, of which 20 per cent were produced locally.

EMPLOYERS AT CORK AIRPORT (1995)

Management, design and planning; construction and maintenance; fire and safety; car parking; shops: Aer Rianta

Flight operators: Aer Lingus, Servisair, Irish Helicopters, Hibernian Flying Club, Cork Aviation Centre

Freight Companies: Lep Transport, Diamond Freight Services, Allied Forwarding, DHL, Sea Sky Express, Redmond International Freight Services

Car Hire Operators: Hertz/Avis, Budget, Murray's Eurocar, Eurodollars, Dan Dooley, Alamo Rent-a-car, Thrifty Car Rental

Fuel Providers: Skyfuel

Banking: Bank of Ireland

Catering: Campbell's Catering

Cleaning: Noonan's Cleaners

Government Services: Customs and Excise, Immigration, Department of Agriculture, Marine Communications, Met Eireann, Air Traffic Services, Engineering Division

Taxis: various

Source: Richard Moloney *et al.*, 'The Economic Value of Cork Airport: An Input–Output Study of the Impact of Cork Airport on its Catchment Area' (Department of Economics, UCC/Aer Rianta, 2001).

Beyond this direct contribution, the study calculated the airport's 'overall impact' in the catchment area:

- Purchases of £5.08 million worth of goods and services, £12.3 million in wages and salaries and 702 full- and part-time jobs

- 234,000 round-trip visitors (non-resident): 40 per cent business, 49 per cent non-business and 11 per cent charter visitors (1995)

- These visitors spent £101 million while in the area and £895 million on goods and services produced in the catchment area. This had an overall impact of £137 million worth of purchases, £23 million in wages and salaries and almost 3,600 full- and part-time jobs.

The authors pointed to the continuing growth of freight-handling facilities and the fact that half of all passenger traffic was business related as indicators of the airport's major role in 'aiding the establishment of industry in the area by providing an important access point for business people and a gateway to foreign markets for actual and potential exporters from the region'. Furthermore, tourists using the airport made a significant contribution to the local economy. Would those tourists not have come anyway? A survey of non-resident passengers in the airport showed that 40 per cent would not have travelled to the region in the absence of the airport.[35]

Spring at Cork Airport, 25 March 1999. GABRIEL DESMOND

Thanks a million!

The long-anticipated 1 million mark was finally passed in 1996 when 1,124,320 passengers passed through Cork Airport. Cross-channel traffic showed the largest increase – up from 590,401 to 698,393 – because of improved frequencies by Aer Lingus, Ryanair and British Airways Express. Air South West operated twice daily to Belfast, while a new fortnightly service to Orlando, Florida, proved popular. New services from Toulouse and Rouen were added to the thriving French charter business, and Italy was added to Austria and Andorra as a destination for ski charters. The increasing traffic led to necessary enlargement of car-parking facilities in 1996. Access was much improved with the upgrading of the main road to the airport from the city to a national primary route, together with the construction of a new roundabout at the entrance. The fire service at the airport welcomed the delivery of a new Timoney fire tender and the completion of an extension to the fire station, incorporating a new watch room and a 10,000-gallon gravity-fill water tank, which speeded up refilling of the tenders. Other physical developments in 1996 included the opening of two new check-in desks and a new 'executive lounge'. A new air-conditioning system was installed, additional seating was provided in the departures area and flight information screens were improved. Also in 1996, Cork become the first Irish airport to go live on the Internet.[36]

In March 1996 Minister for Transport Michael Lowry announced an £18 million capital investment programme for Cork Airport over the following five years. Plans included an overlay and widening of the runways, new approach lighting and ramp edge lighting, new freight facilities and another extension to the duty- and tax-free shop, which continued to thrive.[37] This was despite the looming reality that duty- and tax-free shopping for travellers within the EU were due for abolition in 1999. This issue was raised in the Dáil by Cork Fianna Fáil TD Joe Walsh in October 1996, who pointed out that thirty-five people were directly employed in the duty-free facility and there were an additional hundred jobs in ancillary activities, as well as numerous County Cork industries supplying products to the shop, such as Gubbeen, Milleens, Ahakista and Round Tower cheeses. Walsh correctly stated that the duty-free shop was almost totally responsible for the airport's profitability in recent years.[38] The duty-free business was essential to the profitability of Aer Rianta's three airports, but Cork was particularly vulnerable to the abolition of intra-EU sales because, unlike its sister airports, which had significant non-EU traffic, 95 per cent of all duty- and tax-free sales in Cork were to internal EU passengers, thus calling into question the future viability of the service there.

Revenue losses from the changes to duty-free rules would force Aer Rianta to recoup losses through increasing landing charges. Ryanair had been vociferously criticising the charges, especially at Dublin, though they were not particularly high by international standards and had not been increased in eleven years. However, Aer Rianta began 1997 with the announcement of an incentive scheme for new scheduled services through Dublin, Shannon and Cork. From January that year new services through Cork and Shannon would not be subject to airport charges for the first three years, with a 50 per cent discount applying in years four and five. (In Dublin, a 90 per cent rebate in the first three years was to be followed by a 70 per cent discount in the next two years.) These incentives resulted in additional routes being offered at all airports and, together with the growth spurt in the Irish economy at this time, helped to fuel the continuing growth of air travel in and out of Ireland, and the knock-on profitability of all three airports.

27 July 1999. On the ground is one of DHL's Boeing 727 freighters while a Trans Aer Airbus 300 on a charter from Spain is about to land. GABRIEL DESMOND

Cork benefited from the new discount scheme in 1997 with the introduction of new services to Rotterdam and Frankfurt, and the announcement that direct services to Paris and Amsterdam would be resumed the following year. Passenger numbers continued their upward trajectory, reaching 1,196,261, more than double the numbers of a decade before and a 6.4 per cent increase on 1996. Nine airlines were now using the airport, servicing sixteen scheduled destinations. The French charter market was down in 1997, but this was more than compensated for by the continued growth of the sun and ski charters. Twelve 'sun' destinations were served by a total of twenty-two flights per week from Cork. The new freight terminal that opened in 1995 was paying dividends, as cargo handled in the airport almost doubled from 4,214 tonnes in 1996 to 8,095 tonnes in 1997. The growth of Cork and the surrounding region as a hub of pharmaceutical and electronics multinational investment was aided by the existence of the airport and, in turn, helped to boost the airport's business, especially freight handling, but also in accommodating private company jets. Capital investment in the airport in 1997 amounted to just under £3 million.

A Ryanair Boeing 737-800 at Cork, 14 July 1999. GABRIEL DESMOND

Completed projects included the provision of two new parking stands, new approach lights on the second runway, surface water drainage and additional car parking.[39]

Towards the twenty-first century

There was increased expenditure in the capital investment programme in 1998, when a total of £8 million was spent, mostly on the widening and overlaying of the main runway. This complex project was carried out at night to minimise disruption, and was completed in March 1999. Two new freight buildings and offices for use by DHL and TNT Express Worldwide were opened in 1998, increasing the airport's freight-handling capacity, which was up 58.3 per cent on the previous year. Further extensions to the main and freight ramps were completed also. Business was up again – a 9.9 per cent increase in passenger numbers saw a new record of over 1.3 million travellers pass through, and duty-free sales passed the £8 million barrier. European traffic was up by over 22 per cent. Aer Lingus introduced a daily jet service on its new Amsterdam route, upgraded its

The first phase of the Cork Airport Business Park opened in September 1999. *IRISH EXAMINER*

Cork–Paris service and introduced Airbus A321s on the Heathrow route. Jersey European Airways (which became Flybe in 2002) took over the Belfast and Exeter service abandoned by Air South West, and Cityflyer increased its Cork–Gatwick service to four flights a day.[40]

At the beginning of May 1997 the government had announced the establishment of an enterprise zone (which allowed for significant tax breaks) on lands adjacent to the airport.[41] This cleared the way for the development of the £60 million, 40-acre Cork Airport Business Park, on which work began in March 1998. The development was a joint enterprise between Aer Rianta, ICC Bank and Gerry Wycherley's Marina Commercial Park Ltd. The park was to consist of a mixture of warehousing, light industrial units and high-tech accommodation. It was specifically aimed at airport-related uses and companies running international call centres. Aer Rianta also saw a major change in its status in 1998. The Air Navigation and Transport (Amendment) Act, 1998 put it on the same footing as other state-sponsored bodies, changing its status from an agency to a corporation and making it liable for rates and taxes for the first time. Cork, Dublin and Shannon airports were now fully controlled by the Aer Rianta company, rather than as an agent of the Minister, as had been the case since 1969.[42] Another major event in 1998 was the retirement in March of Barry Roche, who had been general manager of the airport since 1984 and had overseen its spectacular growth since that time. He was replaced by Joe O'Connor, who took up his post as a new long-term development plan was initiated in response to the demands being placed on the airport by the continuing growth in passenger numbers.

By the end of the decade, Cork Airport was, in the words of one journalist, 'bursting at the seams'.[43] The projected growth in passenger numbers had been far outstripped, and the recent expansion was proving insufficient. Passenger numbers passed the 1.5 million mark in 1999, almost double the number of five years previously, and up 14 per cent on 1998. New routes included Jersey European's Birmingham service. European business grew by 24 per cent, driven mainly by Aer Lingus' Paris and Amsterdam routes. The downside was that the long-feared abolition of duty free for internal EU passengers came about at the end of June 1999, which had a devastating affect on sales and profits. Aer Rianta was forced to adapt its retailing strategy in response, introducing Travel Value offers and other incentives. In August, Cork finally became a 24-hour airport.[44] For many years the airport closed for a number of hours after midnight, and crews operated to a two-shift system, changing shifts at 4.00 p.m. on weekdays and 3.00 p.m. on Sundays. In 1999 a three-shift roster was introduced to deal with round-the-clock opening.[45] The overlay of the

main runway and an apron extension were completed, and in September the Cork Airport Business Park was officially opened. It was one of only two digital e-commerce parks in the country, and tenants had been moving in across the year, including leading computer technology, electronics and biomedical firms. The main mover behind the park, Gerry Wycherley, headed up a consortium which unsuccessfully negotiated to take over the airport in a 'public-private partnership' arrangement. The airport was not for sale, according to Aer Rianta, who had engaged the services of international engineering consultants Scott Wilson Kirkpatrick & Company to prepare plans for its development, and in September unveiled a £60 million 'blueprint for the future' of Cork Airport.[46]

As the twentieth century drew to a close and Cork Airport prepared to celebrate forty years in business in 2001, the future looked bright. Even the continuing speculation about the airport being privatised showed how successful it had become, in that few investors would be interested in taking over an operation that was performing badly or had poor prospects. The airport had been showing healthy profits every year since the breakthrough was made in 1985, though the abolition of duty- and tax-free sales for travellers within the EU in 1999 posed enormous challenges for the future in that regard. Passenger numbers in 1999 were over 1.5 million, four and a half times the number in 1985, which was at the time the second highest in the airport's history to date. The new business park that opened in 1999 was a massive boost to the airport's economic profile, and symbolised its continuing centrality to the region's economic well-being. A year-on-year increase of 9 per cent in business travellers reflected the growth of the economy in the southwest region, where export-oriented pharmaceutical and electronics industries in Cork accounted for one-third of regional output. Food processing and tourism accounted for most of the rest, and the existence of a state-of-the-art airport in Cork was essential to this growth.

A tangible example of the connection between it and the broader economy was the hangar leased by the computer multinational EMC[2], which opened a base in Ovens, County Cork, in 1988 and employed 1,100 people; the company used a private jet based at the airport to transport international customers to and from its plant. It seems unlikely that EMC[2], and many more like it, would have located in Cork in the absence of the airport. In 1999 Cork Airport itself employed the equivalent of 913 full-time workers on site, in thirty businesses, while an economic survey, carried out before the opening of the business park, estimated that just under 4,000 jobs were linked to airport activities.[47] With the Irish economy continuing its unusual growth trajectory, the airport was poised to enter the most exciting and challenging phase of its short history.

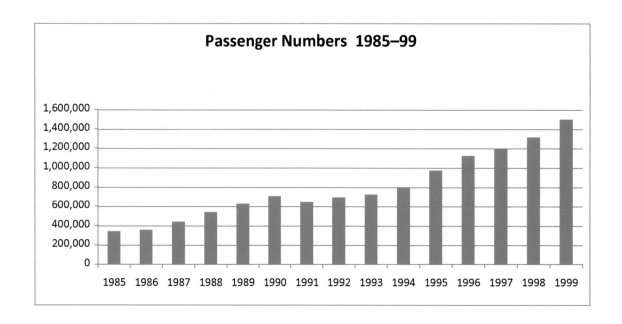

The new terminal at night. CORK AIRPORT

THRUST AND DRAG

2000–11

THRUST AND DRAG are interrelated aeronautical terms, denoting the forward driving force of an aircraft and the resisting force exerted on it respectively. Cork Airport's thrust continued into the first decade of the twenty-first century, but it also experienced significant drag, from the doubts about its future in the early part of the decade, through to the effects of the economic downturn that began in late 2008.

The growth in passenger numbers that Cork had enjoyed since 1992 continued into the new millennium and did not show a decline until 2009, the first full year of the economic recession that began in the second half of 2008. These seventeen consecutive years of growth saw passenger numbers at Cork rise from 692,093 in 1992 to 1.68 million in 2000, and peak at 3.25 million in 2008. Irish people travelled abroad in increasing numbers on leisure and holiday breaks, a taste for foreign travel growing in tandem with an affluence that was based largely on an over-inflated property market and easy credit. The Irish economy grew spectacularly from the mid-1990s and large numbers of immigrants were attracted here, especially from countries in Eastern and Central Europe. There is a very close link between air travel and economic well-being, and while the economy grew, so too did the numbers flying to and from Ireland. Between 2000 and 2007, the number of passengers travelling through the three principal Irish airports rose from 18 million to

In 2003 Cork Airport passed the 2 million mark in passenger traffic for the first time. CORK AIRPORT

over 30 million and there was a consequent need to upgrade and expand aviation infrastructure at those airports. Cork shared in this phenomenal growth and in the first decade of the twenty-first century the airport was upgraded on a scale and to a standard that matched the exuberance of those years. However, the link between aviation and economic well-being also has a negative corollary, and when the Irish economy suffered a series of near calamitous setbacks from the autumn of 2008, there was a parallel impact on air travel.

Terminal plans

The extension and upgrading of the passenger terminal in 1994 had led to a doubling of capacity at Cork Airport, but the steady growth in passenger numbers in subsequent years, and the projected future growth, made further expansion necessary. A long-term development plan was initiated in 1998 and plans for further expansion of the passenger terminal were considered. At that stage it was thought that a major redevelopment would begin in 2000 and be complete by 2003. In September 1999 a £60 million blueprint for future development at Cork was unveiled, with proposals to expand the terminal to cater for 3.5 million passengers, as well as a new pier, air bridges and other ancillary works. The following year the plan still envisaged an extension of the old terminal, effectively doubling its size, and design proposals for the work were invited. In 2000 Cork had the biggest growth of the three principal Irish airports, at 12 per cent. On 19 June of that year, there were shockwaves in Cork when the *Irish Independent* reported that Aer Rianta was shelving the £60 million Cork Airport plan 'on the basis that it cannot afford it', confirming what Aer Rianta chairperson Noel Hanlon had recently suggested to staff at the airport.[1] However, the Minister of State at the Department of Public Enterprise assured Cork deputies in the Dáil that the plans were going ahead, and this was confirmed by the Minister, Mary O'Rourke, later in the year.[2]

On 31 May 2001 Mary O'Rourke officially opened the new Great Southern Hotel at Cork Airport, and in her address she announced that a major upgrade was to begin before year's end and that this work would include an extension to the terminal, new air bridges and a multi-storey car park. In the region of €76 million was earmarked for the work and planning approval was to be sought immediately. Passenger numbers at Cork were expected to reach 2 million by the end of 2003 and a further €50 million was to be spent at the airport before the end of the decade to bring capacity to 5 million.[3] Later in 2001 the plan changed somewhat and a decision was made to build a completely new terminal at the airport. A planning application was made in August for a 25,000m² building and associated developments, estimated to cost €109.2 million.[4] The new plans were broadly welcomed in the Cork region, especially by business interests, but doubts were raised by some as to the viability of such an expanded facility in the light of potentially reduced passenger tariffs and the difficulty of getting a profitable return on such a large investment. The president of the Cork Business Association, James O'Sullivan, reflected the attitude of those in favour of the expanded development: 'As far as we are concerned Dublin and Shannon have been developed and it is important that we pull out all the stops here. The business community is sick of being treated with contempt in relation to this issue.'[5] Bill Prasifka, the first aviation commissioner, said expenditure of about €50 million would be justified on terminal development at Cork but that the scale of the €109 million sanctioned by the Minister for Public Enterprise was about twice that recoverable from landing fees.[6]

Aviation regulation: a challenge for Aer Rianta

The debate and controversy as to the advisability or otherwise of an investment of over €100 million at Cork must be seen in the context of developments in aviation and related issues in Ireland at the time. In 1998 the Air Navigation and Transport (Amendment) Act was passed and complete ownership of the Dublin, Shannon and Cork airports passed to Aer Rianta on 1 January 1999, giving the company greater freedom in deciding strategy and policy, and in funding developments. At the end of June 1999 duty-free sales for those travelling within the EU were ended, resulting in an immediate drop of 35 per cent in profits in the following year. Only 23 per cent of Aer Rianta revenues came from airport charges, the group relying on duty-free sales and its other interests in Ireland and abroad to generate the remainder. Hopes of relying on increases in airport charges to boost income were dealt a blow in 2001 with the establishment of an independent aviation regulatory body.

On 27 February 2001 the Commission for Aviation Regulation came into being and Bill Prasifka was appointed the first aviation commissioner. This body would have responsibility for regulating airport charges, slot allocation and other matters relevant to the functioning of Irish aviation. The scale of charges approved by the Aviation Commissioner in 2001 was lower than Aer Rianta expected and an appeal was lodged by other parties. A revised set of charges was introduced in February 2002, which was accepted by Aer Rianta pending the outcome of a judicial review requested by the company. The new charges introduced at Cork and Shannon were less than half the maximum allowed by the regulator, but the board felt that the reduced rates were necessary at those two airports to counteract 'the strong magnetic effect of a major airport such as Dublin'.[7] The company felt that it would be constrained in undertaking future developments and in servicing its borrowings if it could not increase airport charges to what it saw as an economic level, especially at Dublin. Noel Hanlon, chairman of the Aer Rianta group, argued that there was 'a serious imbalance in the present regulatory regime in favour of the shorter term or immediate needs of the users of airports at the expense of longer term imperatives to provide facilities to meet future growth'.[8]

Ryanair's growth through the 1990s and into the following decade was, to a large extent, built on its ability to drive down costs in all areas of its business. The airline often chose airports on the basis of deals that gave large discounts on landing and other charges. Ryanair lobbied hard for a reduction in charges at Dublin Airport in particular and was quite adept at promoting its message that lower charges would reduce costs, drive growth in passenger numbers and thereby stimulate growth in tourist numbers coming to Ireland. It was felt in Aer Rianta, and later in the Dublin Airport Authority (DAA), that too much credence was being given by government and the Commission for Aviation Regulation to Ryanair's arguments, and that necessary development at Ireland's three principal airports could not be financed if airport charges were kept, as they saw it, at too low a level. As the chairman of the DAA noted in 2004: 'Airports and airlines share a common responsibility for the well-being of their passengers and for providing them with cost effective transport facilities; but their other business goals do not always dovetail neatly.'[9]

The break-up of Aer Rianta: independence for Cork?

Economic growth in Ireland in the later 1990s and into the following decade led to a growing consensus, driven by some commentators and proponents of so-called free-market economics within government and business, that state-owned enterprises such as Aer Rianta would function more efficiently if they were fully or partly privatised. There were regular reports in the media suggesting such a flotation of Aer Rianta and the company believed that a partial flotation, at least, would generate the funds needed to invest in development and service debts. The *Irish Independent* had reported in August 1998 that the company was to be floated on the stock market 'within the next eighteen months'.[10] In 1999, following a recommendation by the Aer Rianta board that an initial public offering of a minority shareholding be made, Minister for Public Enterprise Mary O'Rourke commissioned a report from Warburg, Dillon, Read and presented it to cabinet in February 2000. This report supported the Aer Rianta board's plan and news circulated that a full or partial sell-off of the company was imminent.[11] The possible privatisation of Cork Airport alarmed many and workers at the airport formed a group, Cork Airport Against Breakup, to lobby politicians, business organisations, local authorities and others in an effort to prevent such a sell-off. The group was chaired by Donie Harris of the Airport Police and Fire Service.

Séamus Brennan became Minister for Transport in June 2002 following a general election and took over responsibility for Aer Rianta. The future of the company continued to be debated and Brennan drove the idea of establishing the airports at Dublin, Shannon and Cork as independent entities, though he assured the Dáil that the investment in Cork would proceed, whatever the outcome of his examination of the options for greater autonomy for the airport.[12] In July 2003 Brennan announced that Aer Rianta was to be broken up along those lines. The Minister gave a commitment that the debts of Shannon and Cork would be cleared from their balance sheets and would reside instead on the books of the newly constituted Dublin Airport. While such an arrangement would give the two airports a clean start, eyebrows were raised in some quarters at the prospect of the debt for the building of the new terminal at Cork, by then estimated to be in the region of €140 million, passing to the new Dublin Airport company. Aer Rianta workers at Cork and at the other airports were worried about the security of their jobs following the proposed break-up and there was strong trade union resistance to the proposal. A PricewaterhouseCoopers report on the Brennan plan projected that the profitability of Dublin Airport would be seriously eroded by the interest payments on debt transferred from Shannon and Cork. Brennan remained steadfast, however, saying:

> We can trade figures on this decision until we are blue in the face but, at the end of the day, all they are is projections. This is a strategic Government decision which I think is the right one for Shannon and Cork airports. I take the view that Shannon and Cork airports are better in the long term with new boards, new authorities, clean balance sheets, debt free and to be in a position to grow those airports strongly and that is the correct road forward.[13]

In July 2004 the State Airports Act was passed, providing for the break-up of Aer Rianta and the creation of three airport authorities, one each for Dublin, Shannon and Cork. The new structures were to give the airports the maximum possible responsibility for their own growth and development to enable them to serve their regions and customers in a more effective way. The three new airport authorities were required to draw up detailed business plans as an initial step towards tackling the complex legal and financial issues involved in restructuring the Aer Rianta group. Initially all Aer Rianta assets, liabilities and contracts were to remain with the Dublin Airport Authority (DAA). In August 2004 Séamus Brennan announced the membership of the new Cork Airport Authority (CAA) board, which was to be chaired by Joe Gantly, a former managing director of European operations for Apple. The CAA would have limited powers and would operate essentially in a subsidiary role to the DAA until the final and formal separation of the three airport authorities. Pat Keohane was appointed as chief executive of Cork Airport in 2005 and commercial and marketing executives were also appointed to drive the delivery of the commercial and business objectives necessary to establish Cork as an autonomous and fully independent authority. As the new terminal was being built at Cork, the new CAA was dogged by the question of its debt and whether it would be fully taken over by the DAA as originally planned, or left fully or partially to be serviced by the CAA.

Who's to pay?

In June 2003 the Taoiseach Bertie Ahern turned the sod to mark the beginning of the development of the new terminal at Cork, the most significant undertaking since the airport had been built over forty years before. The work, planned to be completed by 2005, when Cork was designated as European City of Culture, consisted of the building of a 25,000 square metre terminal building, incorporating air bridges, retail and catering space, a fire station, new surface and multi-storey car parks and a new internal road system. The value of the contract was then put at €140 million, about €30 million more than had been anticipated when the initial planning application was made in August 2001. As the work progressed, the break-up of Aer Rianta was announced and plans were set in train for the establishment of three separate airport authorities for Dublin, Shannon and Cork.

On a visit to Cork in July 2003, Séamus Brennan stated that: 'When I establish the independent Shannon and Cork authorities on a statutory basis they will both commence business free of debt. The existing debts associated with both airports, including the debt associated with the major new investment programme at Cork will not be assigned to the new companies but will remain with Dublin Airport.'[14]

While the work at Cork proceeded satisfactorily during 2004, the board of the DAA was informed in November that the original budget of €140 million for the project could overrun by €10 to €30 million.[15] In his review of 2004 Oliver Cussen, acting chief executive of the DAA, remarked: 'The challenge for Cork is to develop its business sufficiently to remunerate this significant investment within the context of a viable business model.'[16] Throughout 2005 debate raged as to how the debt taken on to fund the development at Cork would be serviced, as the DAA became increasingly unwilling to take on a sum that would be over €160 million by the time the work was completed. It was being suggested by some that the CAA would have to take on part or even all of that debt burden. Gary McGann, chairman of the DAA, wrote in 2005: '… it is incumbent on me to highlight that all investments, regardless of scale, must be remunerated and should be remunerated by the users of those facilities.'[17]

Séamus Brennan's successor as Minister for Transport, Martin Cullen, favoured the idea of the CAA sharing the debt with the DAA, but political and business interests in the Cork area campaigned against that proposal. While talks between the CAA and DAA continued through the early months of 2006 it emerged that the total Cork debt was €200 million, made up of about €160 million for development works at the airport and a further €40 million of long-standing debt. A total of €100 million of that would have to be

The new terminal opened for arrivals on 1 August 2006. Arriving passengers were welcomed with champagne and orange juice. GABRIEL DESMOND

borne by the Cork authority under Minister Cullen's proposal, an idea supported by the DAA as it felt it would be overburdened by an additional debt of €200 million. Under the 2004 State Airports Act the full separation of the three airports could only proceed when a detailed business plan for each airport, which demonstrated its sustainable operational and commercial viability, was submitted to the Ministers for Finance and Transport. The unresolved question of the Cork debt was one of the principal issues delaying the completion of those plans.

While the question of responsibility for Cork's debt continued to be debated, work on the new terminal was completed in August 2006. By early 2007 the accumulated debt at Cork was reported to be €220 million, an increase of €20 million on the 2006 figure, and positions on the question were hardening. A general election was due in 2007 and many perceived that the fundamental points at issue would be lost in a game of political point-scoring. Some media commentators, such as John McManus, business editor of *The Irish*

Times, were particularly harsh in their criticism of Cork's position:

You would like to think that the board of Cork Airport Authority would accept all this with some grace and get on with the job they were all hired to do – running Cork as an independent airport. Instead they have allowed themselves to get involved in the sort of whining and special pleading that confirms most business people's prejudices about State companies ... Things are about to get serious and it really is time for the directors of Cork Airport Authority to step up. They were hired with a mandate to operate the airport as an independent business that would compete with Dublin and Shannon. If they really feel that they cannot operate the business with a €100 million debt, then they have no business remaining on the board.[18]

Cork Fine Gael TD Michael Creed told the Dáil in June 2007 that: 'If anything reflects the Pale mentality of the current Government, it is the

On 15 August 2006 all operations at the old terminal ceased. Here spectators view aircraft from the viewing area of the old terminal for the last time. GABRIEL DESMOND

decision on Cork Airport ... The boardroom at Cork Airport is in turmoil and the main losers will be the travelling public who use the airport, which is a brand new facility and a tribute to everybody who contributed to its development, design and opening.'[19]

In November 2007 the CAA resubmitted its business plan in an effort to hasten the separation of the airports at Dublin, Shannon and Cork as set out in the 2004 State Airports Act. As the debt problem at Cork was still unresolved, Noel Dempsey, who had succeeded Martin Cullen as Minister for Transport, asked the former trade union leader Peter Cassels to mediate between the

between the Dublin and Cork authorities 'with a view to reaching agreement on a level of debt that was acceptable to both sides'. Cassels' report was published on 2 April 2008 and recommended that €113 million of the €220 Cork debt be taken on by the CAA and that ownership of land around the airport and a stake in the Business Park, valued at between €50 and €70 million, be transferred from the DAA to the CAA. In addition, he recommended that a payment of €10 million be made to the CAA to meet pension and other funding requirements. The Cassels compromise was accepted at a board meeting of the CAA on 10 April 2008 on the casting vote of the chairman,

Joe Gantly. Following the decision the Minister for Transport announced that the separation of the three airports would go ahead within a year and that a 'process of engagement will now commence with all the relevant parties on implementation and the technical and legal issues involved will be progressed by the airport authorities and my department'.[20] Less than two weeks later Gantly announced that he was to resign the following July, insisting that his resignation was unrelated to his controversial use of his casting vote at the board meeting of 10 April.[21] (Joe Gantly died unexpectedly in May 2009.) In November 2008 Gerry Walsh, former chief executive of Bord Gáis, was appointed as the new chairman of the CAA and it was suggested that a significant move towards the final separation of the three airports was imminent.

However, by that time, the economic and financial difficulties that befell Ireland and many other countries following the collapse of the Lehman Brothers bank in September 2008 were causing great uncertainty. There was a sudden and significant fall in passenger numbers at all Irish airports, and in the light of what he called 'the very significant challenges facing the aviation market, the Minister decided to accept the 'overall conclusion' of the boards of the three airports and defer a decision on separation until 2011.[22]

New terminal opens

The new terminal opened for arrivals on 1 August 2006. The first passengers through the new arrivals hall were from a Ryanair flight from Stansted that landed that morning at 7.20 a.m. They were welcomed with champagne and the first arriving passenger through the new terminal was Martin Davis from Essex in England, on a business trip to Cork, who, according to the *Irish Examiner*, chose to drink orange juice rather than

Details of the new terminal.
CORK AIRPORT

The new terminal, which opened in August 2006. CORK AIRPORT

champagne, given the early hour.[23] At the arrivals gate to greet the first passengers was Sergeant Cornelius Buckley of the airport's police and fire service, the longest-serving employee who had begun work at Cork Airport in 1966. However, the festive atmosphere at the airport that morning was dampened somewhat by a taxi drivers' strike, which saw a number of pickets at the main entrance.

At a Cork City Council meeting the previous week, the opening of the new terminal had caused some controversy when a group of councillors proposed that the CAA name the facility 'Christy Ring Airport' in honour of Cork's greatest hurler, a bronze statue of whom had stood in the concourse of the old terminal. The indications from the CAA were that the proposal would not be considered. During the council debate, one councillor, Mick O'Connell, was critical of the CAA for its treatment of the statue, which had been moved to a location close to the Great Southern Hotel for the duration of the new terminal works. 'Christy Ring has been treated with the utmost contempt,' he said. 'He was kicked in the ass and booted up to the hotel.' Councillor O'Connell believed that the decision not to name the airport after Christy Ring had been taken by the DAA, adding: 'They'll be saddling us with substantial debt in a few weeks. If Christy was here he might fire a few sliothars at them.'[24] The statue was later repositioned outside the entrance to the new terminal.

On the morning of 15 August departures began through the new terminal and all operations ceased at the old facility. The first passengers to depart through the new building were flying to Amsterdam and they were each presented with a box of chocolates to mark the occasion. The first of these passengers, Chris and Michelle Richardson and their sons Lewis and Kyle, also received a

Evening sun on the new terminal.
CORK AIRPORT

177

piece of Waterford Crystal, a bottle of champagne and a bunch of flowers. The transfer of operations took place during the busiest period of the year at the airport and caused no disruption.

The new terminal building, designed to cater for 3 million passengers a year and with the capacity to be expanded to cater for up to 5 million, is about three times the size of its predecessor, and there was some concern that the intimacy and friendliness that many associated with the old building would be lost. However, surveys of airport users have shown that there was a very high level of satisfaction with the new facility initially and that this high satisfaction rating has been maintained during its first five years. Kevin Cullinane, marketing manager for Cork Airport, attributes this not only to the state-of-the-art facilities, but more especially to the ethos of service and commitment of airport staff: 'People are more important than buildings. Many of the staff have worked at Cork for many years and they bring a very personal touch to their work. They have transferred this to the new building and have managed to maintain the unique Cork Airport atmosphere – the spirit, the recognition of regular travellers, a pride in what they do.'[25]

Gary McGann, chairman of the DAA, felt that 'the people of Cork and Munster now have a gateway of which they can be justifiably proud', but also noted that 'the Board [of the DAA] was less than fully satisfied with the overall cost of the redevelopment and the delays in bringing the new terminal into operation'.[26] Minister Cullen, meanwhile, declared that it was important that 'the debate about Cork's future does not obscure this major development for the airport ... The new terminal should be seen as a key component in delivering on Cork's status as a gateway city under the national spatial strategy.'[27]

The best of times, the worst of times: 2000–11

While the corporate restructuring and debates about debt and ownership were proceeding in the background, passenger numbers at the airport continued to grow. The new millennium started very positively with numbers up by 12 per cent in 2000, the highest growth for any of the three principal Irish airports. Traffic to European destinations jumped by 21 per cent and the Cork–Dublin route saw 19 per cent growth, as Aer Arann began daily services and Aer Lingus introduced larger aircraft on the route. The summer charter business also grew significantly and for the first time over 100,000 people were carried to seventeen destinations during the summer holiday period. The following year a number of factors impacted negatively on air travel to and from Ireland but, despite this, growth of 5.7 per cent was achieved at Cork. The outbreak of foot-and-mouth disease in Britain and its spread to Ireland in the first half of 2001, followed by the 9/11 terrorist attacks in the USA caused the growth in air travel to slow noticeably and the American and European economies, including Ireland, contracted somewhat in 2002.

In 2003 Cork again recorded the highest growth of the three Irish airports with passenger numbers passing the 2 million mark for the first time as the airport reported a 16.4 per cent rise in passenger traffic. New routes to Britain were introduced and Aer Arann became the sole operator on the Dublin route in October, operating nine flights per day to the capital.[28] The withdrawal of Aer Lingus from the route disappointed many as the airline had operated the service since the opening of the airport in 1961. Local politicians and others, ever sensitive to the neglect of Cork's needs by Dublin-based decision makers, were quick to criticise the decision. Opposition Fine Gael TD Bernard Allen said

Irish Holstein Friesian cattle being loaded at Cork Airport, en route to Brussels for the Agribex European Championship, 12 February 2004. *IRISH EXAMINER*

'every politician should fight this decision tooth and nail' and Dan Boyle, Green Party TD, characterised the decision as 'a calculated insult and denial of responsibility' by Aer Lingus.[29]

In March 2003 a number of entrepreneurs set up a new airline, Jetmagic, based at Cork with funding of €5 million. The new carrier aimed to carry 200,000 passengers annually and began operating in April with services to Brussels, Barcelona, Nice, Belfast and London City, later adding eight further destinations. The airline used 34- and 49-seater aircraft. Air travellers in the Cork area were most pleased with the additional choice offered by Jetmagic, but by January 2004 the company was in trouble with debts of around €3.5 million. It ceased trading at the end of that month and was wound up. It had carried in the region of 80,000 passengers and its demise was a loss not only for the investors and its hundred or

so employees, but also for the travelling public.[30]

In 2005 Cork enjoyed an unprecedented 21 per cent growth in passenger traffic, with fifteen airlines serving thirty-two scheduled destinations and a further twenty-six destinations served by chartered services. Part of this increased traffic was due to Cork city's designation as European City of Culture for that year. European traffic through Cork increased by a quarter, much of which was due to the increasing traffic to and from Eastern and Central Europe. This continued to grow in the middle years of the decade and Cork acquired connections to Budapest, Prague and five Polish cities. By 2007 traffic to and from continental Europe had grown to over 1.2 million passengers (out of a total of 3.1 million) and 206,000 of those were accounted for by Cork's links to five Polish cities. Forty-two scheduled services were being operated from Cork and holiday charter traffic

The new terminal, which opened in August 2006. CORK AIRPORT

Departure area of the new terminal. *IRISH EXAMINER*

On 31 December Evelyn Slye was the three-millionth passenger to pass through Cork Airport in 2006. Here she is presented with a piece of Waterford Crystal and a €1,000 travel voucher by Kevin Cullinane (left), Marketing Manager at Cork Airport. On the right is Cork Airport Duty Manager, Garrett Lyons. CORK AIRPORT

through the airport continued to grow as increasing numbers flew to twenty-five different destinations. A growing proportion of this charter traffic was to winter ski resorts. The UK, especially London, has always made up the most significant proportion of Cork's traffic and in the 2000s new airlines such as BMI, bmibaby, Easyjet, Jet2.com, as well as the more established operators like Aer Lingus, Ryanair and Aer Arann, served a variety of UK destinations. Competition between operators is always intense, especially on popular routes, and sometimes heats up to a level that is unsustainable, resulting in a short-term benefit to travellers in terms of choice and cost, followed by a reduction in service and higher fares. In 2005, for example, Ryanair and Easyjet launched new

services to London Gatwick and competed aggressively for passengers, driving growth in total London traffic by 27 per cent. Over 1 million passengers travelled between Cork and London that year, one third of Cork's total traffic. The competition between Ryanair and Easyjet could not be sustained and in September 2006 Easyjet ceased operations from Cork. Ryanair later reduced capacity on its services and London traffic fell by 14 per cent overall in 2007. By 2008 traffic on the route returned to a normalised level of just over 900,000, but the severe economic setback that befell the country from the autumn of that year caused a 5 per cent fall in London traffic, while the decline on routes to other British cities was 17 per cent.

During the winter of 2010–11 frequent severe weather caused great disruption to flights. Here a number of aircraft are forced to stay overnight at Cork due to the closure of Dublin Airport. GABRIEL DESMOND

The Dublin route accounts for the overwhelming proportion of domestic services from Cork and during the 2000s there have been some dramatic reversals of fortune on the route. In 2000 domestic traffic through Cork peaked at 310,000 following a number of years of steady growth. Five years of decline followed and by 2005 domestic passenger numbers had fallen to 238,000. Ryanair joined Aer Arann in serving the Dublin route and there followed a jump of 73.5 per cent in passenger numbers travelling between the two cities to over 400,000 in 2006. In 2007 domestic passenger numbers grew by a further 20 per cent to peak at just under 500,000 and at one stage there were fourteen flights per day between Cork and Dublin. In 2008 this traffic fell by 11 per cent and the following year there was a further decline of 24 per cent as a number of services were withdrawn. This decline has continued through

2010 and into 2011 as economic recession and other factors impact. Inter-city rail fares have fallen and the frequency of train services between Cork and Dublin has increased and this, combined with the opening of the completed M8/M7 Cork–Dublin motorway, has had a significant negative impact on domestic air traffic. The disruption caused by the volcanic ash cloud from Iceland in the spring of 2010 also led many potential air passengers to choose to travel again on the improved roads and rail services.

The sudden economic collapse in 2008 is reflected particularly in the decline in passenger numbers on Polish routes to and from Cork. Much of Ireland's economic growth up to that year had been driven by the construction sector and many thousands of workers in that industry had come from Poland to work in Ireland. In 2008 Polish traffic fell by 35 per cent, but so many people from

Wizz Air operates to Vilnius and five Polish locations from Cork. GABRIEL DESMOND

Poland have settled permanently in Ireland that there is a continuing need for services and Polish airline Wizz Air now operates to five Polish cities and opened a new route to Vilnius in Lithuania in 2011. Wizz Air now has an 11 per cent share of all traffic through Cork Airport.

In 2011, the third year of economic recession in Ireland, passenger numbers at Cork are back to 2004 levels. Aviation continues to struggle internationally and many airlines are coming under increasing pressure as costs rise and passenger numbers fall in many sectors of operation. Some airlines have collapsed and there has also been some consolidation and rationalisation, resulting in the withdrawal of some routes and reduced services on others. This consolidation has happened at Cork also and it is particularly noticeable in services to so-called short-break leisure destinations such as Prague, Budapest, Berlin, Barcelona and other European cities that enjoyed profitably high levels of traffic during earlier, more affluent years. In 2011 Cork is served by six scheduled airlines – Aer Lingus, Aer Lingus Regional (a franchise agreement between Aer

Lingus and Aer Arann Regional), Ryanair, Wizz Air, Air Southwest and Jet2.com, a substantial fall from the fifteen airlines operating through the airport in 2005. Aer Lingus now handles approximately 40 per cent of Cork traffic on fifteen year-round routes and it operates a further seven routes in summer and one in winter. Ryanair has a share of about 28 per cent of passengers and flies to four year-round destinations and to another twelve in summer. Wizz Air is Cork's third biggest airline with a share of about 11 per cent of passengers and year-round services to six destinations. Air Southwest serves Newquay and Plymouth and Jet2.com flies to Newcastle.[31]

Tragedy: the loss of Flight NM7100

On Thursday 10 February 2011, Flight NM7100, an SA-227-BC Metro III commuter aircraft operated by Manx2 Airlines, crashed at Cork Airport at 9.50 a.m. while landing in foggy conditions. There were twelve people on board, two crew and ten passengers. Both crewmen died,

Cork Airport Police and Fire Service personnel were praised for their prompt action following the crash of the Manx2 aircraft at the airport on 10 February 2011.
GABRIEL DESMOND

the pilot Jorge Sola Lopez and co-pilot Andrew Cantle, and four passengers were killed: Pat Cullinan, Michael Evans, Brendan McAleese and Richard Nobles. Four of the surviving six passengers were seriously injured.

The plane had left Belfast City Airport that morning at 8.10 a.m. and made its first approach to Runway 17, the main runway, flying in a southerly direction at 8.58 a.m.[32] Conditions at Cork were quite foggy at the time and visibility was reduced. This attempt was abandoned at 9.03 a.m. and the aircraft subsequently made an approach to Runway 35, again the main runway, but on this occasion approaching from the south. This attempt at landing was abandoned at 9.14 a.m. The pilot then requested permission to fly in a holding pattern for fifteen to twenty minutes to await an improvement in weather conditions and visibility. At 9.39 a.m. the pilot elected to make a third attempt at landing, again on Runway 17. As the aircraft neared the runway it rolled to the left and then to the right, causing the right wing tip to hit the runway. The plane then flipped over and came to a halt off the runway, 189 metres from the impact point. Both engines caught fire after impact, but the speedy response of the Cork Airport Police and Fire Service (APFS) prevented the fire spreading to the fuselage and causing an even greater loss of life.

The Regional Major Emergency Plan was activated and the local authority emergency services responded and came to the scene. When fire crews from the Cork City Fire Brigade and from Carrigaline, Ballincollig and Bandon arrived, the immediate need was for cutting equipment to effect the rescue of the survivors, the fire having been extinguished by the Cork APFS. The cooperation between all personnel at the scene was crucial to the minimisation of injury and loss of life. 'In pre-planning, we had done this time and time again. We were on first-name terms with all the airport officers. We all knew exactly what we were doing,' said Declan O'Shea of the Cork Fire Brigade. 'It was a tough job but everyone was working together and that was what made the operation seamless.'[33] Praise for the Cork APFS and local authority emergency services services was universal and a relative of one of the survivors expressed the feelings of many: 'I can't say enough about the emergency services and the doctors, nurses and everybody involved … Every little detail worked. Nobody shrugged off responsibility. Everybody just went and stuck to the plan.'[34]

The broader airport community, though greatly affected by the incident, made every effort to comfort and help the relatives and friends of the dead and injured following the crash, as the traditional Cork Airport spirit united all on what was a dark day in its history.

Onwards

In 2011 Cork Airport celebrates its golden jubilee. Over thirty years of campaigning, broken promises and political intrigue preceded the opening of the airport on 16 October 1961, and half a century has passed since the then Taoiseach, Seán Lemass, declared that the new airport was 'a symbol of our progress and of our purpose'. In its fifty years of operation the airport has grown and flourished in parallel with the progress Ireland has made over that time. The Cork that the airport first served at the beginning of the 1960s was a smaller, quieter, more isolated place. The excitement that accompanied the opening and the almost innocent delight people took in visiting the airport or watching an aircraft pass over the city has disappeared. Air travel has become available to virtually all and flying abroad on business or on holiday is hardly remarked upon. Ireland has matured and is a full and active member of the European Union, as Lemass had wished, and its people are confident, able and equal citizens of that Europe. Cork Airport is one of the southern region's gateways to Europe and to the wider world, a piece of modern aviation infrastructure that has grown to become an essential element of the economic well-being of the south. Its passenger throughput, originally measured in tens of thousands per year, is now measured in millions.

In its first fifty years the airport has prospered and grown, but it has also had its difficult times, its tragedies and setbacks. The first decade of the twenty-first century saw the greatest growth in traffic in its history, but also saw the biggest fall as the economic recession that hit the country in 2008 led to a very challenging period for the aviation industry. The crash of the Manx2 aircraft at the airport in February 2011 was a reminder that certain events can have outcomes for individuals more tragic and painful than an economic downturn, no matter how serious. But airports are also places of joy where returning friends or family are met and embraced, where great journeys begin, where a star of sport or film may be glimpsed, where a head of state is formally welcomed or bid adieu. An interesting event took place in March 2011, when the old terminal building that had been abandoned in 2006 was the venue for a multimedia art event titled 'Terminal Convention', organised by the Cork-based National Sculpture Factory along with the Crawford College of Art and Design and Liverpool's John Moores University School of Art and Design. Curator Peter Gorschlüter (Deputy Director of MMK Museum für Moderne Kunst, Frankfurt am Main) explained the concept:

In 2006 the former Cork International Airport Terminal was decommissioned. A site that saw thousands of passengers passing through arrival and departure halls, duty-free shops and customs controls every day until a few hours earlier, finally closed its doors for the last time.

Now, reopened for a few days after years of abandonment in which the site has preserved the traces of its past and has assumed a personal, almost humanlike identity, flickering technology and infrastructure, personal goods and permanently lost property, airport diaries and broken display cases are being reactivated to unfold new life through the interventions and works by over twenty international artists.[35]

Another unique event, which would have been unimaginable fifty years earlier, occurred on 20 May 2011 when Queen Elizabeth II left Ireland after her historic visit to the country. Having visited Cork on the last day of her stay, the Queen left for home from Cork Airport and was accorded the full formality such a departure demands. A red carpet was laid from the terminal building to the awaiting aircraft and a military guard of honour lined the way as Taoiseach Enda Kenny accompanied the royal guests to the steps of their plane. Never before had Cork seen such levels of security and, as the royal plane took off, the roar of its engines drowned the collective sigh of relief drawn by all, happy that everything had gone to plan and that Cork Airport had done itself proud before the gaze of the world's media.

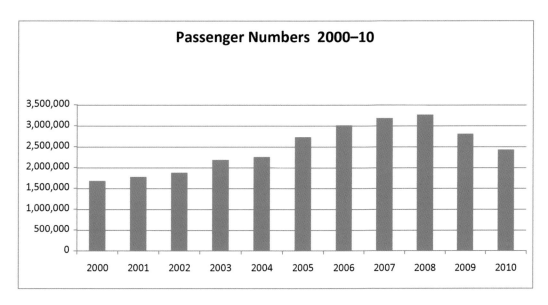

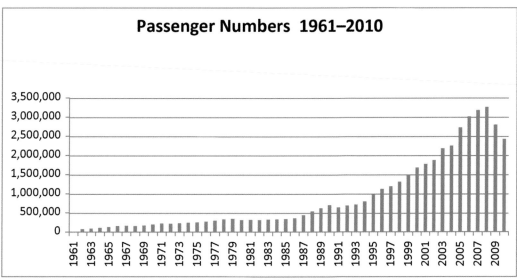

Queen Elizabeth II, accompanied by An Taoiseach Enda Kenny, leaves from Cork Airport on 20 May 2011 following a state visit to Ireland. MAXWELL PHOTO

FIFTY YEARS OF PHOTOGRAPHY AT CORK AIRPORT

Gabriel Desmond remembers

I was not there on the day Cork Airport opened, but I clearly remember catching an envious glimpse from my school desk of two planes, an Aer Lingus Friendship and Viscount, as they flew over the city that October day. Whenever I got the chance, I went to the new airport to see the planes. I developed an abiding interest in aviation and photography and with good friends such as the Frost brothers – Paul, another Gabriel and the late Noel – we had our own information grapevine on what might turn up.

Of course, things were very primitive then by today's standards. I had no air radio, no telephoto lens, no car or mobile phone. I cycled up the long hill to the airport and with luck would ease the journey by grabbing on to the back of a truck of Henry Good of Kinsale winding its way up the hill at a snail's pace. (Kids – don't try this today!)

The cheap cameras we had then were unreliable and prone to shutter failure. They took 35mm film giving thirty-six shots before you had to stop and change the roll. Then came Kodachrome 25 slide film, which I remember cost thirty-four shillings and ten pence. You estimated the exposure from a chart based on how sunny it was and if you got it wrong the photo was ruined. But by the standards of the 1960s Kodachrome was sharp with good colour rendition. Other slides and negatives have faded badly over the decades but some of the Kodachromes have survived well and with digital scanning and restoration can produce fascinating images.

I was mainly interested in the aircraft then but now it is often the incidentals in the photo, the clothes worn or a vehicle, that give the most telling glimpse into the past.

My first flight was not on a scheduled service but in a de Havilland DH89A Dragon Rapide that came in from Dublin offering pleasure flights in October 1963. The Shell fuellers at the airport wanted to go up but the pilot needed a full load. They asked me to join them, but as teenagers of the day didn't normally carry a whole five pounds with them, the Shell men offered to lend me the cash and I happily agreed. We made a graceful circuit of the city as I peered out through the rigging of the 1930s biplane. You never forget your first flight. Interestingly, in England and New

Right: 'In October 1963 I took my first flight and I took this photograph from the de Havilland Rapide biplane as we flew over Cork city that day.'
GABRIEL DESMOND

Left: An Aer Lingus Boeing 747 at Cork Airport, 5 July 1989. At the time this type of plane was the world's largest commercial aircraft.
GABRIEL DESMOND

Zealand today, you can still take a ride in a Rapide. Compared to say, cars, aircraft have quite a long lifespan and since then I've been lucky to fly in and photograph classic aircraft in many countries.

Over the years I've seen many types of aircraft and airlines come and go. In the early years propeller types with piston engines such as the Douglas DC-3 and the new turboprops like the Vickers Viscount were the order of the day. Then came the early jets like the British Aircraft Corporation One Eleven. They were smoky and we were all impressed by their speed and especially by their noise. The take-off of the day's first flight to Dublin at about 8 a.m. served as a free alarm clock and time signal to people all across Cork city. We should be thankful for how relatively quiet jet engines have become.

I have been fortunate to photograph some momentous occasions at Cork Airport. Some were planned or joyous events, others not so. Among the latter were the Air India crash recovery operations in June 1985, the arrival of former Taoiseach and much-loved Cork man Jack Lynch's remains at the airport in 1999 and the great Air Spectacular of 1985, cancelled by Cork's notorious low cloud.

Happier events included the runway extension opening ceremony of 1989, which brought an Aer Lingus Boeing 747 jumbo jet and the Air Corps Silver Swallow display team to Cork on a day of glorious sunshine. It was interesting to watch the smooth transition to Cork's new terminal in August 2006. The snow of 2010 brought extra problems for airport operations but also many unusual photo opportunities.

But for all the changes seen there are some constants. Two operators who have stood the test of time are Aer Lingus and the Irish Air Corps. From the opening day in 1961 Aer Lingus has given unbroken service to the people of Cork on the routes to London Heathrow and Paris. If they carried just half of all passengers, a conservative estimate, that would amount to millions of people carried through Cork. The Irish Air Corps, who flew the Alouette helicopter for forty-four years without serious accident, came to Cork frequently on air ambulance duties, with heads of state and other VIPs, on training or other military missions. Lastly, there has been the great courtesy and assistance I have always received from all the staff when photographing at Cork Airport. For this and for all I have seen there over the years, I am truly grateful.

8

Gerry O'Donnell of Skyfuel refuels a Boeing 747 on 31 March 1991.
GABRIEL DESMOND

FIFTY YEARS HAVE FLOWN

't was a privilege to work there,' Joe O'Connor says of his almost forty years at Cork Airport. Joe worked initially in the Department of Transport and Power in Dublin and in 1966 transferred to Cork where he remained for the next thirty-nine years until his retirement in 2005, having become Airport Manager in 1998.

There was always so much going on, famous people passing through, exciting events. No two days were the same. I can remember my first days at the airport, in our office, looking out on to the ramp. A flight would come in – there weren't many in those days – an Aer Lingus Viscount or maybe a Cambrian DC-3, and there was excitement straight away. It was still like that for me on the last day I worked there – I'd still look out when a plane landed, still feel that excitement.

Lilibeth Horne, now Head of Retailing at Cork and Shannon airports, began work at Cork in 1970 and says, 'The airport is part of my soul, I just love it. There was never a day, ever, that I didn't want to come to work.' Remarks such as these are typical of the many people who spent decades working at Cork. The camaraderie is remembered and valued by all. 'We grew up together there; it was just a fantastic place to work,' remarks Tom Russell. Tom spent forty-one years at the airport having joined first in 1961 when he and ten other men were recruited for the Airport Security and Fire Service team. 'We were nearly all young. There were lads from all parts of Ireland in our section, most of us in our twenties. We all socialised together, we were like a big family.'

Donie Harris, a colleague of Tom's through those years, remembers his interview for the job:

I was twenty-one and I was working as an apprentice electrician in Tralee. I saw the ad in

Joe O'Connor.

Lilibeth Horne.

Donie Harris stands beside the beacon on top of the control tower in 1961.

the paper and went for interview in the GPO in Cork. The interview was fairly general – they asked me about the Berlin crisis, John F. Kennedy, things like that. When I came out there was a big queue of lads waiting to go in. One fellow asked me what the questions were like. When I told him a lot of it had to do with current affairs and general knowledge he ran out to buy the *Echo*!

Donie values the lifelong friendships he made while working at the airport and still regularly meets up with former colleagues. 'We established

something special in Cork,' he says, 'it was friendly and homely. The personal touch was always important.'

Denis McCarthy, who worked with Aer Lingus at Cork Airport from 1964 to 2002, also recalls the special Cork atmosphere. 'There were very few flights in the early days so we had a lot of downtime. A lot of time was spent in the staff canteen and there were always people there from the different departments. It was like a social hub.' The ample 'downtime', allied to the small scale of the airport and the fact that shift work made friendships outside the circle hard to maintain, all

Mick Healy, founding member of Cork Airport Singers.

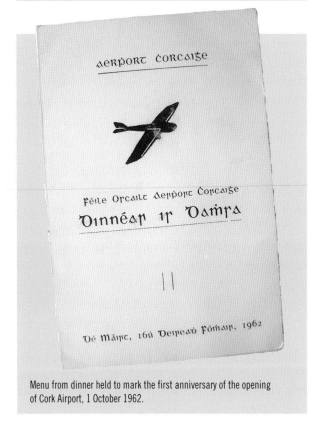

Menu from dinner held to mark the first anniversary of the opening of Cork Airport, 1 October 1962.

helped to strengthen the bonds between workers. Mary Murphy, who worked with Aer Lingus and who was one of many who went on to marry one of her airport colleagues, has fond memories of the parties in the Aeroclub and drinks in the bar after the late shift. Card playing was a central part of the days and nights, and many former airport workers meet weekly to maintain the tradition. Sport was a significant part of airport social life and leisure time – golfing societies, a GAA club with football and hurling teams, soccer teams, a badminton club and an angling club were formed and, given the aviation connection, sporting competition often involved foreign travel. In 1986 the Cork Airport Singers was formed to coincide with the twenty-fifth anniversary celebrations at the airport. The choral group has performed widely and has published recordings of its work.

'Aviation had an air of romance about it. That's probably what attracted me to it. I can remember thinking that air hostesses were the most glamorous people you could imagine. And pilots? Well, they were, like, as high as you could go,' recalls another member of the early Aer Lingus team at Cork. 'Working at the airport was considered a "plum job", good money, great travel concessions and a great lifestyle.' The airport was such an attractive place to work that when Lilibeth Horne went for interview in 1970 for a job at the Aer Rianta information desk, she was one of over 300 people who were interviewed for the position over a two-week period. The airport was also a place to see and meet celebrities. Lilibeth remembers being rendered speechless when she was introduced to film star Kevin Costner in the VIP lounge: 'I was awe-struck. He was so charismatic … I met Liam Neeson there too, and he was very charming and handsome, but not like Kevin Costner.' Joe O'Connor recalls that it was the custom to muster a guard of honour of security personnel when Bishop of Cork and Ross Cornelius Lucey travelled from Cork Airport.

Aer Lingus Cork soccer team, 1974. Back row, l–r: Tom Kerrigan, Barry Murphy, Jim Kearney, Patsy Dorgan, Rom Hyde, John Prendergast, Jerry O'Carroll, Eddie Hegarty and John Buckley. Front row, l–r: Dan Scanlan, Noel Bradley, Mick O'Mahony, Jerry Lane and Jerry Crowley. BARRY MURPHY

Barry Roche took over from Gerry Holohan as Airport Manager in 1984 and he served in that capacity until his retirement in 1998. He is fondly remembered as a great leader, an imaginative and creative manager who put Cork and Cork Airport before everything. 'He had vision,' a former colleague remembers:

Barry was the face of Cork Airport for so many people. Everyone recognised him, smiling, with the pipe in his mouth. He saw how a business park at the airport would work. He always thought outside the box, he had a gut instinct for marketing and marketing opportunities. But he delivered too.

Lilibeth Horne worked closely with Barry Roche after the duty-free shop at the airport opened in 1979:

Barry was always around, always visible, trying something new, looking for a new opportunity to improve business. I was in the duty-free shop one day when a party of around twenty golfers came through, heading back to England. They spent a little time browsing in the shop, but not buying anything. Barry spotted them and suddenly I heard him announce that if every member of the party bought something in the shop, I would give each man a kiss! They were unsure at first, but then one of them bought something and came over for his kiss. I gave him a peck on the cheek. The plan worked, because they all bought something and I kissed them all. You wouldn't get away with anything like that today!

Training session on Fire Tender Rescue 7 at the airport on 6 February 1990. GABRIEL DESMOND

Many Cork people found work with Fords in Dagenham in England and over the years many stories have been told about the exploits of the 'Dagenham Yanks', as these people were known when they returned on holidays to Cork, often with a newly acquired English accent. After the airport opened the Cork workers at Dagenham often chartered planes at holiday times, flying from Luton back to Cork. Joe O'Connor recollects the fun and excitement at the airport when the Dagenham Yanks arrived, and the even greater fun as they departed.

I remember one Sunday when a Dagenham charter was flying back to Luton. A huge crowd came up to the airport to see them off. The bar was packed and could hardly cope. Jack Harrington, who had the bar and catering concession, had planned for a busy afternoon but in spite of that he ran out of beer completely. He had to send down to some pubs in the city for extra supplies. Eventually the plane was boarded and they headed off. Afterwards I heard that things got so boisterous on the flight back that the two air hostesses had locked themselves in the toilet for the duration of the journey. As the plane approached Luton there was a knock on the cockpit door. The co-pilot opened the door and a passenger handed in a handkerchief, full of money. The passengers, no doubt feeling a little guilty, had had a collection for the crew of the plane!

A number of former airport employees recall a regular occurrence at the airport in the 1960s and 1970s that sadly captures the harsh situations some Irish emigrants found themselves in:

197

(L–r): Derek Coughlan, Karen Roche, James Kelly, Anthony Healy, Tony Murphy (AFO), Terence O'Connor, Neville Doyle, Padraig McCarthy and Ciaran Walsh. CORK AIRPORT

Back in the early days the morning flight from London would come in. These planes didn't carry very many people so you'd notice anything out of the ordinary. Sometimes you'd see a girl, a young woman, getting off with a small baby in her arms. She'd be nervous, looking around her a bit, but keeping the head down too. She'd be met by some nuns who'd have driven up in a Morris Minor. The girl would go off with them. Later that day you'd see that girl getting on the evening flight back to London, but without the baby this time. I suppose they were Irish girls who had gone to England and got into trouble, or maybe they were daughters of Irish families that had emigrated, coming back to have their babies adopted.

For all who worked at the airport in 1968 the loss of the Aer Lingus Viscount near Tuskar Rock on 24 March that year is a traumatic memory. One of those killed in the crash, Hannah Burke, managed the cafeteria at the airport and was well known to all there. Before she boarded the plane that morning Joe O'Connor remembers speaking to her as he and some of his colleagues joked with her about the hat she was wearing for the journey. The first news that something was wrong came from the tower. Word spread quickly that there was an alert, that radio contact with the plane had been lost. All recall vividly the sense of shock, the fear and dread that grew as time passed and people's worst fears were confirmed. Everyone who worked at the airport helped in the effort to comfort relatives. 'It was as if all the years at the airport up to then had never happened, as if that

Five Cork Airport baggage handlers photographed on 13 April 1995. (L–r): Jim Finn, Martin Walsh, John Cronin, Pat Whyte and John Burns. GABRIEL DESMOND

was just fun or something,' a retired airport employee says. 'It was like hearing about the sudden death of a family member or a friend, it was awful. I'll never forget it. We all knew Hannah Burke and a lot of us knew others who were on the plane too.'

In 1985 more trauma was visited on the airport in the aftermath of the loss of Air India Flight 182 off the south coast of Ireland with the loss of 329 people on 23 June. Cork Airport became the centre of the recovery operation and helicopters ferried the recovered bodies to the airport over the following days. Indian and Canadian air investigators as well as representatives of those governments also had to be accommodated in addition to the many relatives of those killed who travelled to Cork. This strained the capacity of Cork Airport but employees across all sections

rallied and worked long and exhausting shifts to cope with the added traffic of aircraft and people. A media centre was set up and extra telephone lines and telex machines were provided and every effort was made to manage the unprecedented nature of the event effectively, keeping normal flight operations functioning as well as all the traffic generated by the disaster. 'In some ways the Air India crash was harder than the Tuskar crash,' a member of the airport security team recalls:

With Tuskar we didn't have to handle the rescue or deal with the bodies. Air India was completely different. None of us had ever had to deal with anything like that before. Apart altogether from the thousands of people, television crews, photographers and all that, we were dealing with all those bodies coming in.

199

Anthony Healy, Eoin Calnan and Seán McCarthy pose by the *Iolar* on 5 June 1998. GABRIEL DESMOND

It was terrible. Lots of children. It was like a war zone. It was the hardest part of my time at Cork Airport, but on the other hand the way everybody worked together was amazing. We just wanted to do our best.

When the Manx2 aircraft crashed at Cork Airport on 10 February 2011 with the loss of six lives, the current airport staff experienced the type of shock and trauma remembered by so many from 1968 and 1985. One member of staff describes how she came to realise what happened:

I was in my office in the old terminal. It was a foggy morning. I heard the noise and I just knew something had happened. I put on my hi-vis jacket and headed for the new terminal. Suddenly the fog cleared and I looked across and saw the plane, saw what had happened. That was the most gut-wrenching moment of my time at the airport.

Former employees remember different things in reflecting on the decades they spent at Cork Airport. Dan Callanan, who worked in Air Traffic

Control from 1969 to 2003, recalls the easier time they had in the airport's first decades. With only a limited schedule there were long periods of the working day when very little of consequence happened. This was compounded when fog closed the airport to traffic, sometimes for periods of two or even three days. Airport and airline staff were frequently assailed with complaints regarding delays and diversions on foggy days, but were powerless to help. Barry Murphy worked with Aer Lingus at Cork for thirty years and remembers frustrated passengers saying 'We have schedules too. It's not just the airlines.' The diversion rate at Cork up to 1989 was relatively high and a cause of constant complaint. Urban myths grew up around the fact that the airport was situated on a hilltop prone to fog, with stories circulating about political chicanery in the 1950s leading to the Ballygarvan site being chosen despite its apparent unsuitability. With the extension to the main runway in 1989 and the upgrade to Category II status the diversion rate at Cork has fallen dramatically and is now a fraction of the pre-1989 figure.

Cork Airport people have a great love for their airport. Turnover of staff has traditionally been quite small, many people spending all of their working lives there. At different times in its fifty years of operation it has been sometimes perceived and occasionally suggested that the airport was under threat – about to be sold off to private sector interests or possibly downgraded or even closed. Threats like these, real or otherwise, have rallied the Cork Airport spirit, brought workers together from all sections to cooperate, lobby and fight for 'their' airport. 'We had to fight hard for everything we got,' says a retired employee. 'The business community were great to come in behind us and help, lobby politicians and put our case.' The controversy over the debts of Cork Airport and the possibility that upwards of €100 million of debt would fall on the shoulders of an independent

Dan Callanan, who worked in Air Traffic Control, 1969–2003.

John Drennan, who came to Cork in May 1961 to oversee the electrical work during the airport's construction, and remained on to become Electrical Maintenance Manager until his retirement in 1997.

The new terminal at Cork Airport from the south. The old terminal buildings and tower are in the left foreground. KEVIN DWYER

Cork Airport Authority annoyed many, especially as the government minister responsible for aviation had promised in 2003 that this would not happen. In the difficult economic and social conditions of the current period new challenges have presented themselves and Cork, like many other airports, has to fight hard to maintain routes and passenger numbers, thereby securing jobs at the airport and in the broader community, and giving the people of Cork and the southern region a continuing air link to the wider world.

Half a century has passed since Cork Airport opened for business on 16 October 1961, and millions of journeys have since begun and ended there. Ireland has fundamentally changed over that period and travelling by air has come within the reach of a far greater number of people. Much of the romance of air travel has gone and a journey by air, once an adventure, has become commonplace and unremarkable. For aviation, for Ireland, and most especially for Cork Airport, fifty years have flown.

202

References

Chapter 1: Aviation in Ireland: the Cork Connection, 1784–1939

1 *Hibernian Chronicle*, 29 March 1784.

2 *Freeman's Journal*, 5 September 1816.

3 *Ibid.*, 10 September 1816.

4 Orville Wright, 'Kitty Hawk', *Flying* magazine, December 1913, reprinted in John Carey (ed.), *The Faber Book of Science* (London, 1995), pp. 236–40.

5 *Flight*, 23 August 1913.

6 *Cork Examiner (CE)*, 11 July 1914.

7 *Ibid.*, 10 July 1914.

8 *Ibid.*

9 Quoted in *CE*, 14 July 1914.

10 *Flight*, 7 August 1914.

11 AIR/76/76, National Archives (UK).

12 *The Irish Times (IT)*, 9 April and 8 September 1925.

13 *Ibid.*, 25 October and 30 November 1925.

14 M. C. O'Malley, *Military Aviation in Ireland, 1921–45* (Dublin, 2010), p. 7.

15 General Staff, 6th Division, 'The Irish Rebellion in the 6th Divisional Area', General Strickland Papers, Imperial War Museum, London.

16 *CE*, 16 August 1920.

17 *Ibid.*, 12 February 1921.

18 *IT*, 18 April 1921.

19 O'Malley, *Military Aviation*, p. 21.

20 *Ibid.*, p. 53.

21 *IT*, 5 December 1922.

22 Donal McCarron, *Wings Over Ireland: The Story of the Irish Air Corps* (Leicester 1996), p. 19.

23 O'Malley, *Military Aviation*, p. 48.

24 Department of Transport and Power memo, 1962, CA 56/69, National Archives of Ireland (NAI).

25 *Ibid.*

26 *CE*, 6 July 1933.

27 *Ibid.*

28 *Ibid.*

29 For air shows in Ireland, see Madeleine O'Rourke, *Air Spectaculars: Air Displays in Ireland* (Dublin, 1989).

30 *Ibid.*, 7 July 1933.

31 Michael Barry, *The Story of Cork Airport* (Fermoy, 1986), pp. 26 and 28.

Chapter 2: A Long Approach: the 'Prehistory' of Cork Airport, 1921–57

1 'Cork's Airport' (text of speech by Seamus Fitzgerald, n.d. [1950s], and assorted correspondence, Seamus Fitzgerald Papers (SFP), PR/6/880, Cork City and County Archives (CCCA).

2 *Seanad Debates*, vol. 10, no. 31, cols. 1345–1348, 24 October 1928.

3 *Cork Examiner (CE)*, 17 October 1961.

4 M. C. O'Malley, *Military Aviation in Ireland, 1921–45* (Dublin, 2010), p. 19

5 Charles Russell to Alex Healy, 19 October 1928, SFP, PR/6/880, CCCA.

6 *CE*, 29 September 1928.

7 Quoted in Bernard Share, *The Flight of the Iolar: The Aer Lingus Experience, 1936–1986* (Dublin, 1986), p. 4.

8 Michael Barry, *The Story of Cork Airport* (Fermoy, 1986), p. 15.

9 'Aircraft station near Cork Harbour' – report by the Cork Harbour Engineer and Cork Harbour Master to the Harbour Commissioners, 31 August 1929, copy in SFP, PR/6/880, CCCA.

10 Barry, *Cork Airport*, p. 16.

11 Share, *Iolar*, p. 8.

12 'Cork Terminal Airport', Richard F. O'Connor plans, 4 July 1933 (copy in SFP, PR/6/880, CCCA; plan published in full in the *Cork Examiner*, 6 July 1933 and *Flight*, 20 July 1933.

13 *The Irish Times (IT)*, 2 August 1933.

14 *CE*, 7 July 1933.

15 *Ibid.*, 24 and 26 October 1933.

16 O'Connor to E. J. Smyth, Industry and Commerce, 2 February 1934, SFP, PR/6/882(5), CCCA.

17 T. B. Carr to O'Connor, 8 March 1934, SFP, PR/6/882(4), CCCA.

18 Quoted in Share, *Iolar*, p. 9.

19 *IT*, 23 May 1934.

20 Share, *Iolar*, p. 11.

21 'Scheme for establishing a commercial aviation company, "Aerlingus Éireann, Teoranta"', 3 July 1934, SFP, PR/6/882, CCCA.

22 Share, *Iolar*, p. 69.

23 Fitzgerald to Lemass, 4 April 1934, SFP, PR/6/885, CCCA.

24 *Dáil Debates*, vol. 56, cols. 526-7, 8 May 1935.

25 'Report on Seaplane and Aeroplane Bases, Cork', 19 June 1936, SFP, PR/6/882(10), CCCA.

26 Share, *Iolar*, pp. 3 and 25.

27 See correspondence in SFP, PR/6/882, CCCA.

28 *Dáil Debates*, vol. 66, col. 270, 1 April 1937.

29 *IT*, 19 July 1938.

30 Share, *Iolar*, p. 33; Fitzgerald, 'Cork's Airport'; Barry, *Cork Airport*, p. 39.

31 Department of Industry and Commerce memo for government, 'Cork Airport Project', 9 October 1952, Department of Transport and Tourism (D/TT), CA 16/3/1, National Archives of Ireland (NAI).

32 *IT*, 5 August 1942.

33 *Ibid.*, 12 August 1942.

34 SFP, PR/6/901, CCCA.

35 'Cork Airport Project', 9 October 1952, D/TT, CA 16/3/1, NAI.

36 Lemass to Fitzgerald, 20 October 1943, SFP, PR/6/901, CCCA.

37 *IT*, 20 December 1947.

38 *Dáil Debates*, vol. 109, col. 144, 27 November 1947.

39 *Dáil Debates*, *ibid.*, col. 490, 22 February, 1990.

40 *IT*, 15 October 1952.

41 'Cork Airport Project', 9 October 1952, D/TT, CA 16/3/1, NAI.

42 CE, 27 November 1952; *Dáil Debates*, vol. 135, col. 481, 3 December 1952.

43 'Cork Airport Project', 9 October 1952, D/TT, CA 16/3/1, NAI.

44 Cormac Ó Gráda, *A Rocky Road: The Irish Economy Since the 1920s* (Manchester, 1997), p. 227.

45 McElligott to de Valera, 11 September 1952, D/TT, CA 16/3/1, NAI.

46 Aer Rianta, 'Commercial potentialities of air services to and from Cork', 12 February 1952, *ibid.*

47 Department of Industry and Commerce Memoranda for Government: 'Cork Airport Project', 6 January 1954 and 18 May 1957, *ibid.*

48 'Report on the selection of a Site for an Aerodrome at Cork', 15 July 1953, *ibid.*

49 'Report of Meeting (16 October 1953): Provision of Airport for Cork', 19 October 1953, *ibid.*

50 *Dáil Debates*, vol. 142, col. 1403, 4 November 1953.

51 Department of Industry and Commerce Memorandum for Government: 'Cork Airport Project', 6 January 1954, D/TT, CA 16/3/1, NAI.

52 'Cork Airport Project', 18 May 1957, *ibid.*

53 *Dáil Debates*, vol. 160, cols. 21–22, 24 October 1956.

54 *Southern Star*, 1 October 1955.

55 J. J. McElligott had been replaced as Secretary of Finance by Owen Redmond in 1953, but Dr No's spirit still prevailed.

56 'Cork Airport Project: Observations of the Minister for Finance', 6 December 1956, D/TT, CA 16/3/1, NAI.

57 'Cork Airport Project', 18 May 1957, *ibid.*

58 See, for example, a letter to the daily newspapers from Jean Davey, Cork Airways Company secretary, 23 April 1956.

59 *IT*, 18 October 1956 and 26 September 1957.

60 Barry, *Cork Airport*, p. 50.

61 Quoted in CE, 5 January 1960.

62 *Dáil Debates*, vol. 119, col. 487, 22 February 1950.

63 Quoted in Barry, *Cork Airport*, p. 55.

64 *Dáil Debates*, vol. 123, col. 2001, 7 December 1950.

65 *Ibid.*, vol. 127, col. 1665, 28 November 1951.

66 *IT*, 15 October 1952.

67 'Report on the selection of a Site for an Aerodrome at Cork', 15 July 1953; 'Cork Airport Project', 6 January 1954 and 18 May 1957, D/TT, CA 16/3/1, NAI.

68 Quoted in *CE*, 16 December 1955.

69 *IT*, 23 April 1956.

70 *Ibid.*, 19 November 1956.

71 *CE*, 2 March 1957.

72 George Heffernan to Minister for Transport and Power, 27 June 1960, quoted in Barry, *Cork Airport*, pp. 67–8.

73 Heffernan to Lemass, 13 September 1963, D/T S 15402C/63, NAI.

74 Interview with Ogie O'Callaghan, 20 April 2011.

Chapter 3: Delayed Arrival: Cork Airport is Born, 1958–61

1 *The Irish Times* (*IT*), 10 February 1958.

2 *Ibid.*, 15 February 1958.

3 Michael Barry, *The Story of Cork Airport* (Fermoy, 1986), p. 69.

4 *Ibid.*, pp. 71–2.

5 *Ibid.*, pp. 72–3.

6 Government notices, 21 July and 12 August 1959, *IT* and *Cork Examiner* (*CE*); *IT*, 4 November 1959; *Dáil Debates*, vol. 180, col. 1472, 6 April 1960.

7 *CE*, 5 November 1959.

8 *Dáil Debates*, vol. 184, col. 627, 3 November 1960.

9 T. L. Hogan and M. B. Clancy, 'Runways and Associated Works at Cork Airport', *Transactions of the Institution of Civil Engineers of Ireland*, vol. 90, 1964, pp. 135–6.

10 *CE*, 31 March 1960.

11 Hogan and Clancy, 'Runways and Associated Works at Cork Airport', p. 135.

12 *Dáil Debates*, vol. 182, col. 818, 8 June 1960.

13 *Evening Echo* (*EE*), 15 June and *CE*, 18 June 1960.

14 *Sunday Review*, 14 August 1960.

15 *EE*, 13 July and *IT*, 14 July 1960.

16 *Ibid.*, 11 August 1960.

17 *CE*, 3 September and 19 October 1960.

18 *Dáil Debates*, vol. 184, col. 38, 26 October, 1960.

19 Barry, *Cork Airport*, p. 83.

20 *CE*, 3 January 1961.

21 *IT*, 17 January and 28 February 1961.

22 *Ibid.*, 27 April 1961.

23 Hogan and Clancy, 'Runways and Associated Works at Cork Airport', pp. 136–7.

24 *Dáil Debates*, vol. 190, col. 194, 14 June 1960.

25 *The Kerryman*, 8 April 1961.

26 *CE*, 16 June 1961.

27 Department of Transport and Tourism (D/TT), correspondence, June 1961, CA 31/5/3, National Archives of Ireland (NAI).

28 *The Irish Press*, 17 October 1961; Barry, *Cork Airport*, p. 87.

29 *IT*, 28 July 1961.

30 D/TT, Memo from Fanning, 17 May 1961, CA 31/5/3, NAI.

31 *Ibid.*, 17 October 1961.

32 Barry, *Cork Airport*, pp. 87–8.

33 *CE*, 17 October 1961; Barry, *Cork Airport*, pp. 88 and 90.

34 Barry, *Cork Airport*, p. 90.

35 *CE*, 17 October 1961.

36 *Ibid.*, 17 October 1961.

37 *Ibid.*

38 *IT*, 17 October 1961.

39 *CE*, 17 October 1961.

40 *Ibid.*

Chapter 4: Airborne, 1961–69

1 *Cork Examiner* (*CE*), 31 October 1961.

2 *Ibid.*, 9 November 1961.

3 *Ibid.*, 1 November 1961.

4 *Ibid.*, 26 October 1961.

5 *Ibid.*, 6 November 1961.

6 BKS Air Transport Ltd., Derby Aviation Ltd., Starways Ltd., East Anglian Flying Services Ltd. and Jersey Airlines had also been granted operating rights to and from Cork, but did not initially exercise them (Department of An Taoiseach (D/T), S 15402, 9 October 1961).

7 *Cork Examiner* (*CE*), 23 March 1961.

8 Fanning to Civil Aviation Division, 15 September 1964, Department of Transport and Tourism (D/TT), CA 47/1/2, NAI.

9 Bernard Share, *The Flight of the* Iolar: *The Aer Lingus Experience, 1936–1986* (Dublin, 1986), p. 124.

10 For example, Fanning to Civil Aviation Division, 20 November 1965 and 3 November 1966, D/TT, CA 47/1/2, NAI.

11 Speech by P. J. Brennan, Secretary of Aer Lingus, reported in *CE*, 25 March 1960.

12 *The Irish Times* (*IT*) and *Evening Echo* (*EE*), 14 September 1960 and *CE*, 15 September 1960.

13 Share, *Iolar*, p. 130.

14 'Cork Airport – Second Anniversary', press release, October 1963, D/TT, CA 56/21, NAI.

15 Chavesse to Minister, 20 September 1962, D/TT, CA 56/39, NAI.

16 McGillycuddy to Manager, 9 August and 14 November, 1962, *ibid*.

17 Alley to Manager and reply, 27 and 30 August 1962, *ibid*.

18 *The Kerryman*, 12 May 1962.

19 Michael O'Toole, *Cleared for Disaster: Ireland's Most Horrific Air Crashes* (Cork, 2006), pp. 182–97; Michael Barry, *Cork Airport: An Aviation History* (Cork, 2001), pp. 64–8.

20 *CE*, 10 August 1964.

21 *Ibid*., 26 March 1968.

22 *CE* and *IT*, 25, 26 and 27 March 1968.

23 *CE*, 25 and 27 March 1968.

24 *Accident to Viscount 803 Aircraft EI-AOM near Tuskar Rock, Co. Wexford on 24th March, 1968: Report on an Investigation made under Regulation 7 of the Air Navigation (Investigation of Accidents) Regulation 1957*, (Department of Transport and Power, 1970), hereafter referred to as the 1970 report.

25 *Ibid*., p. 10.

26 *Review of Irish & UK files on the loss of the Aer Lingus Viscount St. Phelim Registration EI-AOM on 24 March 1968* (Department of Public Enterprise Report, No. 2000/003, 2000), hereafter referred to as the 2000 report.

27 *Ibid*., Conclusion No. 29.

28 *Ibid*., Conclusion No. 23.

29 *Ibid*.

30 *Report following the study performed at the request of the Minister in charge of the Department for Public Enterprise on the Aer Lingus Viscount EI-AOM accident – occurred on March 24th, 1968, near Tuskar Rock, Ireland* (Department of Public Enterprise, 2002), hereafter referred to as the 2002 report. A detailed summary of and commentary on this report is given in Mike Reynolds, *Tragedy at Tuskar Rock* (Dublin, 2003)

31 *Southern Star*, 4 January 1969.

32 *Irish Independent*, 7 August 1969.

Chapter 5: Turbulence, 1970–84

1 *Aer Rianta Annual Report*, 1970.

2 *The Irish Times* (*IT*), 6 and 28 August, 1971.

3 *Dáil Debates*, vol. 247, col. 249, 27 May 1970.

4 *IT*, 5 August 1970.

5 *Ibid*., 8, 13 and 14 October 1970.

6 *Ibid*., 13 October 1971; *Cork Examiner* (*CE*), 14 October 1971.

7 *IT*, 17, 26 January and 15 September 1972.

8 *Ibid*., 22 November 1972.

9 *IT*, 17 July 1973.

10 Michael Barry, *Cork Airport: An Aviation History* (Cork, 2001), p. 315.

11 Information from Gabriel Desmond.

12 *IT*, 20 October 1976.

13 *Ibid*. and 8 November 1977; *CE*, 20 October 1976.

14 *IT*, 29 April 1977.

15 *Ibid*., 26 March 1980.

16 *CE*, 12 June 1980.

17 *Seanad Debates*, vol. 94, no. 9, col. 949, 18 June 1980.

18 *Ibid*, col. 952.

19 *Aer Rianta Annual Report*, 1980; *IT*, 26 March 1980.

20 *IT*, 6 April 1980.

21 *Aer Rianta Annual Report*, 1981.

22 *Evening Echo*, 18 October 1982.

23 *IT*, 14 October 1982.

24 *Aer Rianta Annual Report*, 1982.

25 *Ibid*., 1983.

26 *IT*, 3 March, 23 April and 19 May 1983.

27 *Ibid.*, 7 February 1984.

28 *Aer Rianta Annual Report*, 1984; *IT*, 14 March 1984.

29 *Aer Rianta Annual Report*, 1984.

30 *CE*, 20 December 1984.

Chapter 6: The Only Way is Up! 1985–99

1 *Cork Examiner* (CE), 13 March and *The Irish Times* (IT), 20 March 1985.

2 Daily press, general, 19 August 1985.

3 Information from Gabriel Desmond.

4 *Aer Rianta Annual Report*, 1985.

5 *Dáil Debates*, vol. 355, col. 2144, 12 February 1985.

6 *Ibid.*, vol. 357, col. 2148, 1 May 1985.

7 *Air India Flight 182: A Canadian Tragedy. Final Report of the Commission of Inquiry into the Investigation of the Bombing of Air India Flight 182* (Canadian Government Publishing, 2010).

8 *Aer Rianta Annual Report*, 1986.

9 Information from Gabriel Desmond.

10 *CE* and *IT*, 29 January 1987.

11 *Dáil Debates*, vol. 372, 14 May 1982, col. 2034; *Aer Rianta Annual Report*, 1987.

12 *Aer Rianta Annual Report*, 1987.

13 *Ibid.*, 1988.

14 *Dáil Debates*, vol. 384, cols. 1233–4, 22 November 1988.

15 *Aer Rianta Annual Report*, 1989.

16 Information from Gabriel Desmond.

17 *Aer Rianta Annual Report*, 1989.

18 *IT*, 28 November 1989.

19 *Aer Rianta Annual Report*, 1990.

20 *Southern Star*, 2 March 1991.

21 *Irish Independent*, 26 February 1991.

22 *IT*, 24 July 1991.

23 *Aer Rianta Annual Report*, 1991.

24 *IT*, 12 January 1991.

25 *Aer Rianta Annual Report*, 1991.

26 *Dáil Debates*, vol. 418, col. 432, 2 April 1992.

27 *Ibid.*, vol. 418, col. 432, 2 April 1992; vol. 467, col. 2024, 2 July 1996.

28 *IT*, 3 September 1992.

29 *Aer Rianta Annual Report*, 1992.

30 *Ibid.*, 1993.

31 *Ibid.*, 1994.

32 *Dáil Debates*, vol. 438, col. 110, 1 February 1994; *IT*, 26 October 1994.

33 *Aer Rianta Annual Report*, 1995.

34 Richard Moloney *et al.*, 'The Economic Value of Cork Airport: An Input–Output Study of the Impact of Cork Airport on its Catchment Area' (Department of Economics, UCC/Aer Rianta, 2001).

35 Ella Kavanagh, Eoin O'Leary and Edward Shinnick, 'The role of airport infrastructure in regional development: the case of Cork Airport' in Eoin O'Leary (ed.), *Irish Regional Development* (Dublin, 2003), p. 186.

36 *Aer Rianta Annual Report*, 1996.

37 *Ibid.*, IT, 29 March 1996.

38 *Dáil Debates*, vol. 469, col. 1073, 2 October 1996.

39 *Aer Rianta Annual Report*, 1998.

40 *Ibid.*

41 *Dáil Debates*, vol. 479, col. 17, 8 May 1997.

42 *Ibid.*, vol. 481, cols. 895–898, 15 October 1998.

43 Dick Hogan, *IT*, 16 March 1999.

44 *Aer Rianta Annual Report*, 1999.

45 Information from Gabriel Desmond.

46 *IT*, 9 June, 30 August, 3 and 11 September 1999; *The Examiner*, 3 and 11 September 1999; *Aer Rianta Annual Report*, 1999; *Dáil Debates*, vol. 508, col. 114, 6 October 1999.

47 Kavanagh *et al.*, 'The role of airport infrastructure', pp. 184–8.

Chapter 7: Thrust And Drag, 2000–11

1 *Irish Independent*, 19 June 2000; *Dáil Debates*, vol. 521, col. 922, 20 June 2000.

2 *Dáil Debates*, vol. 521, col. 923, 20 June 2000, and vol. 524, cols. 934–5, 19 October 2000.

3 *The Irish Times* (IT) and *Irish Examiner* (IE), 1 June 2001.

4 *IT*, 29 August 2001.

5 *Ibid.*

6 *Ibid.*, 5 September 2001.

7   Chief Executive's Review, *Aer Rianta Annual Report*, 2003.

8   *Ibid.*

9   *Dublin Airport Authority Annual Report*, 2004.

10 *Irish Independent*, 13 August 1998.

11 *Ibid.*, 1 February 2000; *Aer Rianta Annual Report*, 2000.

12 *Dáil Debates*, vol. 556, col. 854, 5 November 2002.

13 *IT*, 8 November 2003.

14 Quoted by Deirdre Clune, *Dáil Debates*, vol. 637, col. 773, 27 June 2007.

15 *IT*, Quoted by Deirdre Clune, *Dáil Debates*, vol. 637, col. 773, 27 June 2007. November 2004.

16 *Dublin Airport Authority Annual Report*, 2004.

17 *Ibid.*, 2005.

18 *IT*, 5 March 2007.

19 *Dáil Debates*, vol. 637, col. 774, 27 June 2007.

20 *IT*, 12 April 2008.

21 *IE*, 22 April 2008.

22 *Dublin Airport Authority Annual Report*, 2009; *Dáil Debates*, vol. 673, col. 131, 5 February 2009.

23 *IE*, 2 August 2006.

24 *Ibid.*, 27 July 2006.

25 Interview with Kevin Cullinane, 1 June 2011.

26 *Dublin Airport Authority Annual Report*, 2006.

27 *Seanad Debates*, vol. 183, col. 742, 26 April 2006.

28 *Aer Rianta Annual Reports*, 2000–03.

29 *IT* and *IE*, 24 July 2003.

30 *Dublin Airport Authority Annual Report*, 2004.

31 The information for the foregoing paragraphs comes from a combination of Dublin Airport Authority Annual Reports, various newspaper reports and Kevin Cullinane of Cork Airport.

32 The details of the flight, of the approaches at Cork, and of the crash itself come from *Air Accident Investigation Unit Ireland: Report No. 2011-055*, published 16 March 2011.

33 *IE*, 11 February 2011.

34 *Ibid.*, 14 February 2011.

35 www.terminalconvention.com – accessed 2 May 2011.

Bibliography

PRIMARY SOURCES

Archives

Aer Lingus Archives, Dublin Airport: Aer Lingus staff magazine, *Aer Scéala*

Cork City and County Archives, Cork: Seamus Fitzgerald Papers and Cork City Council Minute Books

Cork Harbour Commissioners: CHC Minute Books

Imperial War Museum, London: General Strickland Papers

National Archives of Ireland, Dublin: Files of the Department of An Taoiseach; Department of Industry and Commerce; Department of Transport and Tourism

National Archives (UK), Kew: Records of the Royal Air Force

Cork Airport: Press Cuttings Book 1959–62; Engineers' Photograph Album 1960–61; 25th Anniversary Photograph Album.

Heffernan's Travel, Cork: Cork Airways Company Press Cuttings Album

Published

Accident to Viscount 803 Aircraft EI-AOM near Tuskar Rock, Co. Wexford on 24th March, 1968: Report on an Investigation made under Regulation 7 of the Air Navigation (Investigation of Accidents) Regulation 1957 (Department of Transport and Power, 1970)

Aer Rianta Annual Reports and Accounts, 1970–2003

Air Accident Investigation Unit Ireland: Report No. 2011-055, 16 March 2011

Air India Flight 182: A Canadian Tragedy. Final Report of the Commission of Inquiry into the Investigation of the Bombing of Air India Flight 182. (Canadian Government Publishing, 2010)

Dublin Airport Authority Annual Reports and Accounts, 2004–2010

Dáil Éireann Debates

Report following the study performed at the request of the Minister in charge of the Department for Public Enterprise on the Aer Lingus Viscount EI-AOM accident – occurred on March 24th, 1968, near Tuskar Rock, Ireland (Department of Public Enterprise, 2002)

Review of Irish & UK files on the loss of the Aer Lingus Viscount St. Phelim Registration EI-AOM on 24 March 1968 (Department of Public Enterprise Report, No. 2000/003, 2000)

Seanad Éireann Debates

Interviews

Mary Blyth
Dan Callanan
Brendan Clancy
Kevin Cullinane
Gabriel Desmond
John Drennan
Donie Harris
Lilibeth Horne
Pat Keohane
Denis McCarthy

Mary Murphy

Barry Murphy

Ogie O'Callaghan

Joe O'Connor

Tom Russell

Ray Shanahan

Newspapers and journals

Aviation

Aviation Ireland

Cork Examiner/The Examiner/Irish Examiner

Evening Echo

Flight

Freeman's Journal

Hibernian Chronicle

Irish Air Letter

Irish Independent

The Irish Press

The Irish Times

Kerryman

Southern Star

Sunday Independent

Sunday Review

Sunday Tribune

BOOKS, THESES AND ARTICLES

Anon., *Aviation on the Shannon* (Dublin, 1985)

Anon., *The Flying Fields of Cork: A History of Aviation in the County of Cork* (Dublin, 1988)

Barry, Michael, *Cork Airport: An Aviation History* (Cork, 2001)

— *The Story of Cork Airport* (Fermoy, 1986)

— *Great Aviation Stories, vol. 1* (Fermoy, 1983)

— *Great Aviation Stories, vol. 2* (Fermoy, 1997)

Browne, Vincent (ed.), *The Magill Book of Irish Politics* (Dublin, 1981)

Butler, P. H., *Irish Aircraft: A History of Irish Aviation* (Liverpool, 1972)

Byrne, Liam, *History of Aviation in Ireland* (Dublin, 1980)

Carey, John (ed.), *The Faber Book of Science* (London, 1995)

Crean, P. J., *et al.*, *Cork Airport: The First Twenty-One Years, 1961–1982* (Cork, 1982)

Cronin, Mike, *Doesn't Time Fly? Aer Lingus – Its History* (Cork, 2011)

Crowley, John, *et al.* (eds), *An Atlas of Cork City* (Cork, 2005)

Daly, Mary, *Industrial Development and Irish National Identity, 1922–1939* (New York, 1992)

Fanning, Ronan, *The Irish Department of Finance 1922–58* (Dublin, 1978)

Fitzgerald, E. J., *A Look at Some Aspects of the Weather at Cork Airport* (Dublin, 1980)

Garvin, Tom, *Judging Lemass* (Dublin, 2009)

Hayes, Karl, *A History of the Royal Air Force and the United States Naval Air Service in Ireland, 1913–1923* (Dublin, 1988)

Hill, J. R. (ed.), *A New History of Ireland VII, 1921–84* (Oxford, 2003)

Hogan, T. L. and M. B. Clancy, 'Runways and Associated Works at Cork Airport', *Transactions of the Institution of Civil Engineers of Ireland*, vol. 90, 1964

Horgan, John, *Seán Lemass: The Enigmatic Patriot* (Dublin, 1997)

Kavanagh, Ella, Eoin O'Leary and Edward Shinnick, *The Role of Cork Airport in Regional Development: Strategic Opportunities*, Report Commissioned by Aer Rianta, Cork Airport (2001)

— 'The role of airport infrastructure in regional development: the case of Cork Airport', in Eoin O'Leary (ed.), *Irish Regional Development* (Dublin, 2003)

Keogh, Dermot, *Twentieth Century Ireland: Nation and State* (Dublin, 1994)

— *Jack Lynch: A Biography* (Dublin, 2008)

Keogh, Dermot, Finbarr O'Shea and Carmel Quinlan (eds), *The Lost Decade: Ireland in the 1950s* (Cork, 2004)

Lee, J. J., *Ireland 1912–1985: Politics and Society* (Cambridge, 1988)

Lenihan, Michael, *Hidden Cork: Charmers, Chancers and Cute Hoors* (Cork, 2009)

Loftus, Paul, 'The crisis years: the second inter-party government and the politics of transition in Ireland, 1954–1957' (unpublished PhD thesis, UCC, 2008)

MacCarron, Donal, *Wings over Ireland: The Story of the Irish Air Corps* (Leicester 1996)

— *A View from Above: 200 Years of Aviation in Ireland* (Dublin, 2000)

McCarthy, Patrick J., 'The RAF and Ireland 1920–22', *The Irish Sword*, vol. 17, 1987–90

McCullagh, *A Makeshift Majority: the First Inter-party Government, 1948–51* (Dublin, 1998)

Moloney, Richard, *et al.*, 'The Economic Value of Cork Airport: An Input–Output Study of the Impact of Cork Airport on its Catchment Area' (Department of Economics, UCC/Aer Rianta, 2001)

Ó Gráda, Cormac, *Ireland: A New Economic History, 1780–1939* (Oxford, 1994)

— *A Rocky Road: The Irish Economy Since the 1920s* (Manchester, 1997)

O'Malley, M. C., *Military Aviation in Ireland, 1921–45* (Dublin, 2010)

Oram, Hugh, *Dublin Airport: The History* (Dublin, 1990)

O'Rourke, *Madeleine, Air Spectaculars: Air Displays in Ireland* (Dublin, 1989)

O'Toole, Michael, *Cleared for Disaster: Ireland's Most Horrific Air Crashes* (Cork, 2006)

Reynolds, Mike, *Tragedy at Tuskar Rock* (Dublin, 2003)

Share, Bernard, *The Flight of the Iolar: The Aer Lingus Experience, 1936–1986* (Dublin, 1986)

Skinner, Liam, and Tom Cranitch, *Ireland and World Aviation: The Complete Story* (Dublin, 1988)

Sweeney, Valerie, *Shannon Airport: A Unique Story of Survival* (Shannon, 2004)

Turner, Paul St John, *UK and Eire Commercial Airports* (Hounslow, 1974)

Warner, Guy and Jack Woods, *In the Heart of the City: The History of Belfast's City Airport, 1938–1998* (Belfast, 1998)

Weldon, Niall, *Pioneers in Flight: Aer Lingus and the Story of Aviation in Ireland* (Dublin, 2003)

Index

Pages with illustrations or photographs are indicated by page numbers in bold.